VAMPIRONICA®

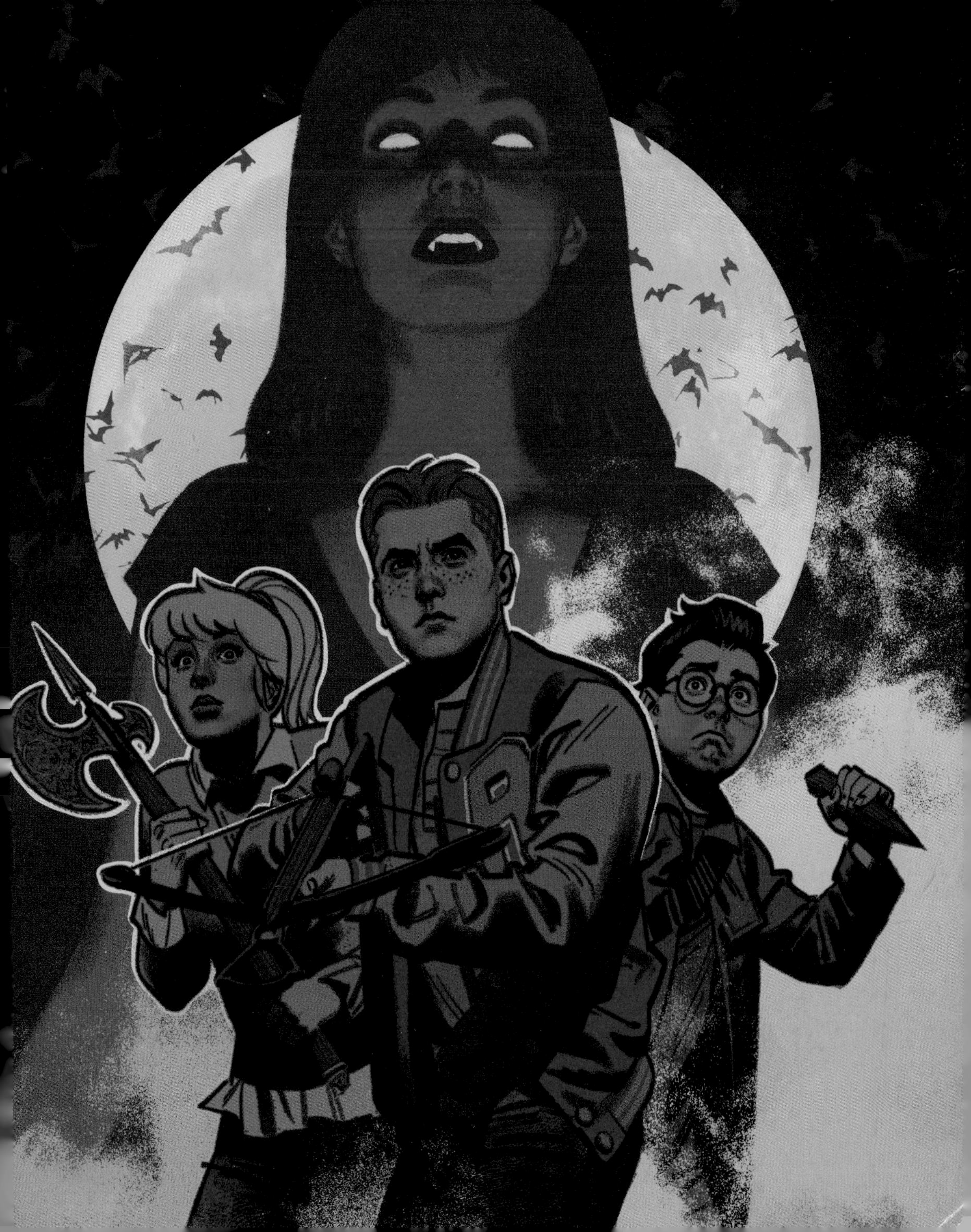

VAMPIRONICA®

Story by
GREG SMALLWOOD
& MEG SMALLWOOD

Art by
GREG SMALLWOOD (ISSUES 1-3)
GREG SCOTT (ISSUES 4-5)

Lettering by
JACK MORELLI

Coloring by
MATT HERMS (ISSUES 4-5)

Creative Consultant
JESSE GOLDWATER

Graphic Design
KARI McLACHLAN

Editor-in-Chief
VICTOR GORELICK

Publisher
JON GOLDWATER

Editors
ALEX SEGURA &
JAMIE L. ROTANTE

Associate Editor
STEPHEN OSWALD

Assistant Editor
VINCENT LOVALLO

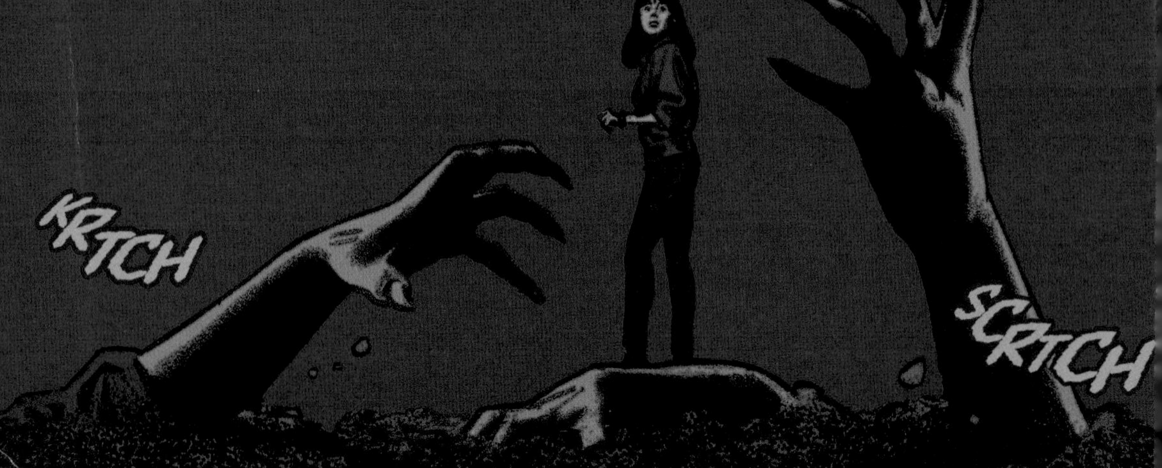
KRTCH
SCRTCH

THE VERONICA CHRONICLES

One thing you learn, early on, when editing comics is that things sometimes find a way of lining up perfectly. It doesn't always happen, but when it does—you really appreciate it.

Take, for example, the story of Vampironica. The idea of Veronica Lodge—Riverdale's favorite social deb—taking on a vampiric form wasn't new. Dan Parent had played with the concept years before in an issue of *Betty & Veronica*, and we'd toyed with it here and there a few times since. But in the wake of Archie Horror successes like *Afterlife with Archie*, *Chilling Adventures of Sabrina* and *Jughead: The Hunger*, the once funny idea took on a darker, much more menacing tone. It was too perfect. It had to be the next Archie Horror hit. And it would be. If we found the right team, that is.

Greg Smallwood is an artist I've long admired, from his debut stint on *Dream Thief* to his lengthy, versatile run on Marvel's *Moon Knight*. He'd graced a number of Archie and Dark Circle titles with iconic and jaw-dropping covers, so we had all become familiar with Greg's attention to detail, spot-on design sense and professionalism. When he emailed me to inquire about maybe doing a one-shot as writer and artist, my interest was piqued. It was more than a coincidence. It had to be fate.

I talked over the idea with our CEO/Publisher Jon Goldwater and we figured it was worth a shot. I bounced the basic "Veronica as a vampire!" idea by Greg and he hunkered down. When he returned, it was with a lushly-illustrated pitch in town—and a co-writer, too. Meg Smallwood, Greg's sister and a lifelong Archie fan, joined the team—helping craft a story loaded with teen drama, humor and plenty of blood-spilling violence. But it wasn't just the action and laughs that make VAMPIRONICA special, mind you. The Smallwoods—in tandem with letterer extraordinaire Jack Morelli and fill-in artist Greg Scott and fill-in colorist Matt Herms—created a tale steeped in monster lore, weaving a narrative that felt totally modern but also literary and historical in its approach.

Kind of the definition of "instant classic," right?

I hope you enjoy your trip down the dark streets of Riverdale. Just keep that garlic and holy water handy. You'll need it.

Alex Segura
Editor, Vampironica

CHAPTER ONE

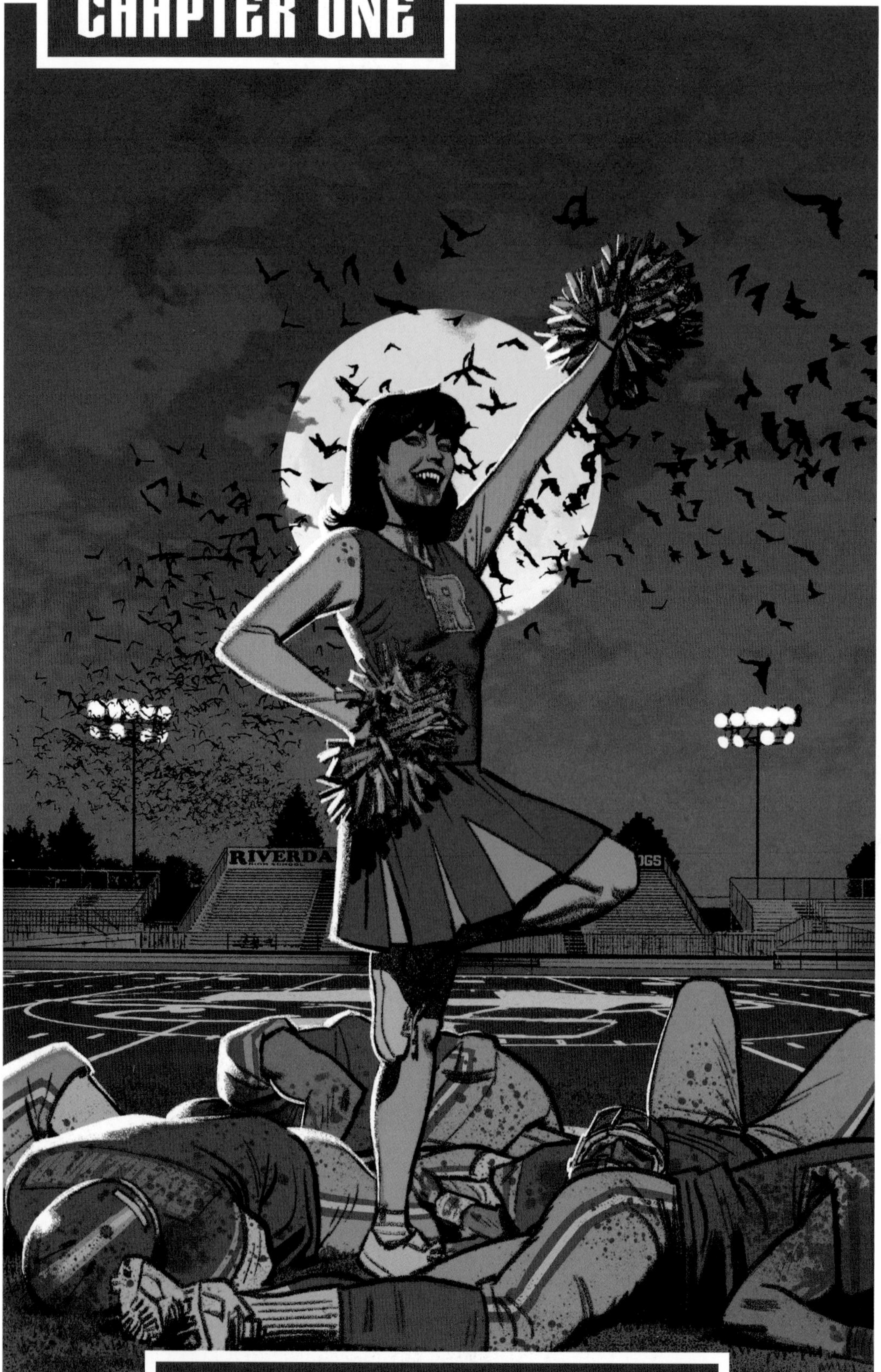
RIVERDA

COVER ART BY **GREG SMALLWOOD**

EMBROOKE ESTATES.

ALRIGHT, EVERYBODY...

...WHO'S UP FOR SOME *BODY SHOTS?!*

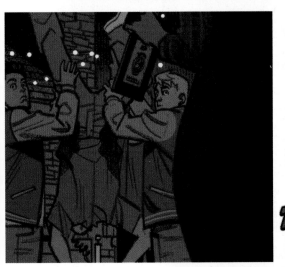

EASY, BOYS. THERE'S PLENTY FOR--

THUD

...EVERYONE.

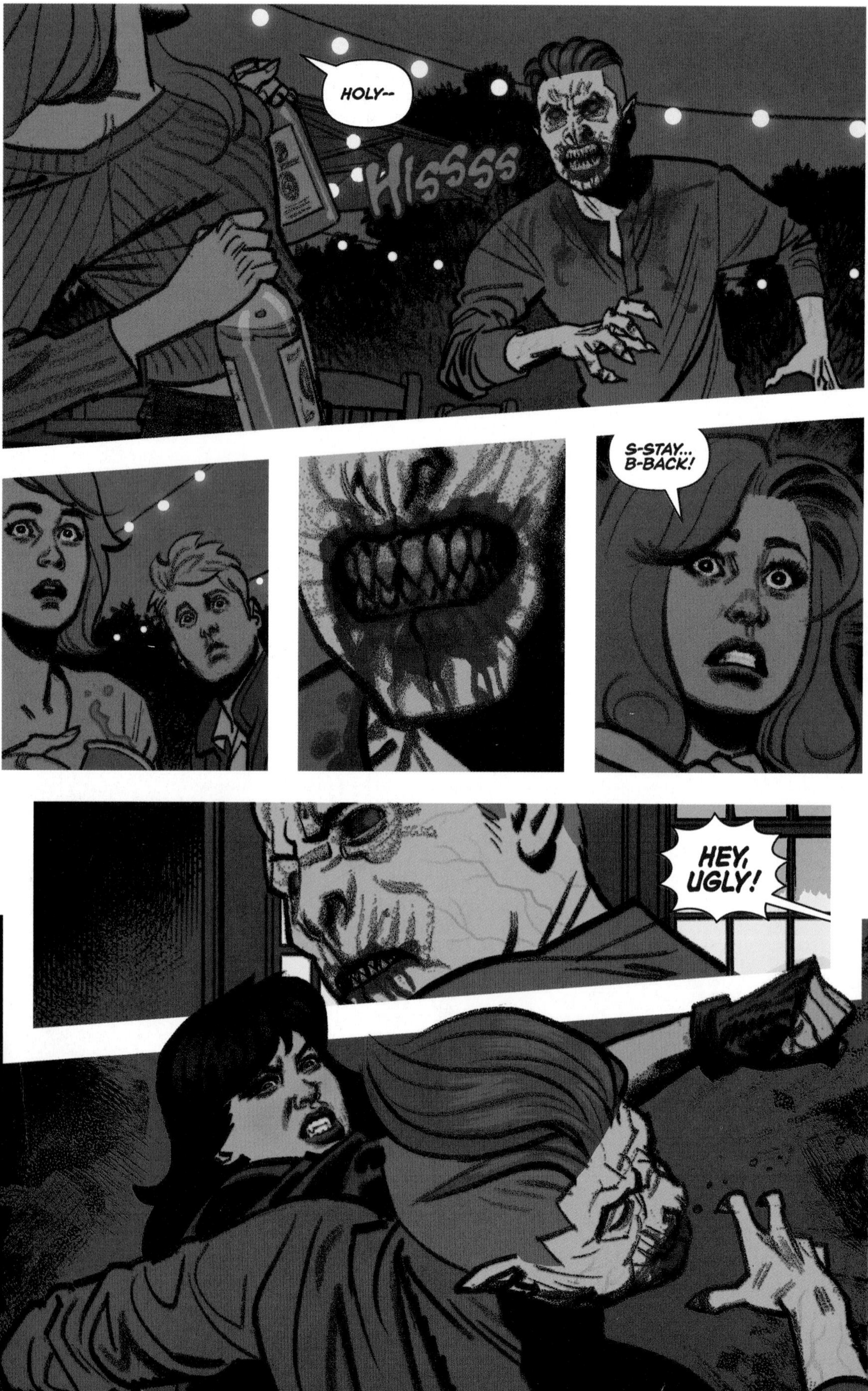
HOLY--
HISSSS
S-STAY... B-BACK!
HEY, UGLY!

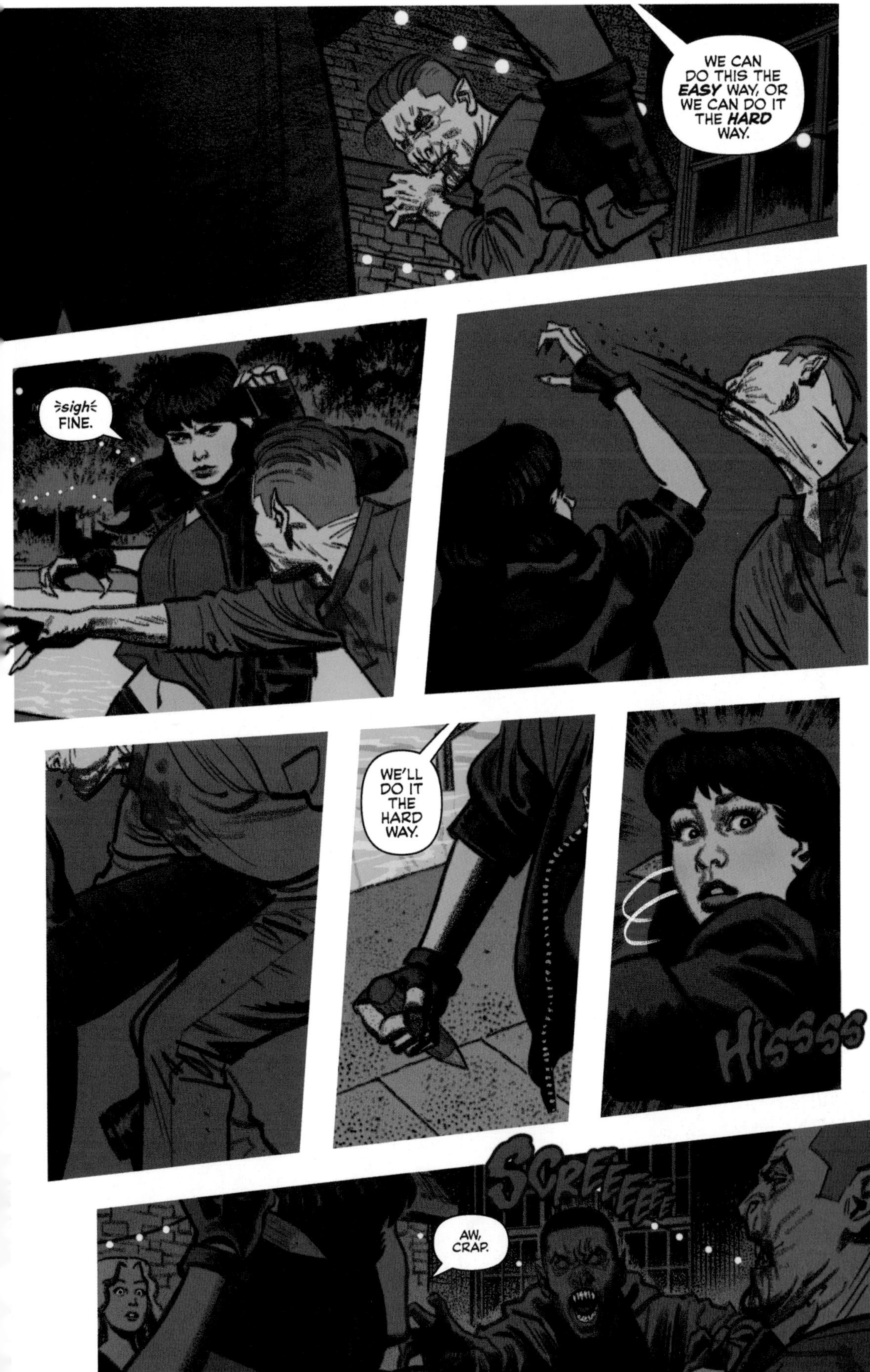

WE CAN DO THIS THE EASY WAY, OR WE CAN DO IT THE HARD WAY.
sigh FINE.
WE'LL DO IT THE HARD WAY.
HISSSS
SCREEEEE
AW, CRAP.

SPLASH

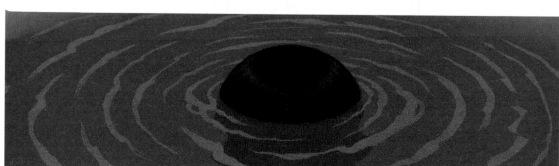

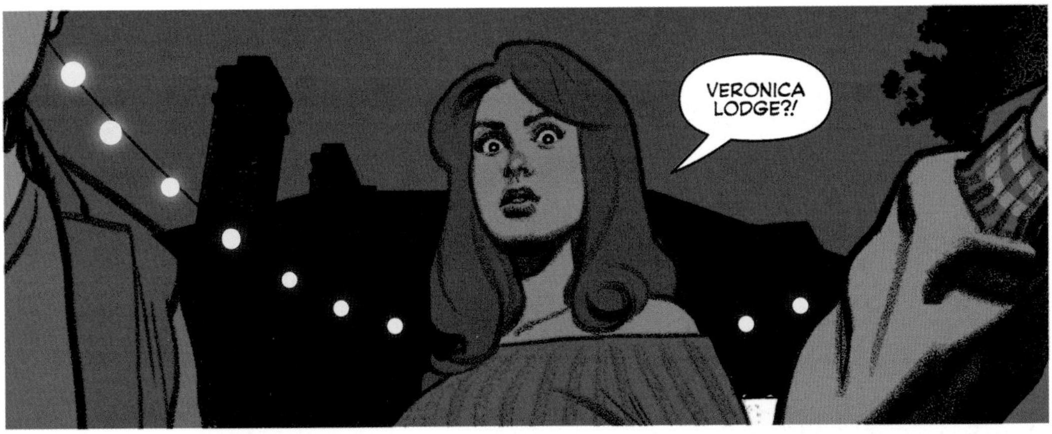
VERONICA LODGE?!

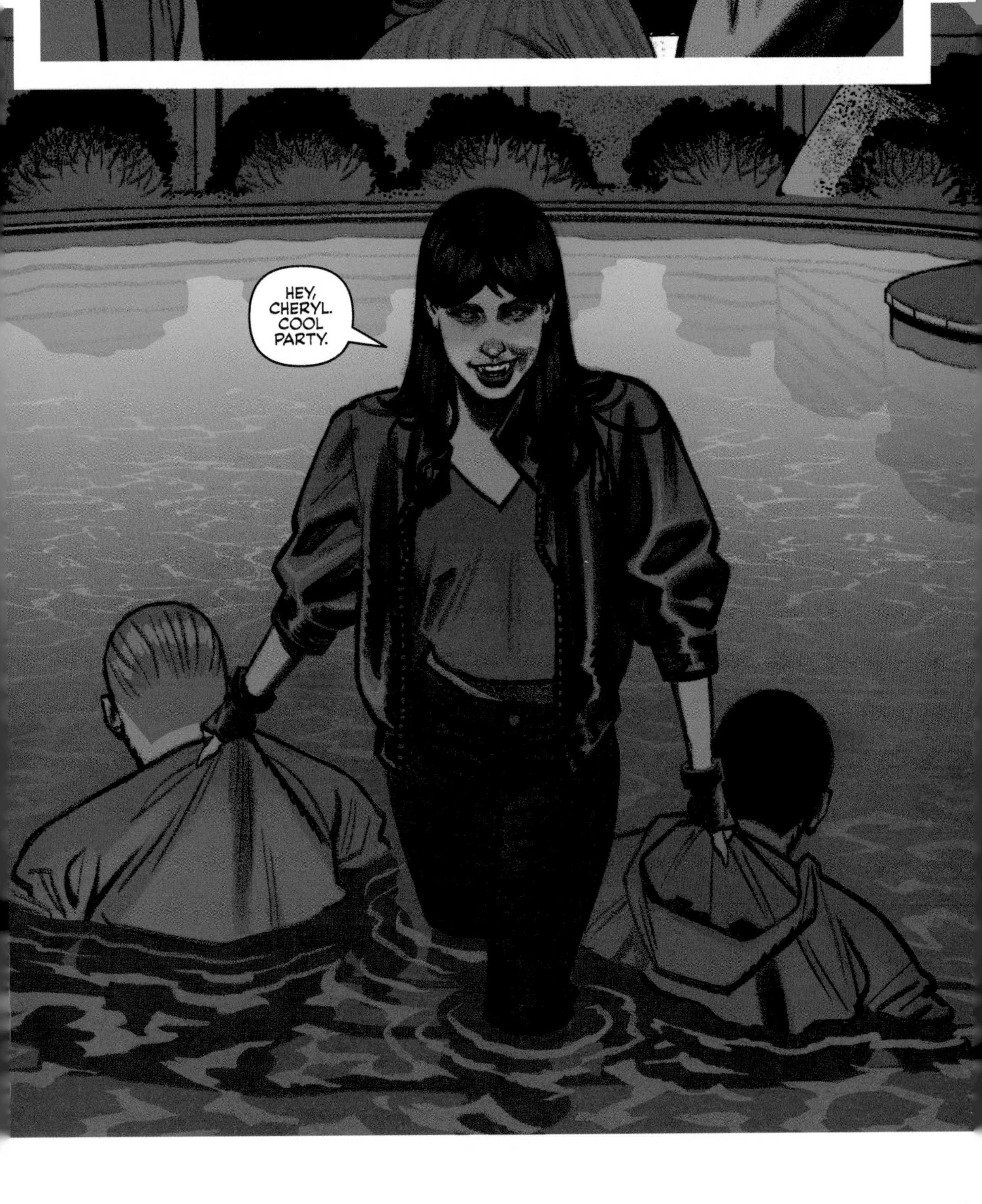
HEY, CHERYL. COOL PARTY.

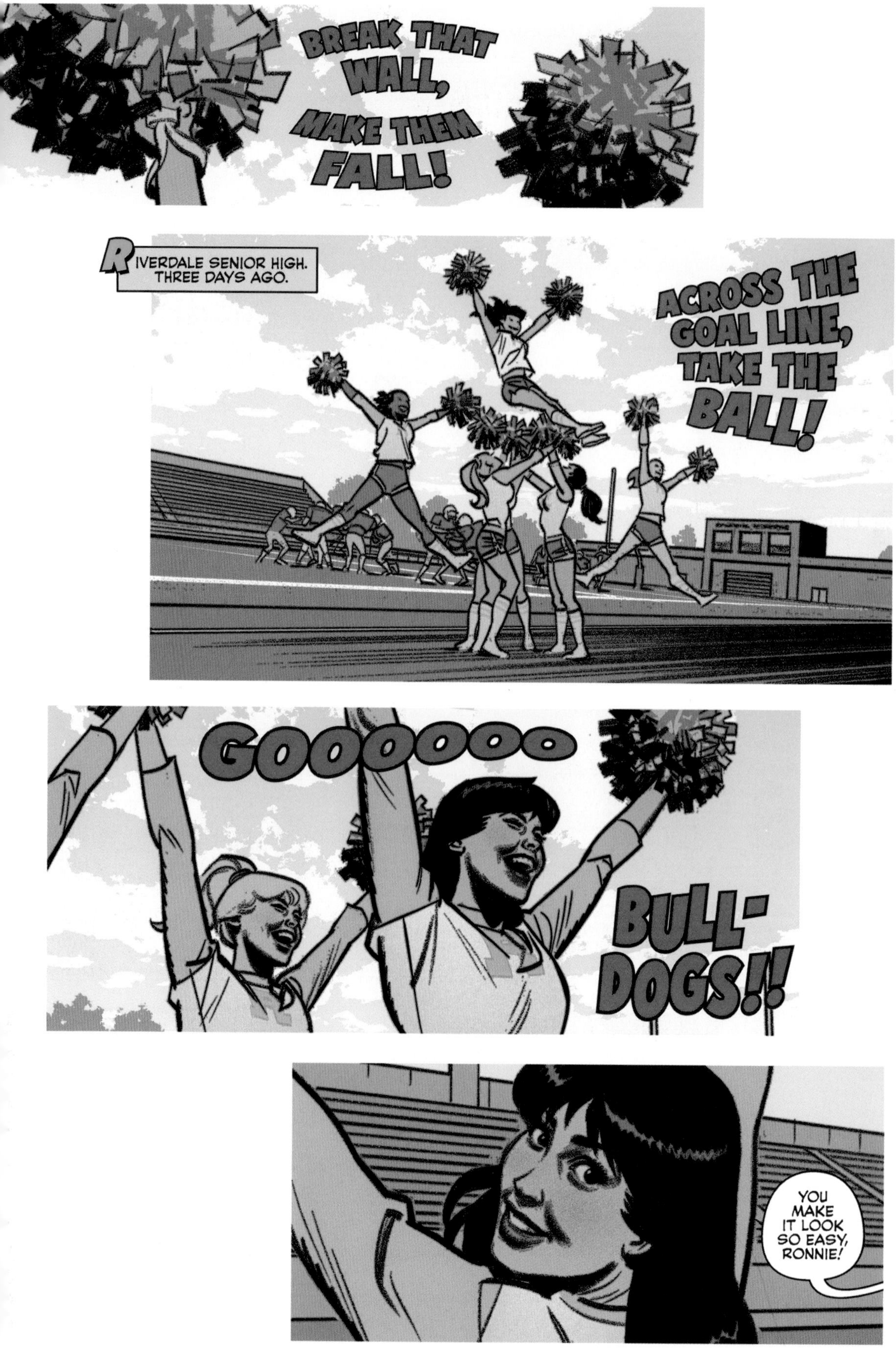
BREAK THAT WALL, MAKE THEM FALL!
RIVERDALE SENIOR HIGH. THREE DAYS AGO.
ACROSS THE GOAL LINE, TAKE THE BALL!
GOOOOOO
BULL-DOGS!!
YOU MAKE IT LOOK SO EASY, RONNIE!

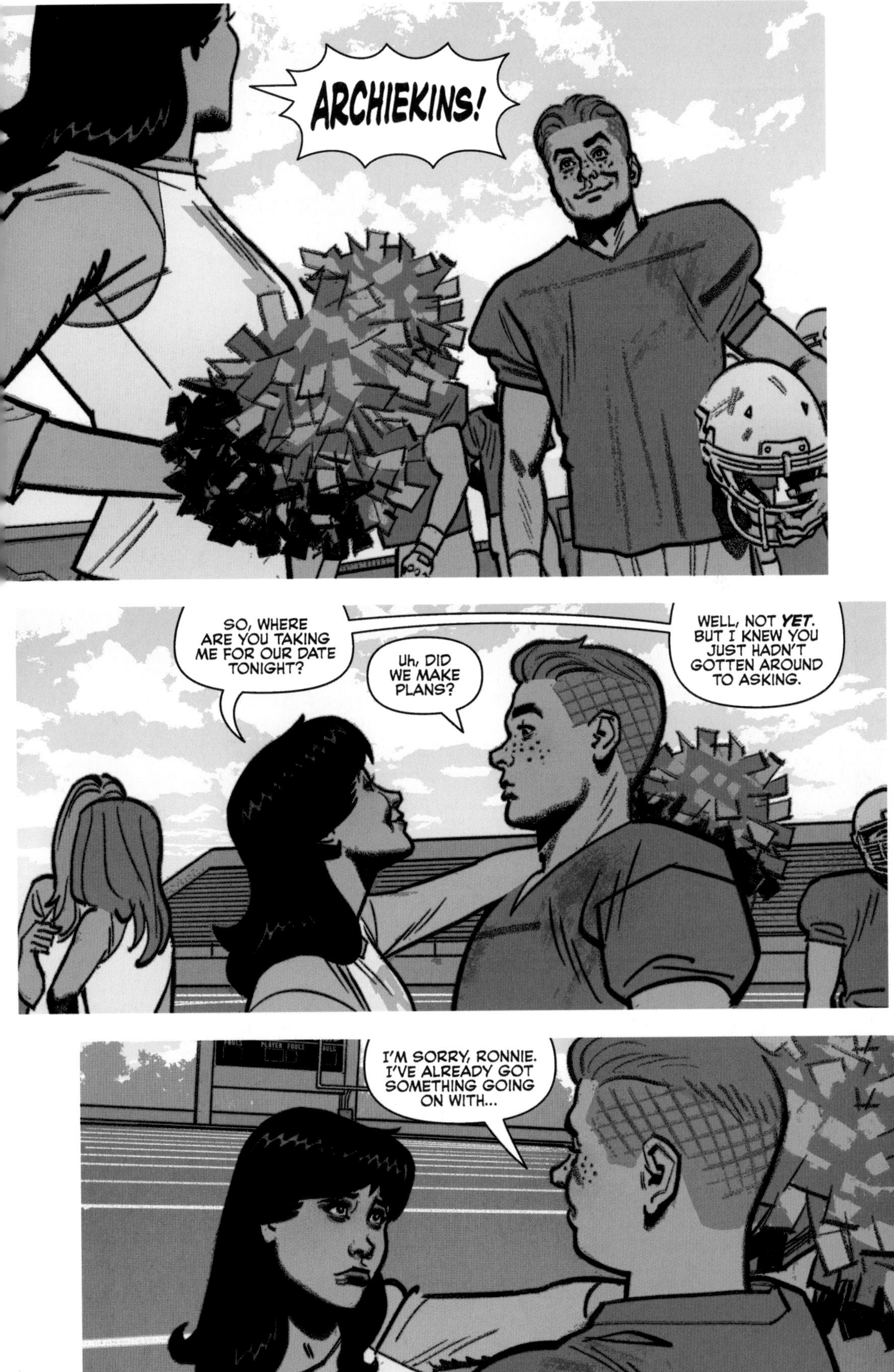
ARCHIEKINS!
SO, WHERE ARE YOU TAKING ME FOR OUR DATE TONIGHT?
Uh, DID WE MAKE PLANS?
WELL, NOT *YET*. BUT I KNEW YOU JUST HADN'T GOTTEN AROUND TO ASKING.
I'M SORRY, RONNIE. I'VE ALREADY GOT SOMETHING GOING ON WITH...

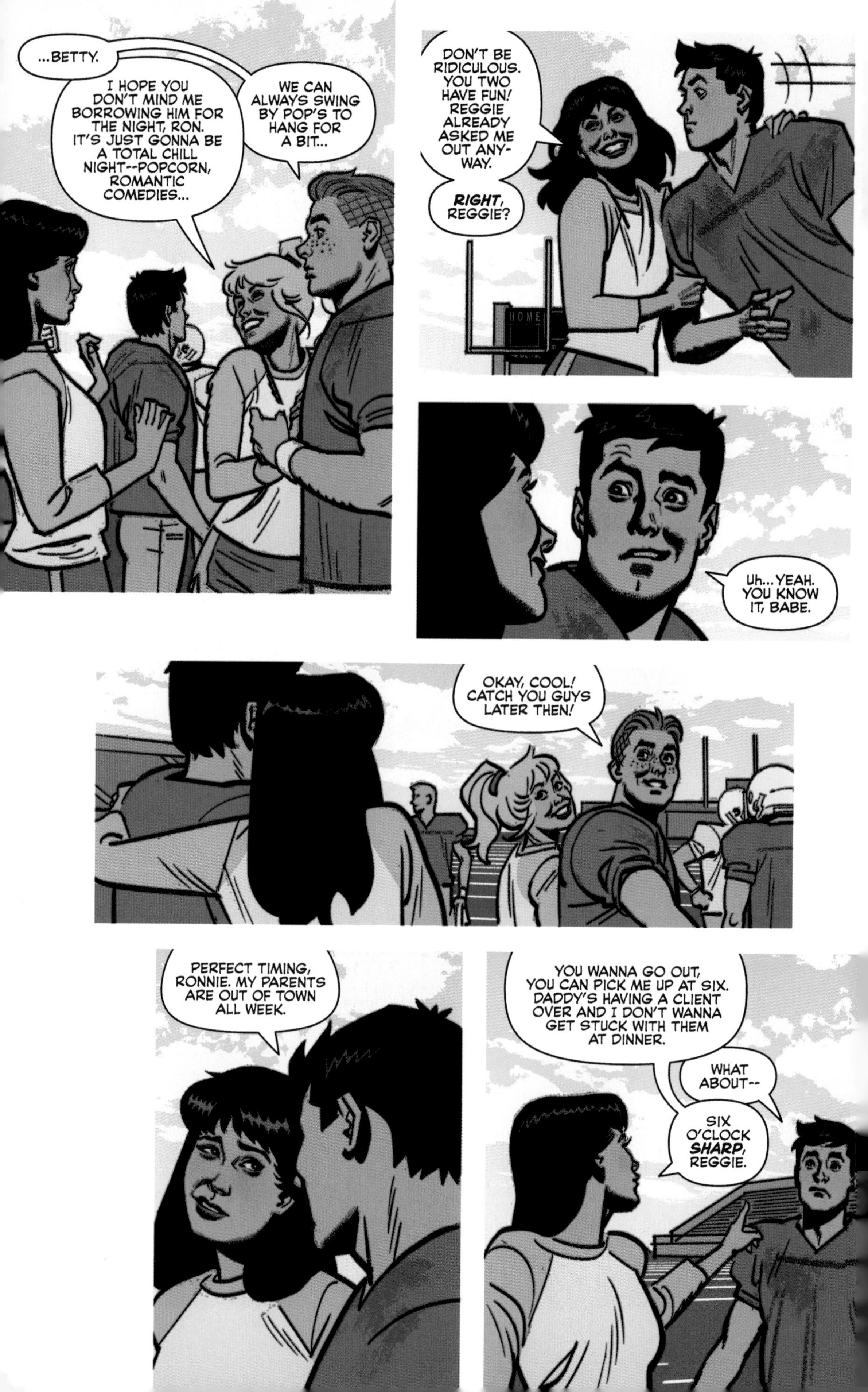
...BETTY.
I HOPE YOU DON'T MIND ME BORROWING HIM FOR THE NIGHT, RON. IT'S JUST GONNA BE A TOTAL CHILL NIGHT--POPCORN, ROMANTIC COMEDIES...
WE CAN ALWAYS SWING BY POP'S TO HANG FOR A BIT...
DON'T BE RIDICULOUS. YOU TWO HAVE FUN! REGGIE ALREADY ASKED ME OUT ANY-WAY.
RIGHT, REGGIE?
HOME
Uh...YEAH. YOU KNOW IT, BABE.
OKAY, COOL! CATCH YOU GUYS LATER THEN!
PERFECT TIMING, RONNIE. MY PARENTS ARE OUT OF TOWN ALL WEEK.
YOU WANNA GO OUT, YOU CAN PICK ME UP AT SIX. DADDY'S HAVING A CLIENT OVER AND I DON'T WANNA GET STUCK WITH THEM AT DINNER.
WHAT ABOUT--
SIX O'CLOCK *SHARP*, REGGIE.

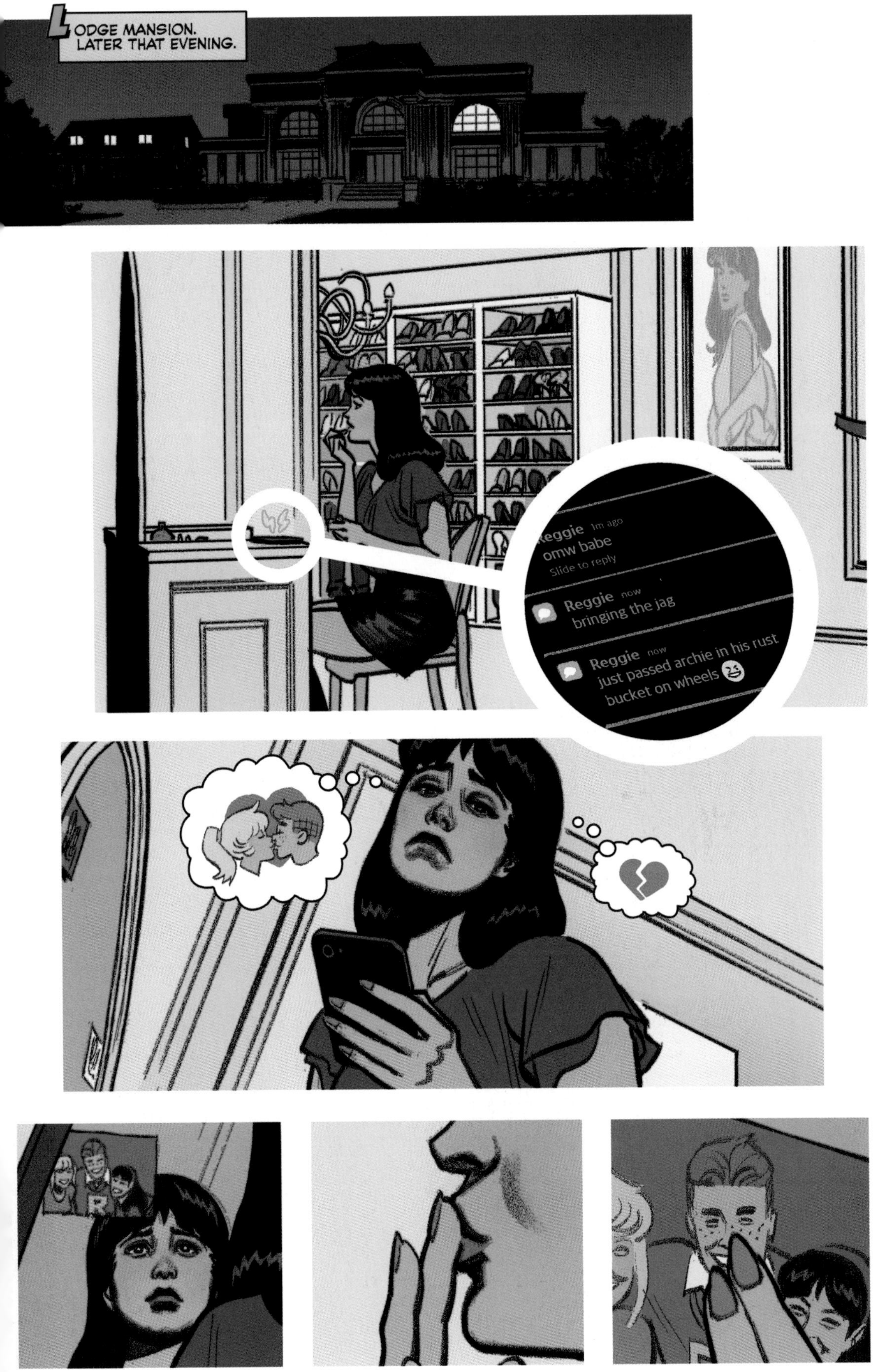
LODGE MANSION.
LATER THAT EVENING.
Reggie 1m ago
omw babe
Slide to reply
Reggie now
bringing the jag
Reggie now
just passed archie in his rust bucket on wheels

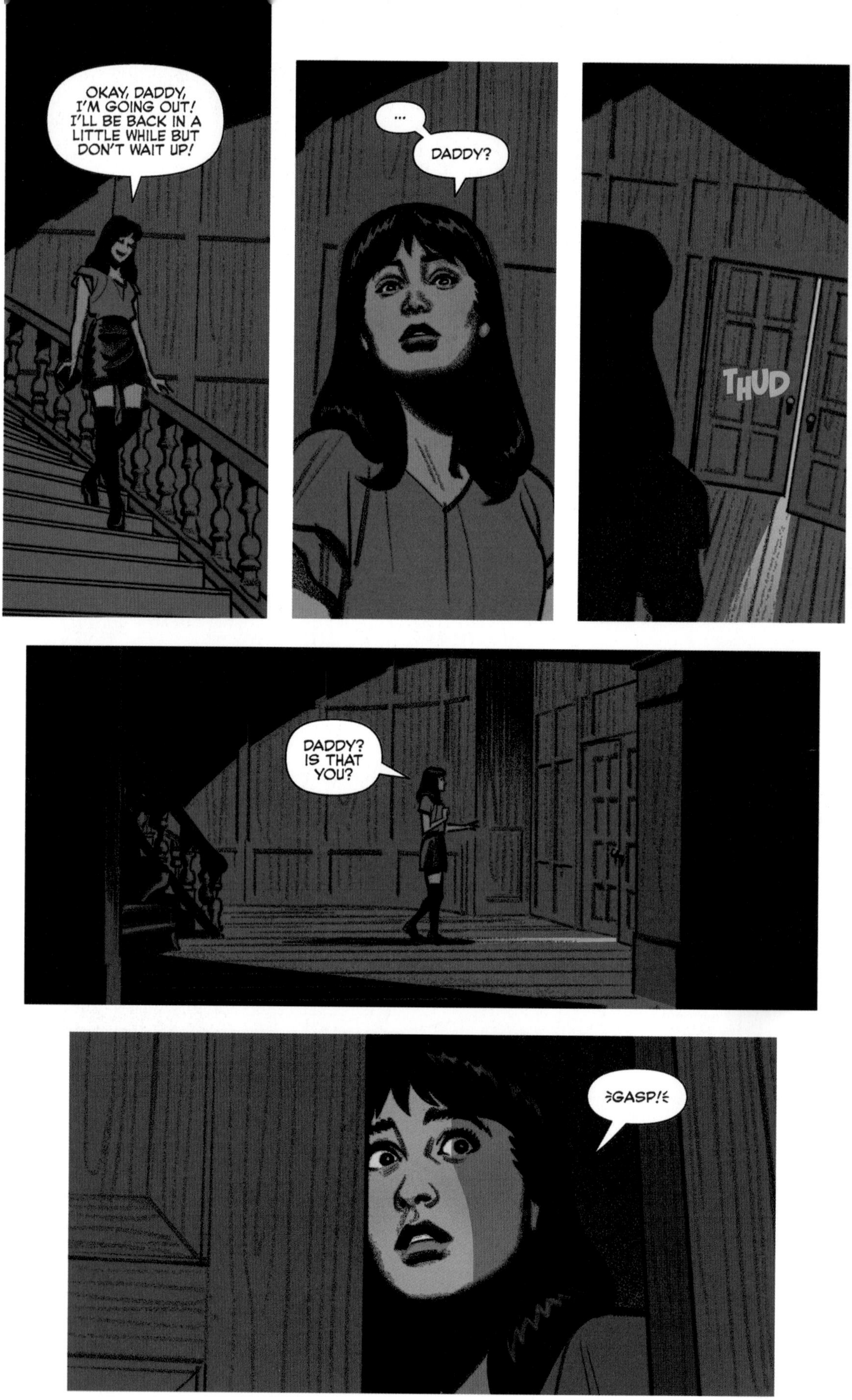
OKAY, DADDY, I'M GOING OUT! I'LL BE BACK IN A LITTLE WHILE BUT DON'T WAIT UP!
...
DADDY?
THUD
DADDY? IS THAT YOU?
GASP!

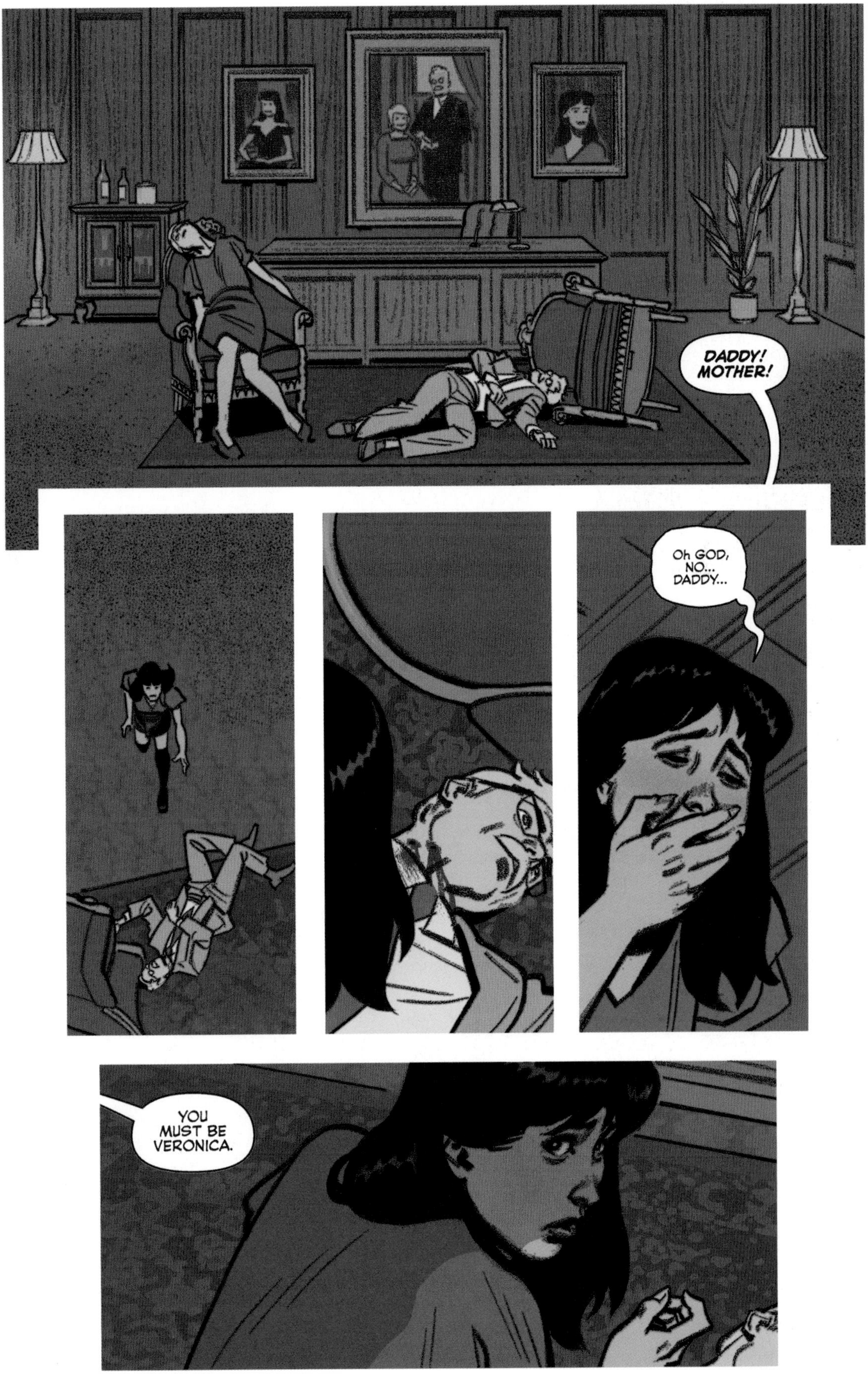
DADDY! MOTHER!
Oh GOD, NO... DADDY...
YOU MUST BE VERONICA.

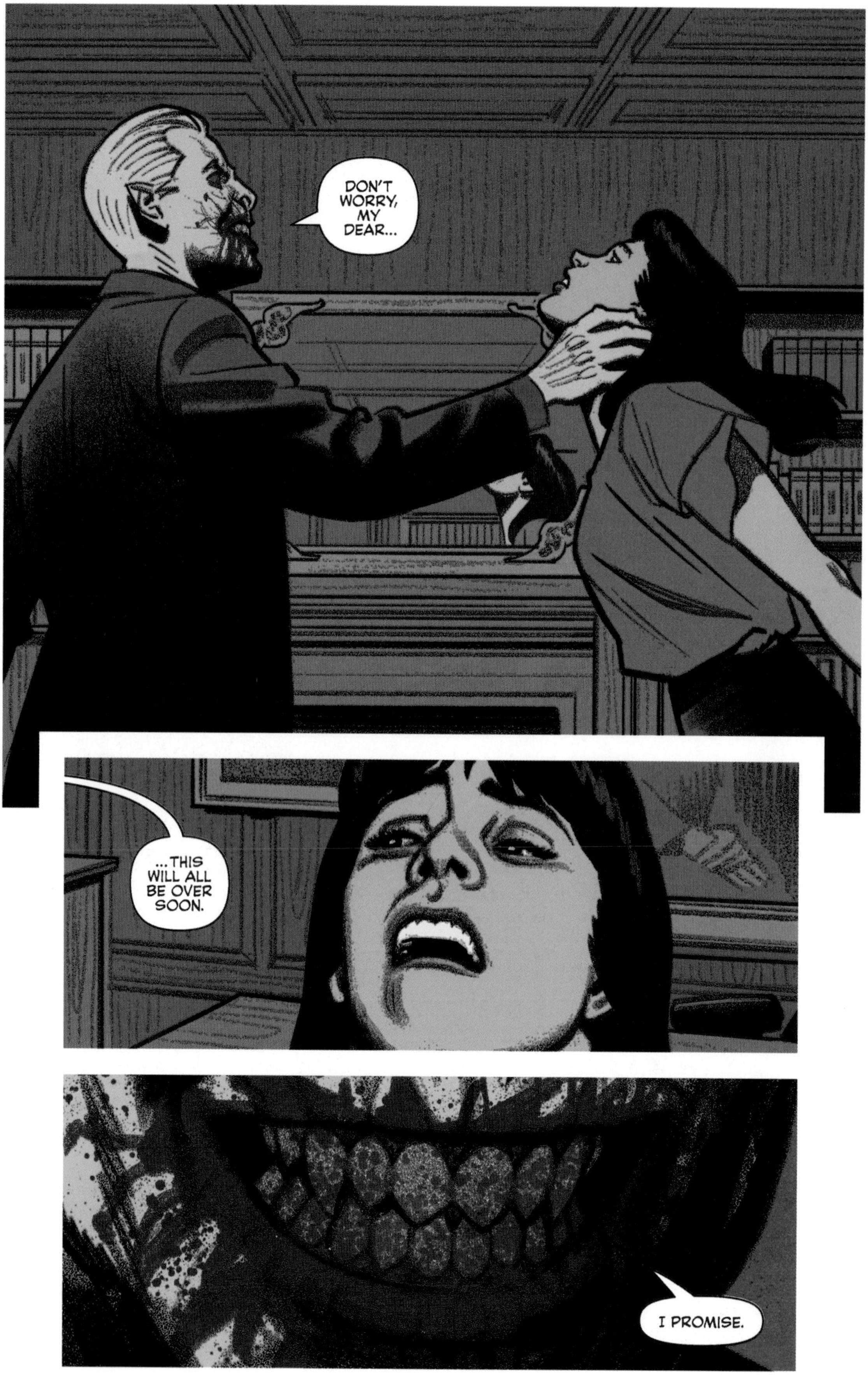
DON'T WORRY, MY DEAR...
...THIS WILL ALL BE OVER SOON.
I PROMISE.

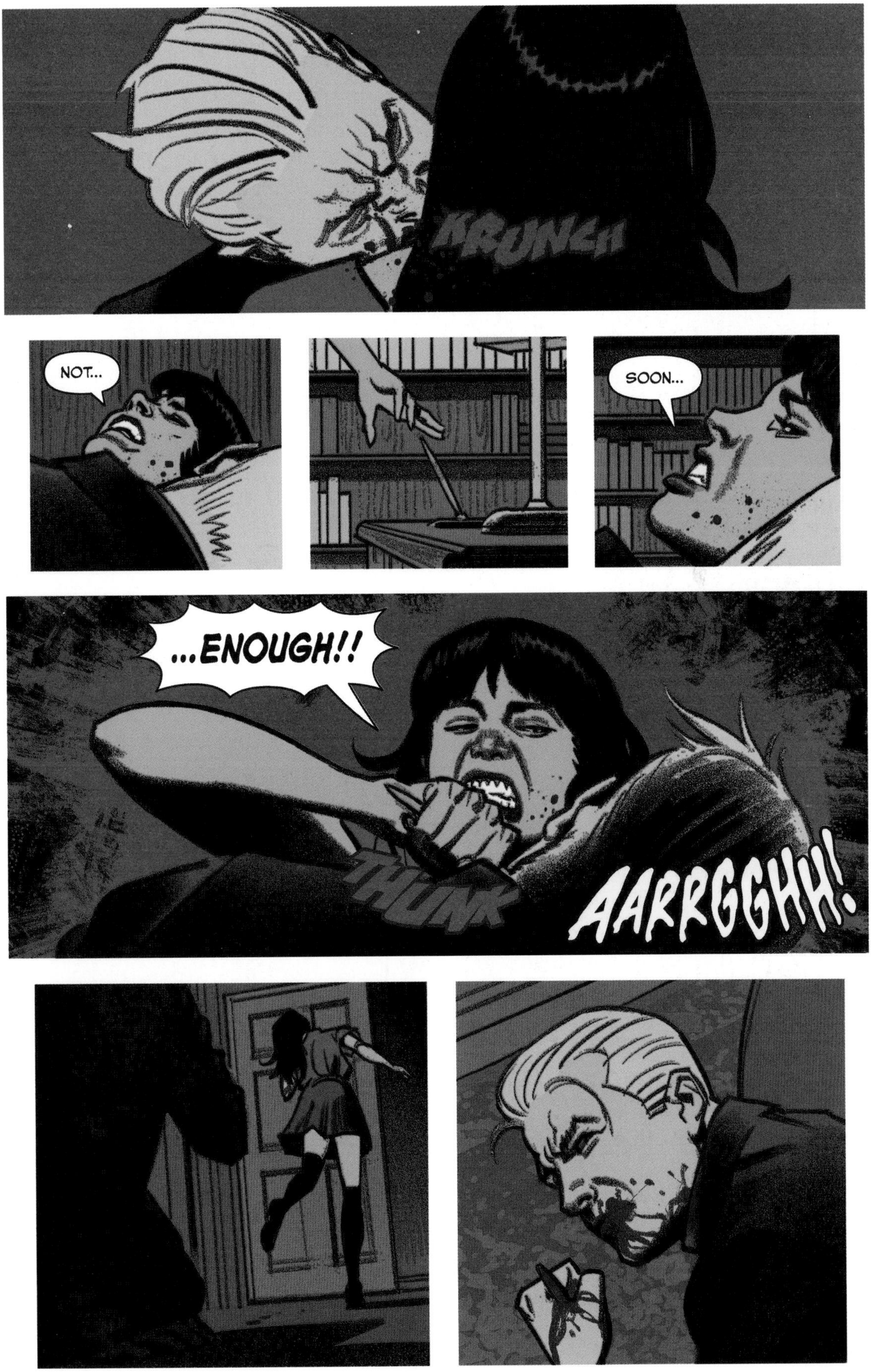
KRUNCH
NOT...
SOON...
...ENOUGH!!
THUNK
AARRGGHH!

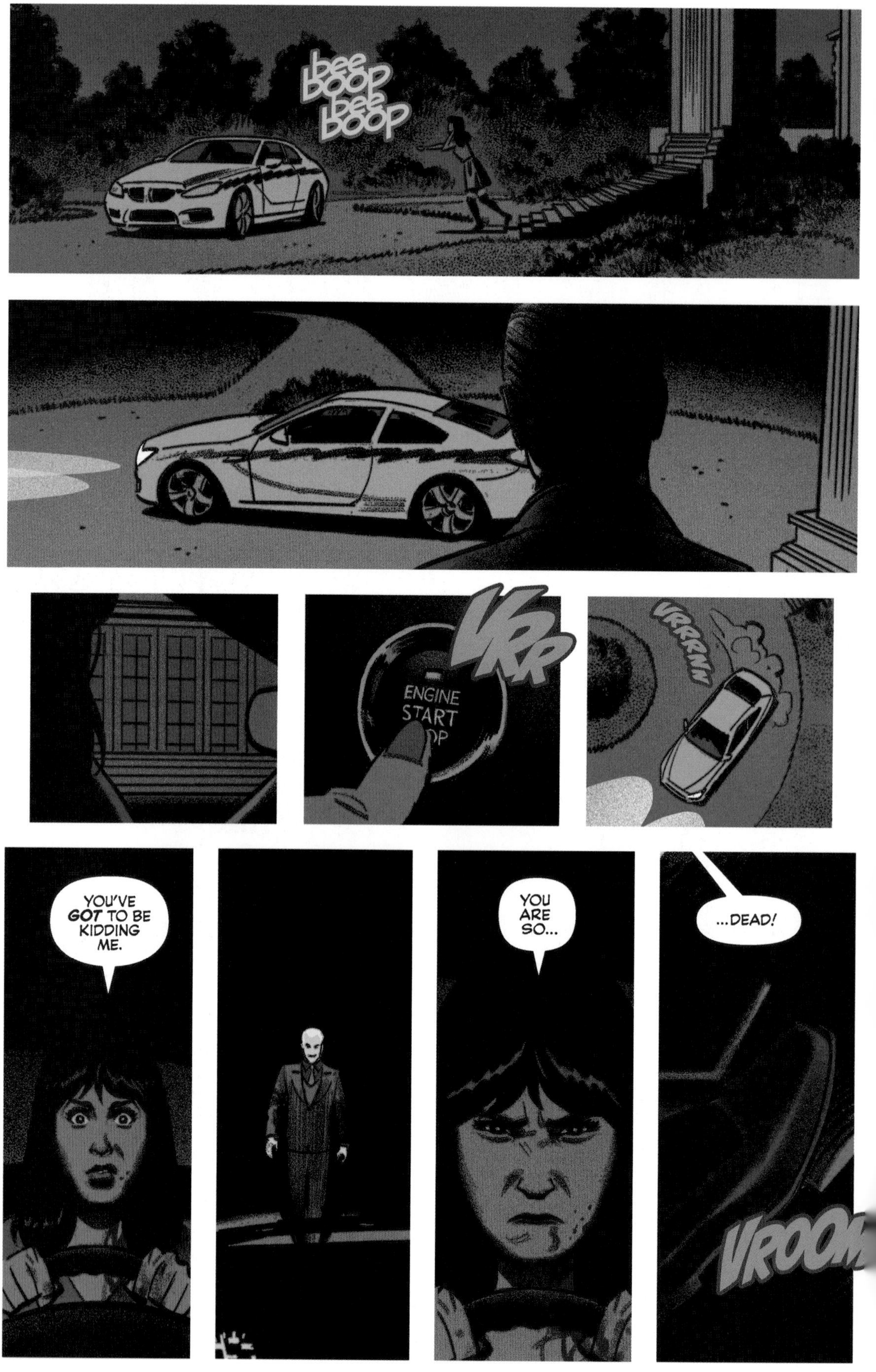
bee boop bee boop
VRR
ENGINE START
VRRRNN
YOU'VE GOT TO BE KIDDING ME.
YOU ARE SO...
...DEAD!
VROOM

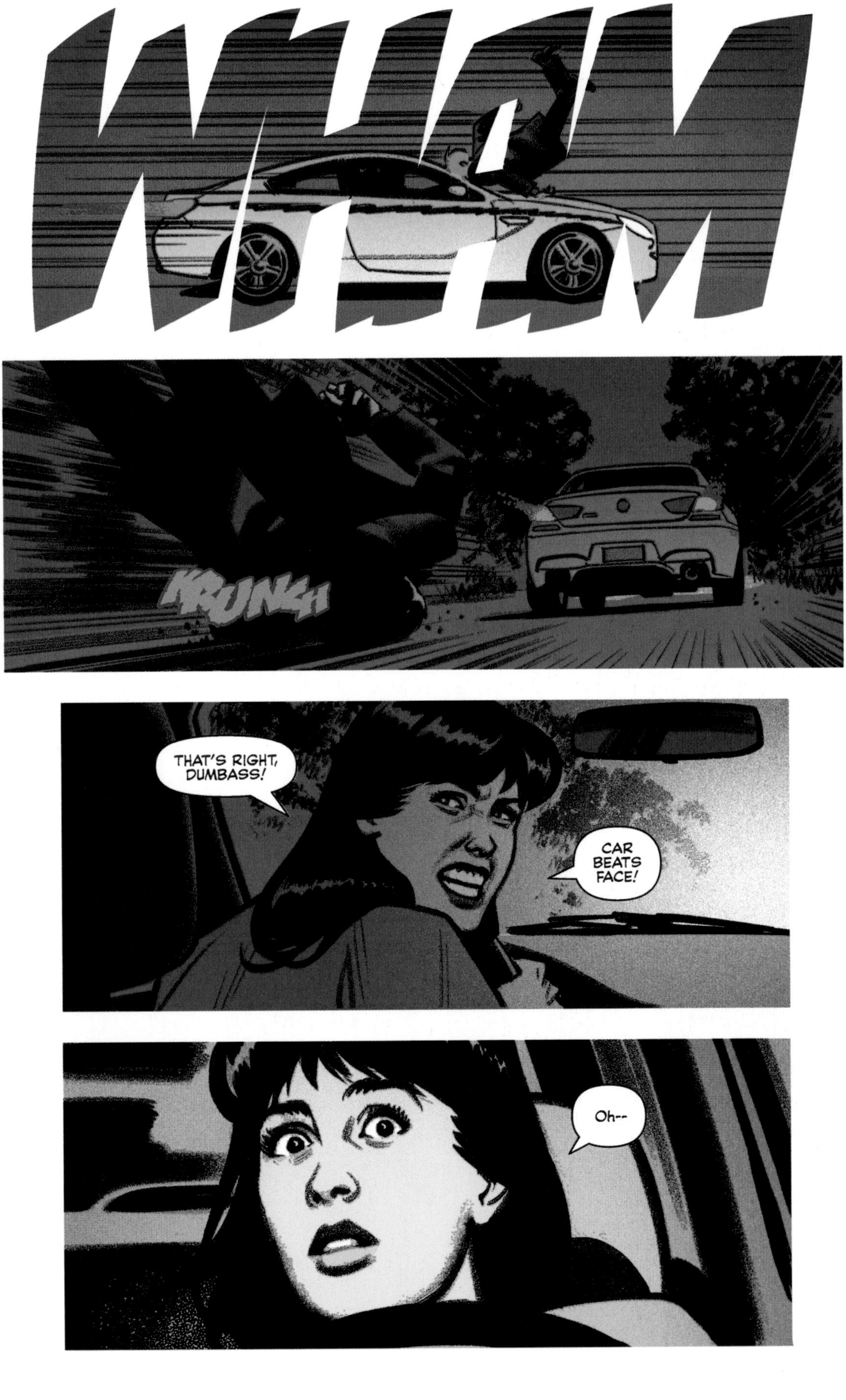
WHAM
KRUNCH
THAT'S RIGHT, DUMBASS!
CAR BEATS FACE!
Oh--

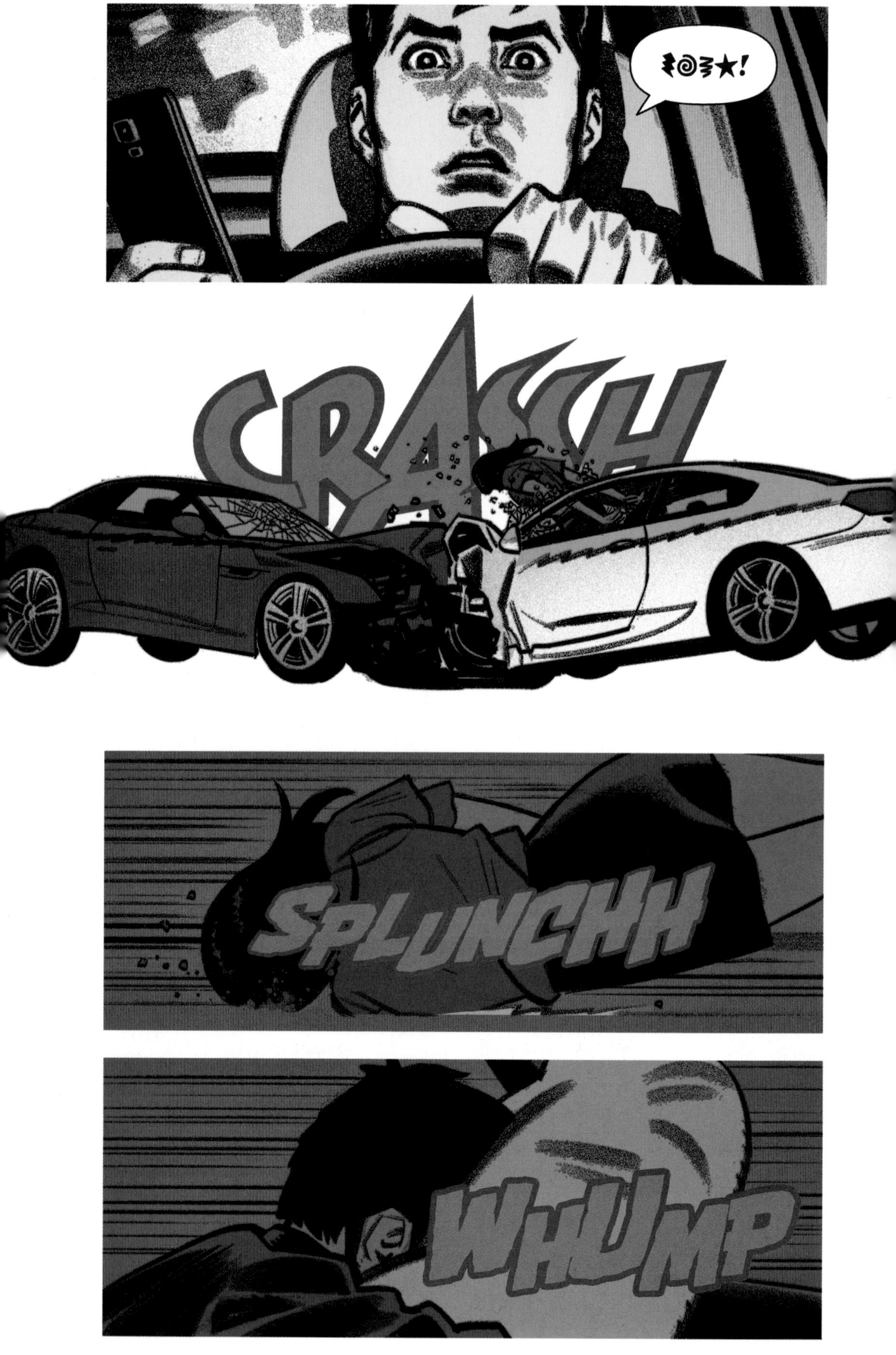
CRASH
SPLUNCHH
WHUMP

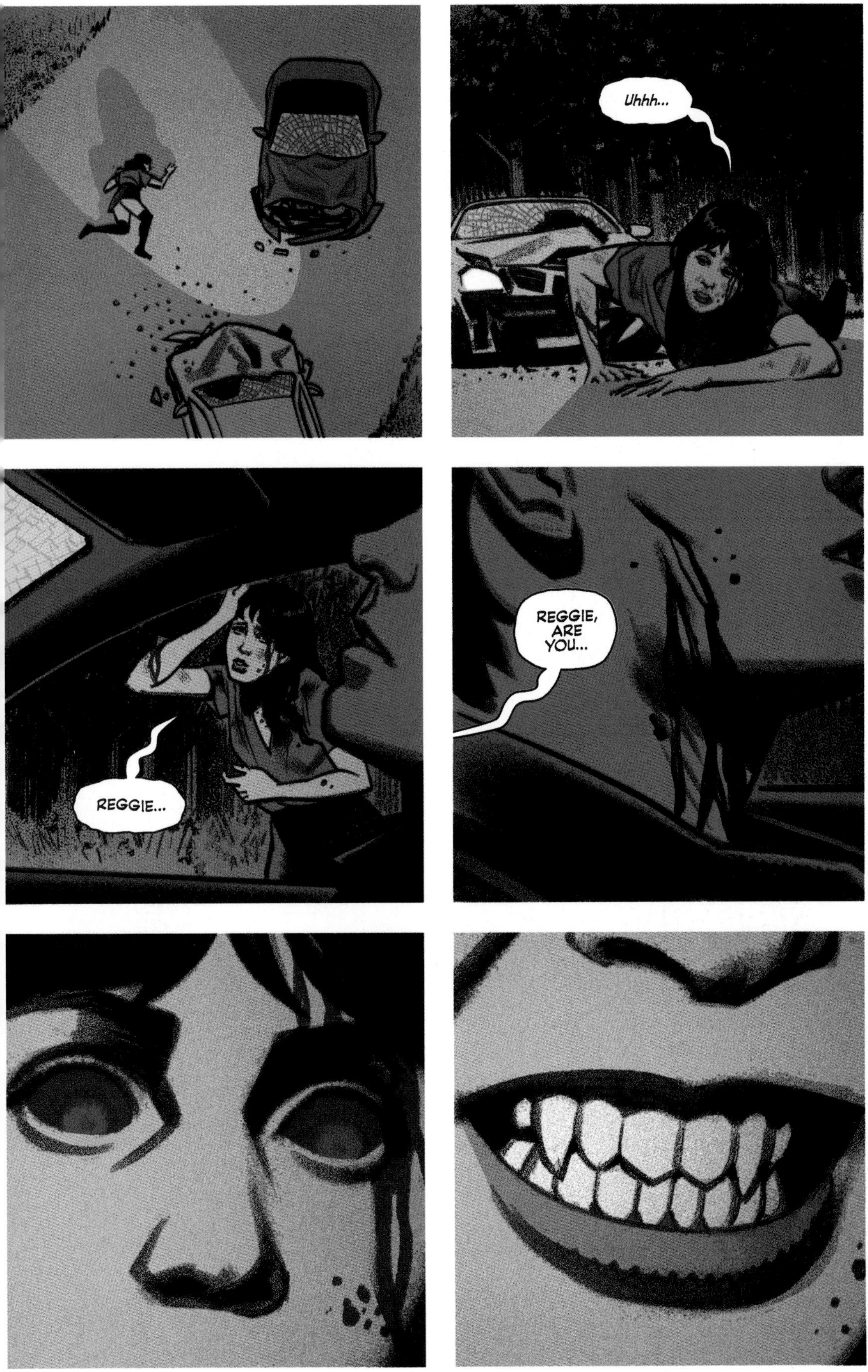
Uhhh...
REGGIE...
REGGIE, ARE YOU...

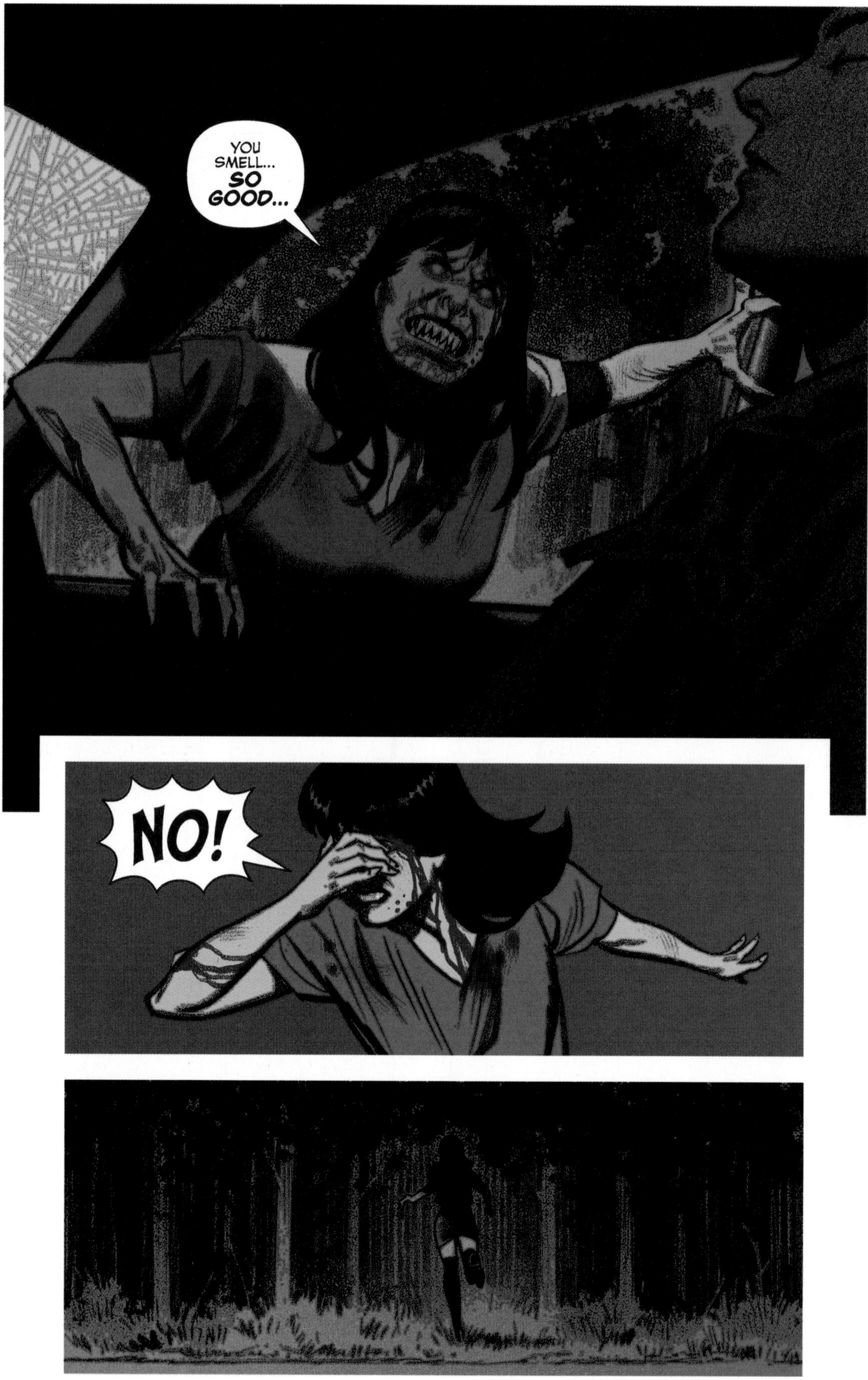

YOU SMELL... SO GOOD...
NO!

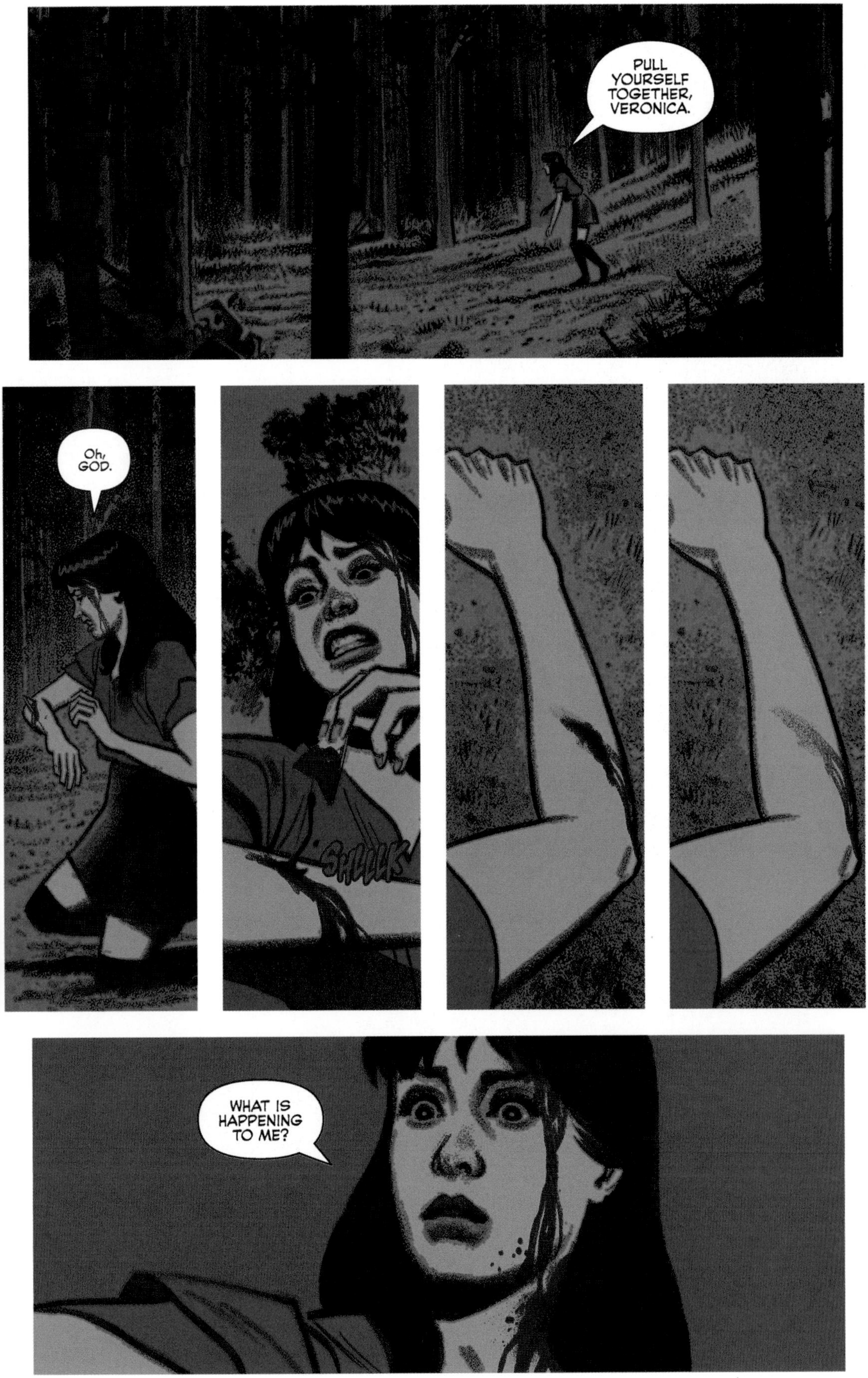
PULL YOURSELF TOGETHER, VERONICA.
Oh, GOD.
WHAT IS HAPPENING TO ME?

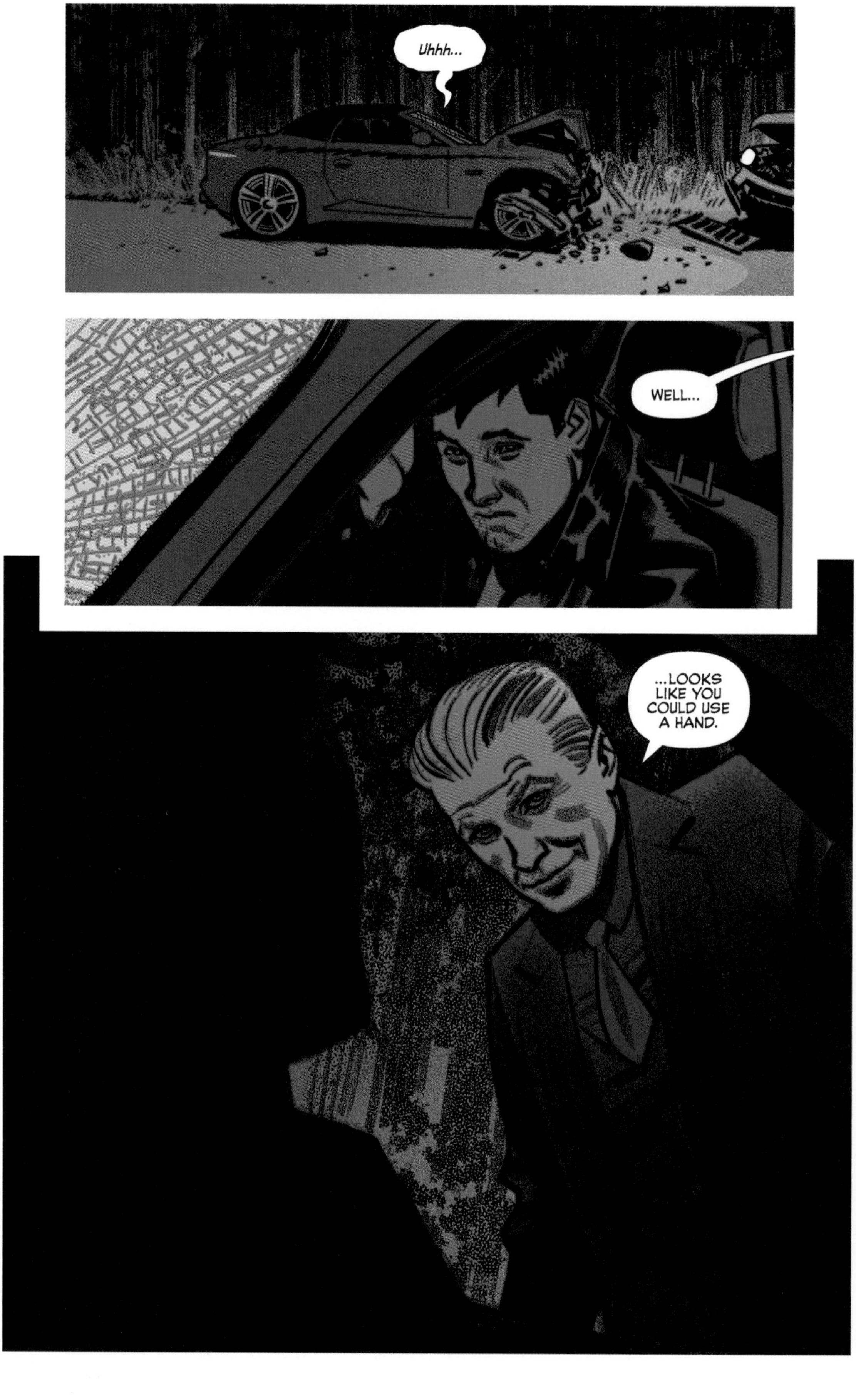
Uhhh...
WELL...
...LOOKS LIKE YOU COULD USE A HAND.

TO BE CONTINUED

CHAPTER TWO

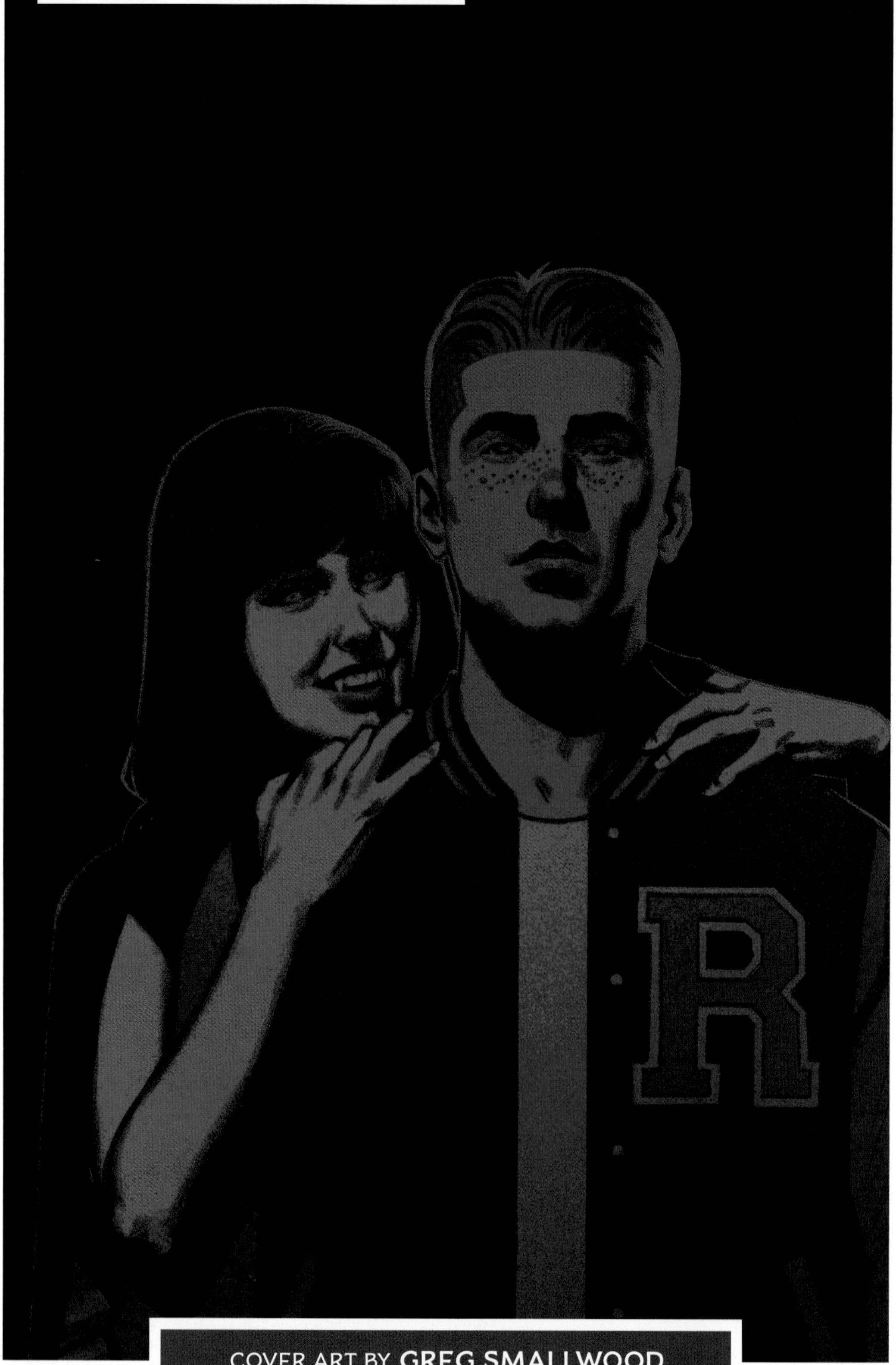

COVER ART BY **GREG SMALLWOOD**

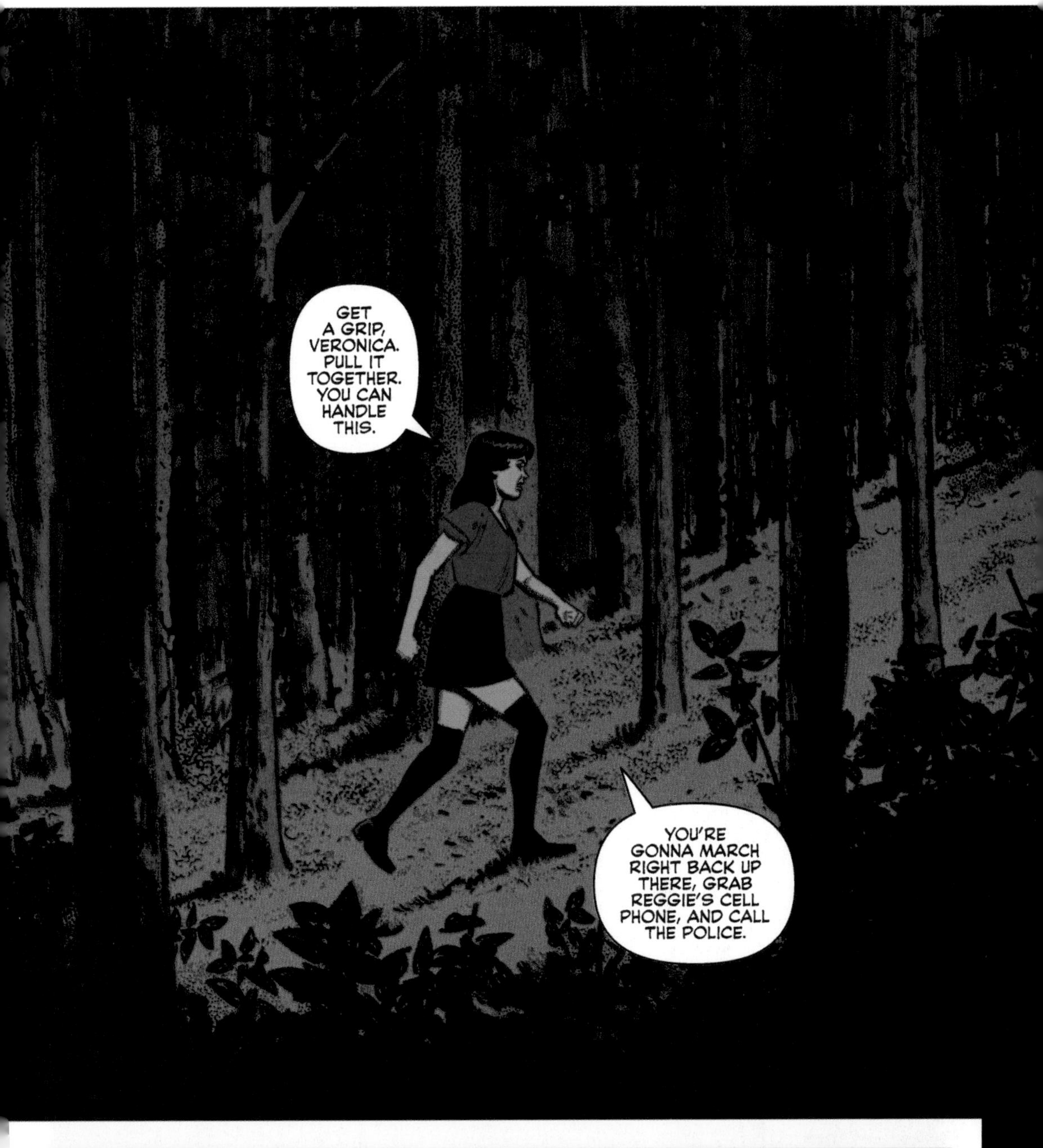
GET A GRIP, VERONICA. PULL IT TOGETHER. YOU CAN HANDLE THIS.
YOU'RE GONNA MARCH RIGHT BACK UP THERE, GRAB REGGIE'S CELL PHONE, AND CALL THE POLICE.

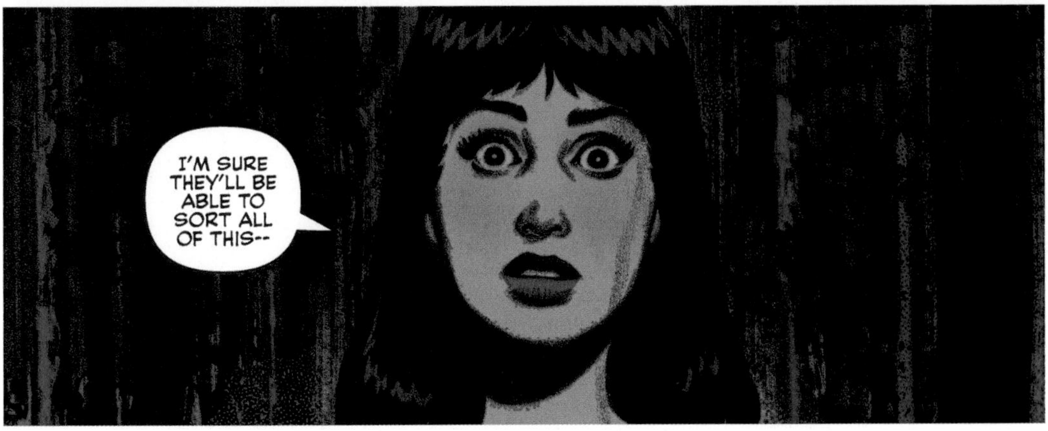
I'M SURE THEY'LL BE ABLE TO SORT ALL OF THIS--

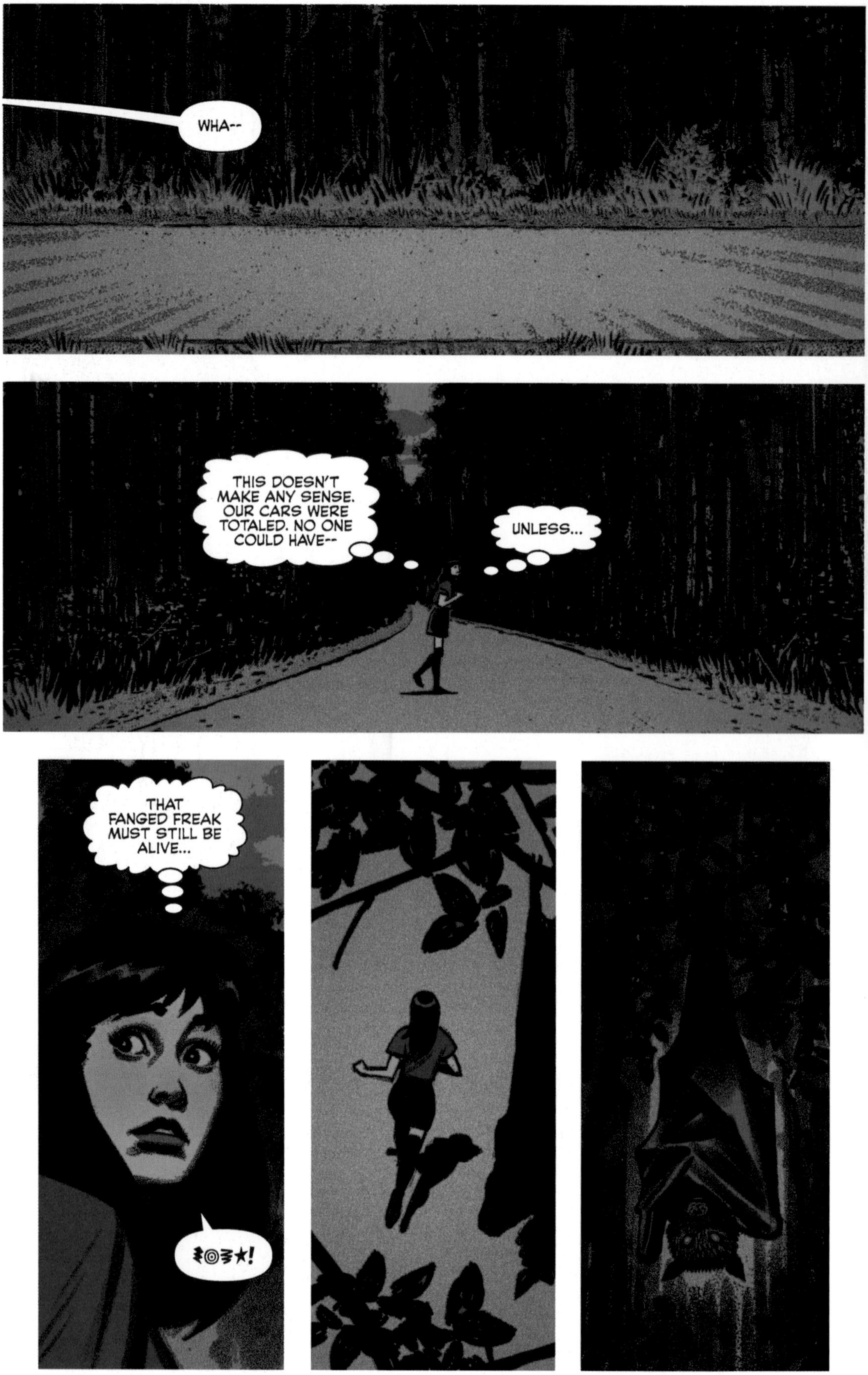
WHA--
THIS DOESN'T MAKE ANY SENSE. OUR CARS WERE TOTALED. NO ONE COULD HAVE--
UNLESS...
THAT FANGED FREAK MUST STILL BE ALIVE...

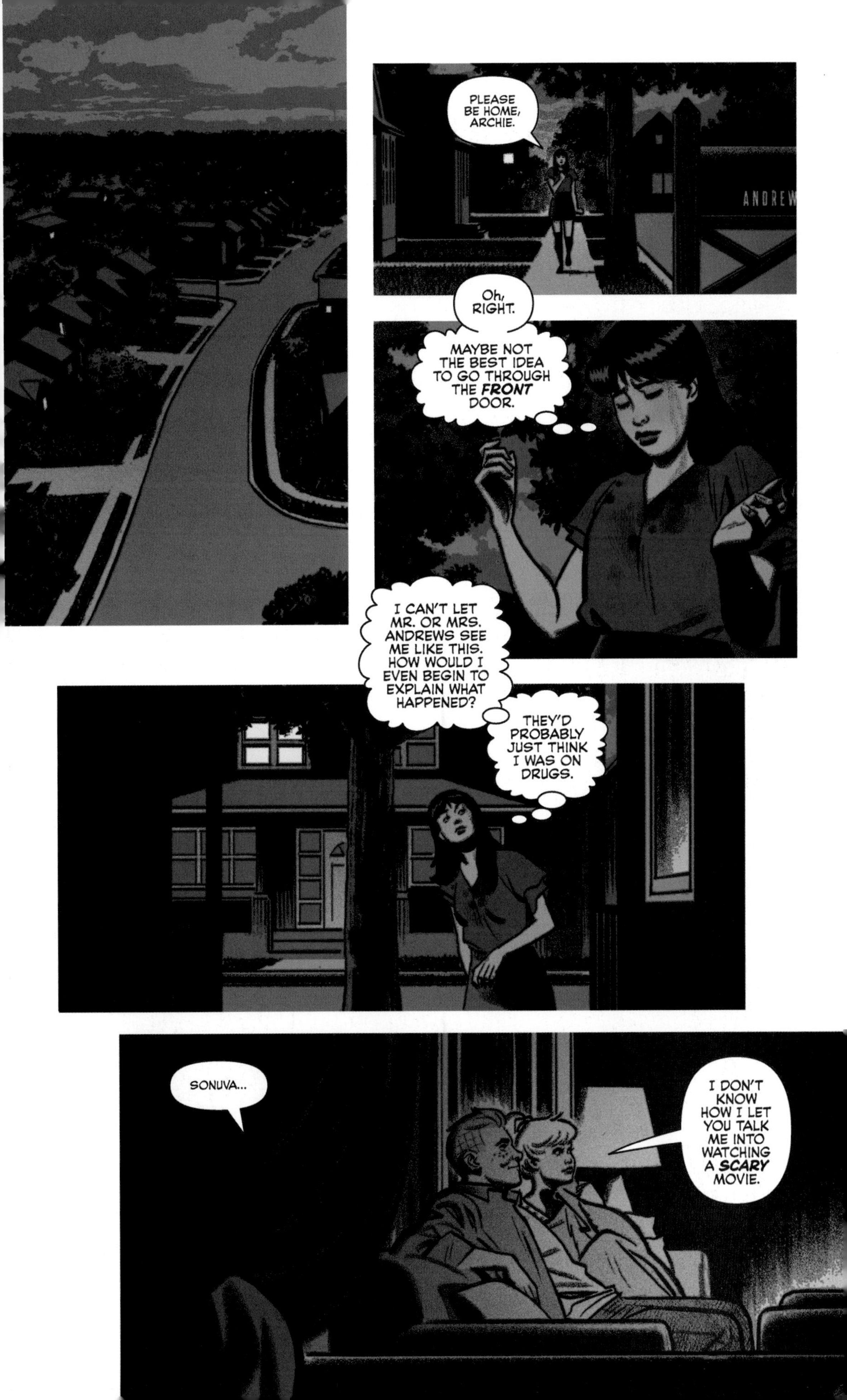
PLEASE BE HOME, ARCHIE.
ANDREW
Oh, RIGHT.
MAYBE NOT THE BEST IDEA TO GO THROUGH THE *FRONT* DOOR.
I CAN'T LET MR. OR MRS. ANDREWS SEE ME LIKE THIS. HOW WOULD I EVEN BEGIN TO EXPLAIN WHAT HAPPENED?
THEY'D PROBABLY JUST THINK I WAS ON DRUGS.
SONUVA...
I DON'T KNOW HOW I LET YOU TALK ME INTO WATCHING A *SCARY* MOVIE.

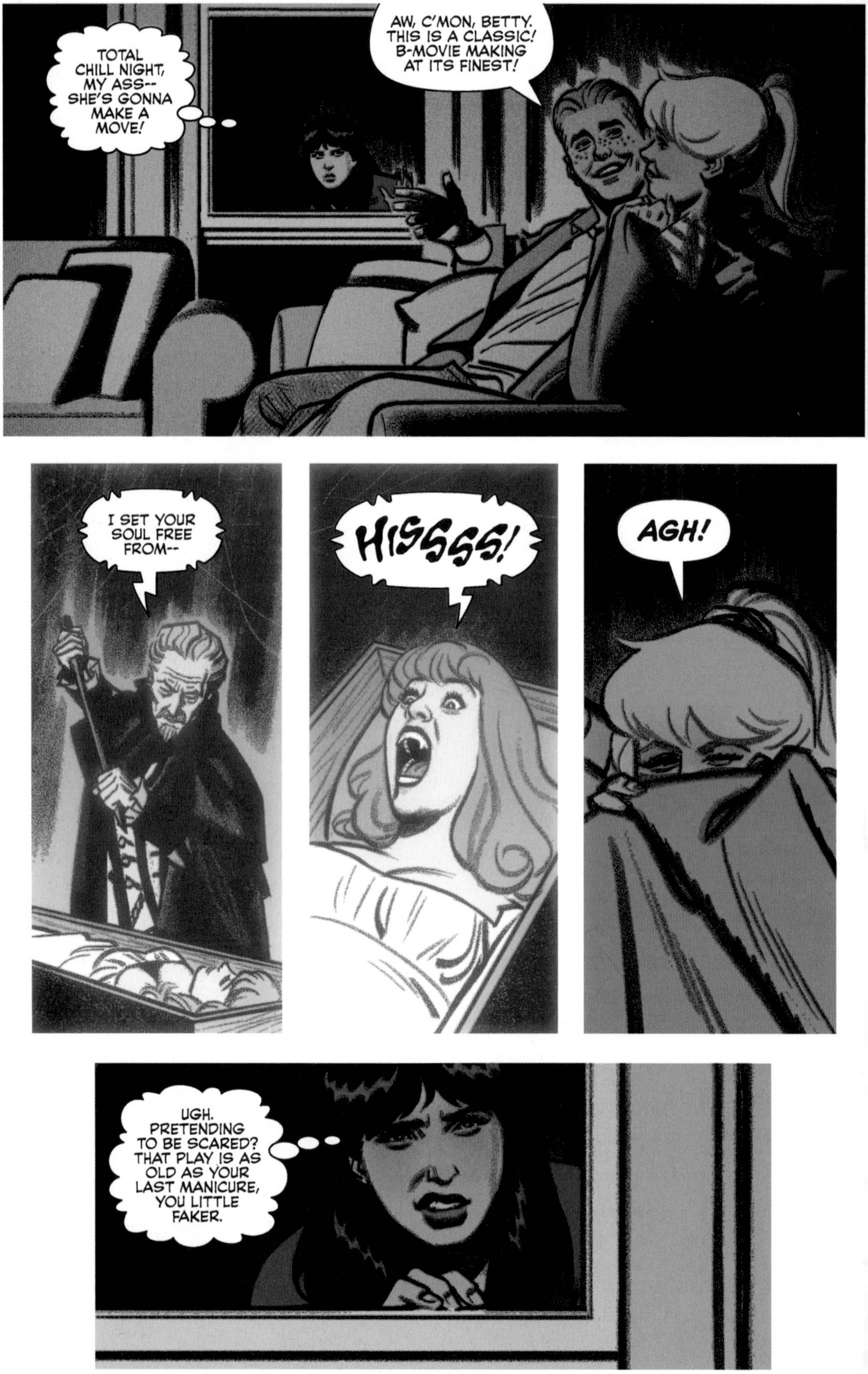
TOTAL CHILL NIGHT, MY ASS-- SHE'S GONNA MAKE A MOVE!
AW, C'MON, BETTY. THIS IS A CLASSIC! B-MOVIE MAKING AT ITS FINEST!
I SET YOUR SOUL FREE FROM--
HISSSS!
AGH!
UGH. PRETENDING TO BE SCARED? THAT PLAY IS AS OLD AS YOUR LAST MANICURE, YOU LITTLE FAKER.

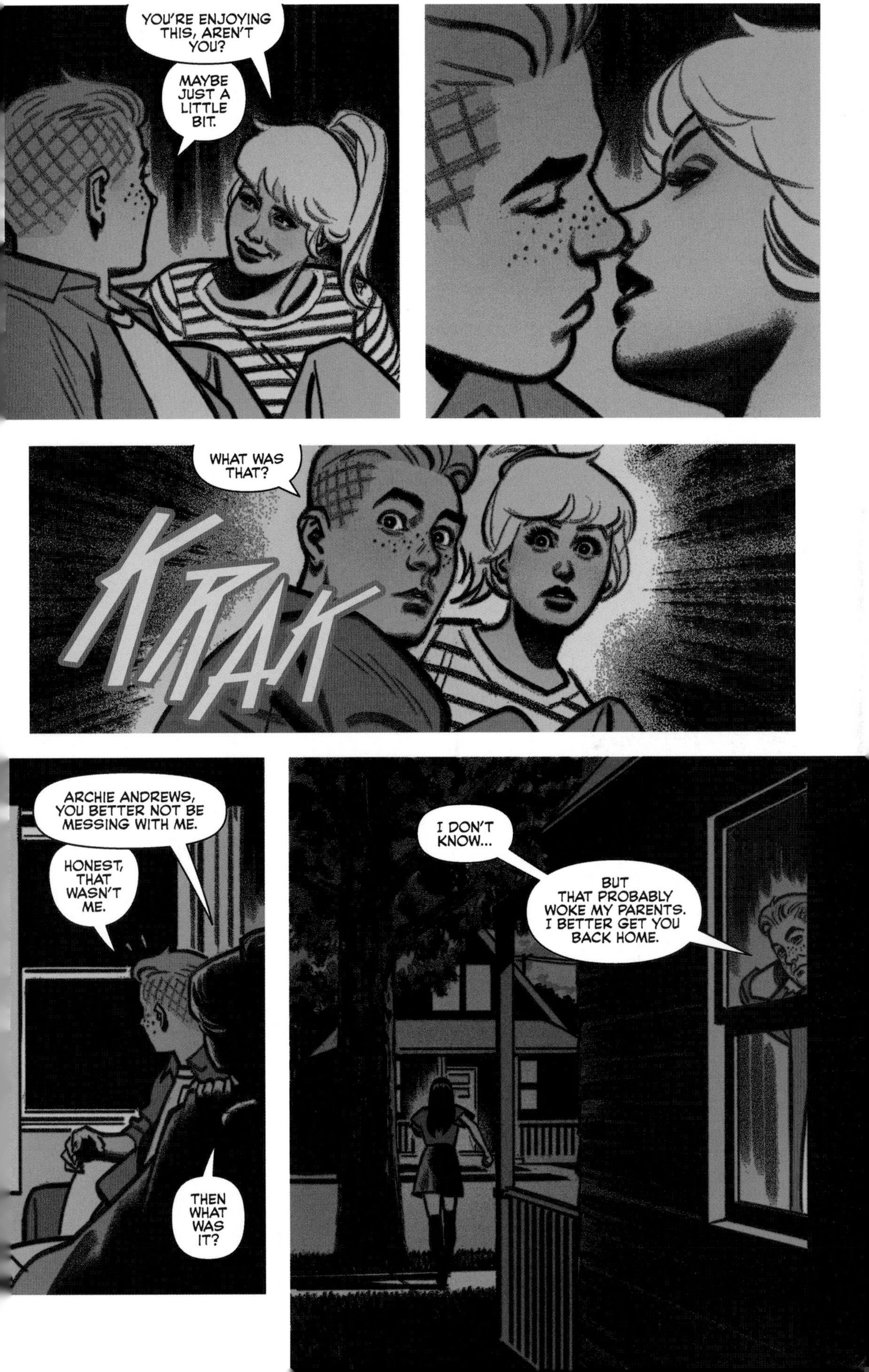
YOU'RE ENJOYING THIS, AREN'T YOU?
MAYBE JUST A LITTLE BIT.
WHAT WAS THAT?
KRAK
ARCHIE ANDREWS, YOU BETTER NOT BE MESSING WITH ME.
HONEST, THAT WASN'T ME.
THEN WHAT WAS IT?
I DON'T KNOW...
BUT THAT PROBABLY WOKE MY PARENTS. I BETTER GET YOU BACK HOME.

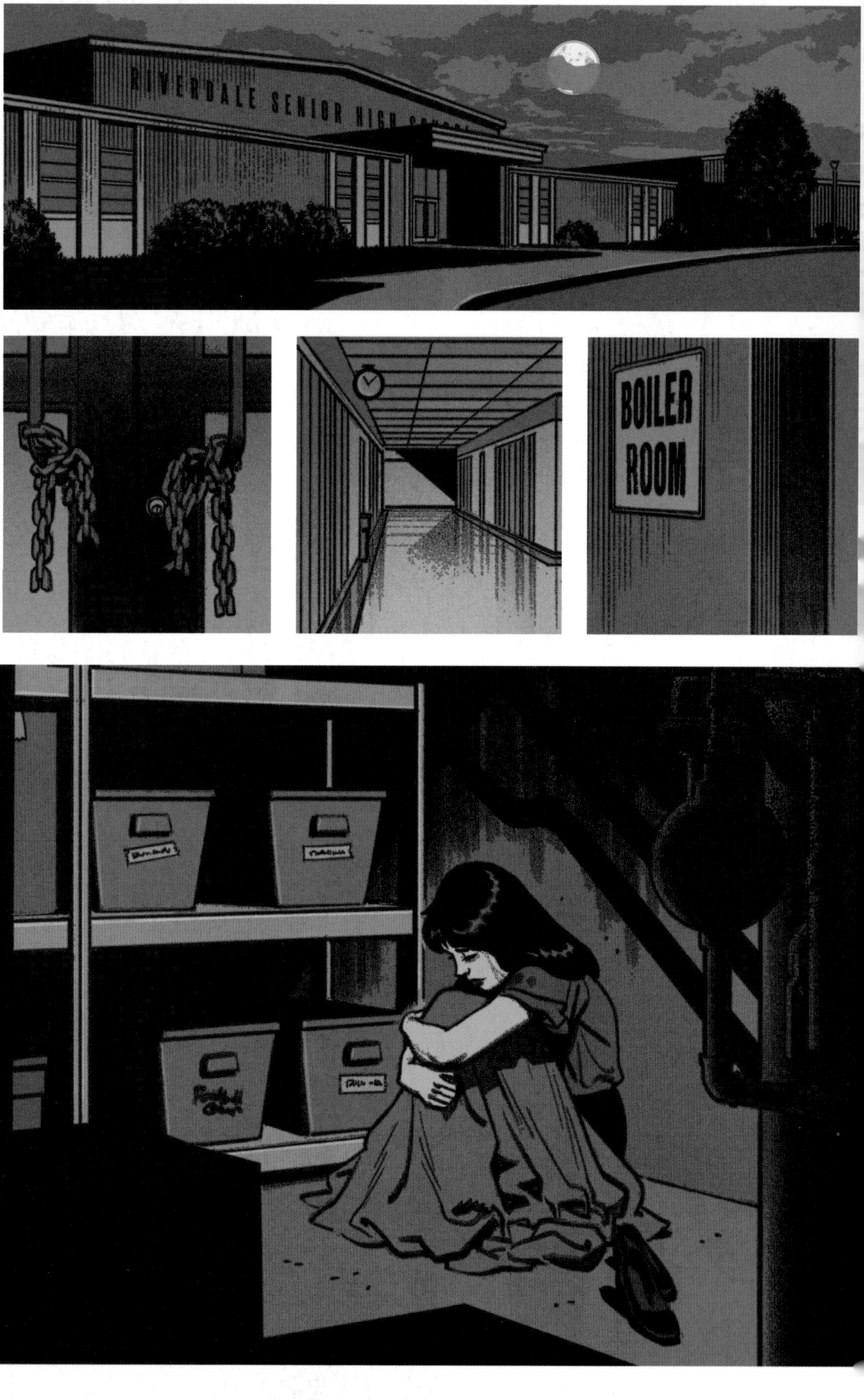
RIVERDALE SENIOR HIGH
BOILER ROOM

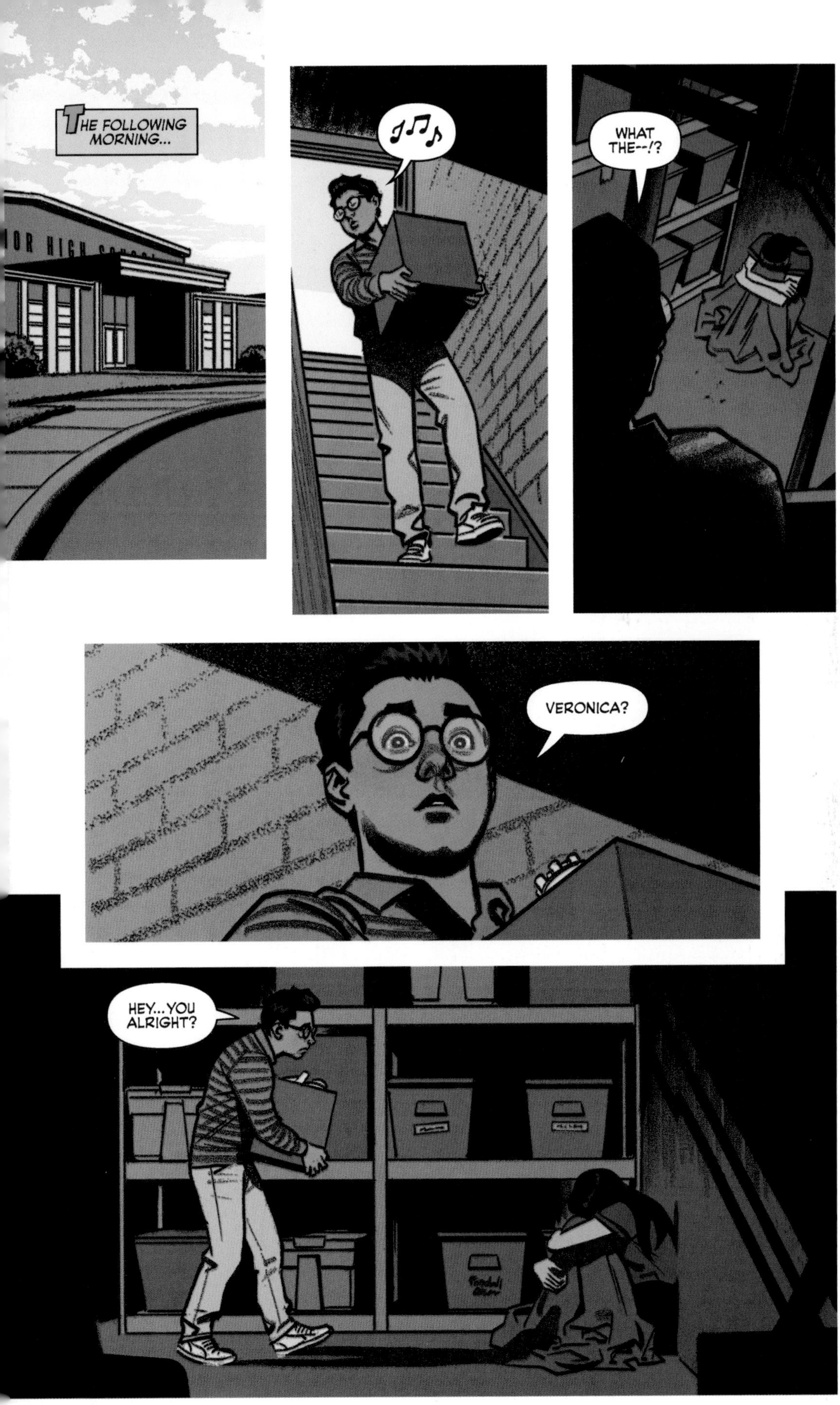
THE FOLLOWING MORNING...
♪♫♪
WHAT THE--!?
VERONICA?
HEY...YOU ALRIGHT?

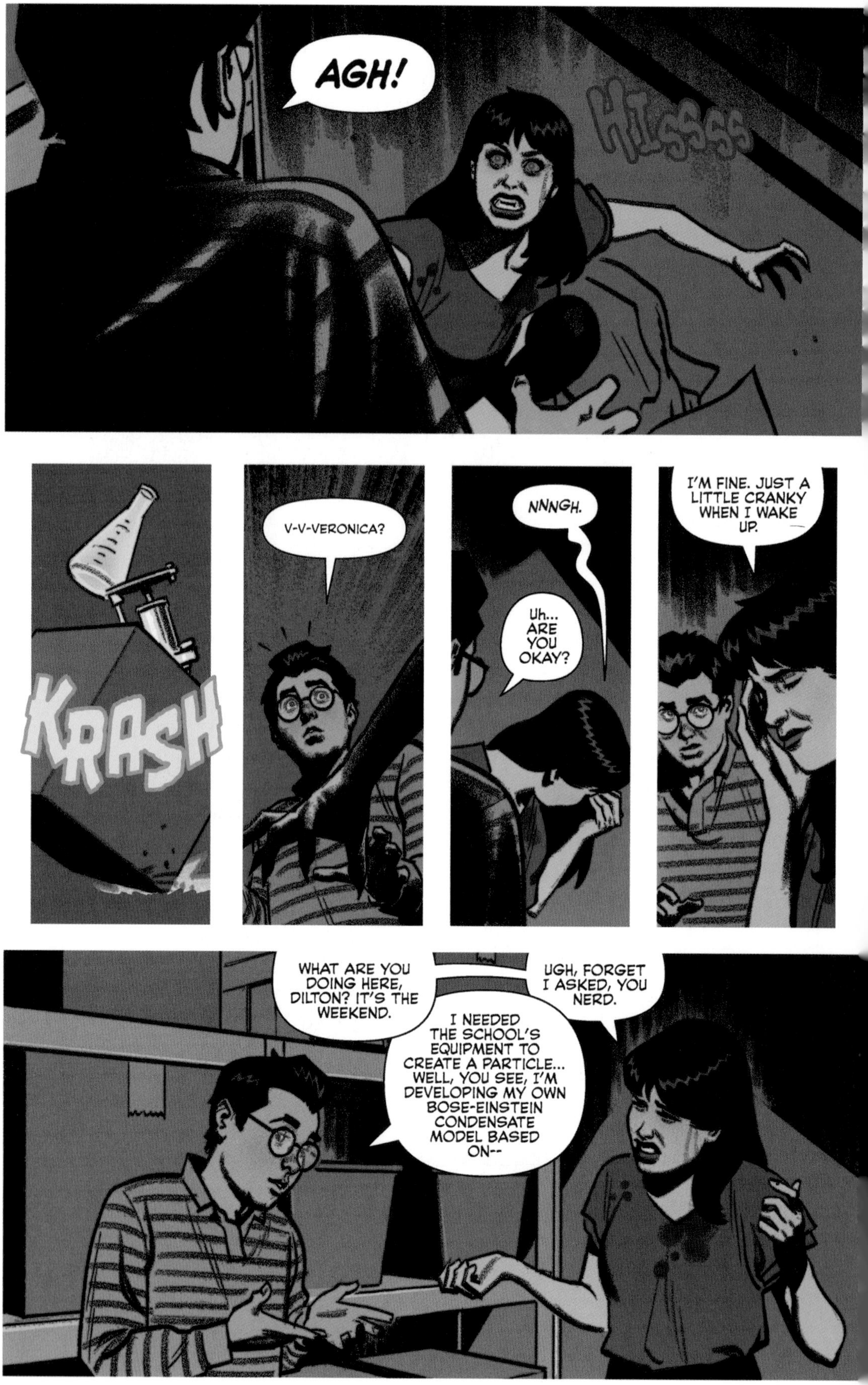
AGH!
HISSSS
KRASH
V-V-VERONICA?
NNNGH.
Uh... ARE YOU OKAY?
I'M FINE. JUST A LITTLE CRANKY WHEN I WAKE UP.
WHAT ARE YOU DOING HERE, DILTON? IT'S THE WEEKEND.
I NEEDED THE SCHOOL'S EQUIPMENT TO CREATE A PARTICLE... WELL, YOU SEE, I'M DEVELOPING MY OWN BOSE-EINSTEIN CONDENSATE MODEL BASED ON--
UGH, FORGET I ASKED, YOU NERD.

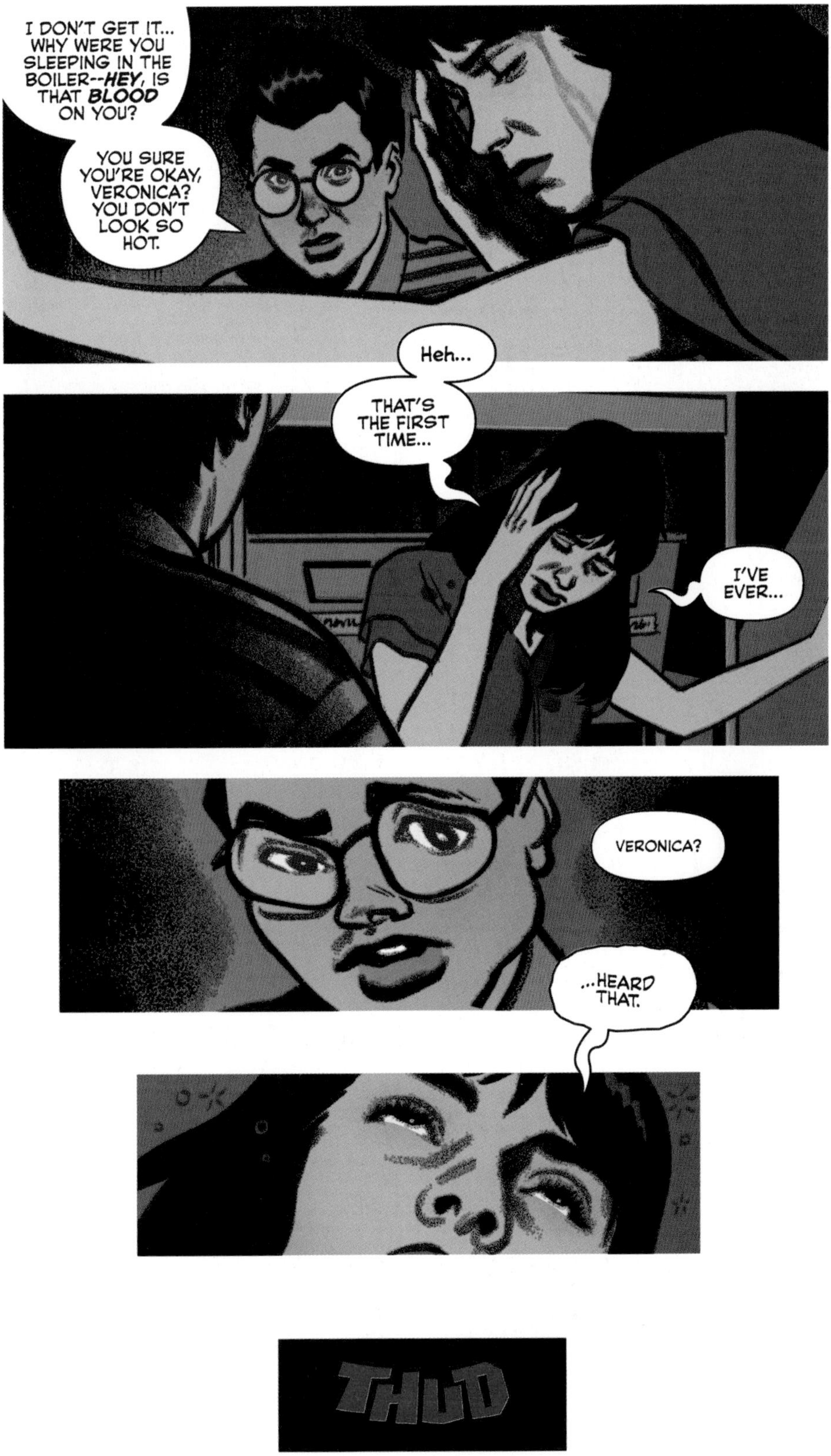
I DON'T GET IT... WHY WERE YOU SLEEPING IN THE BOILER--*HEY*, IS THAT *BLOOD* ON YOU?
YOU SURE YOU'RE OKAY, VERONICA? YOU DON'T LOOK SO HOT.
Heh...
THAT'S THE FIRST TIME...
I'VE EVER...
VERONICA?
...HEARD THAT.
THUD

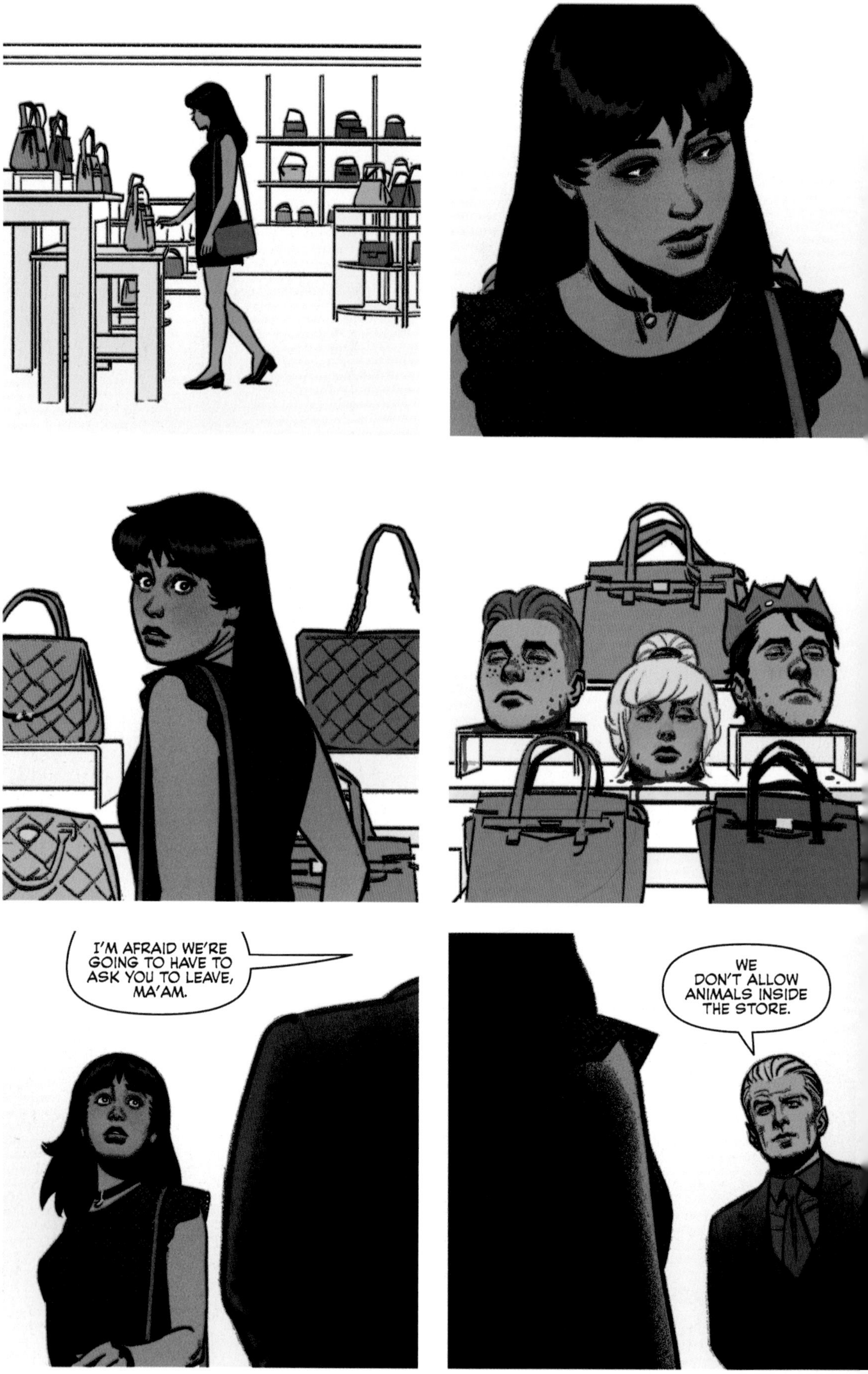
I'M AFRAID WE'RE GOING TO HAVE TO ASK YOU TO LEAVE, MA'AM.
WE DON'T ALLOW ANIMALS INSIDE THE STORE.

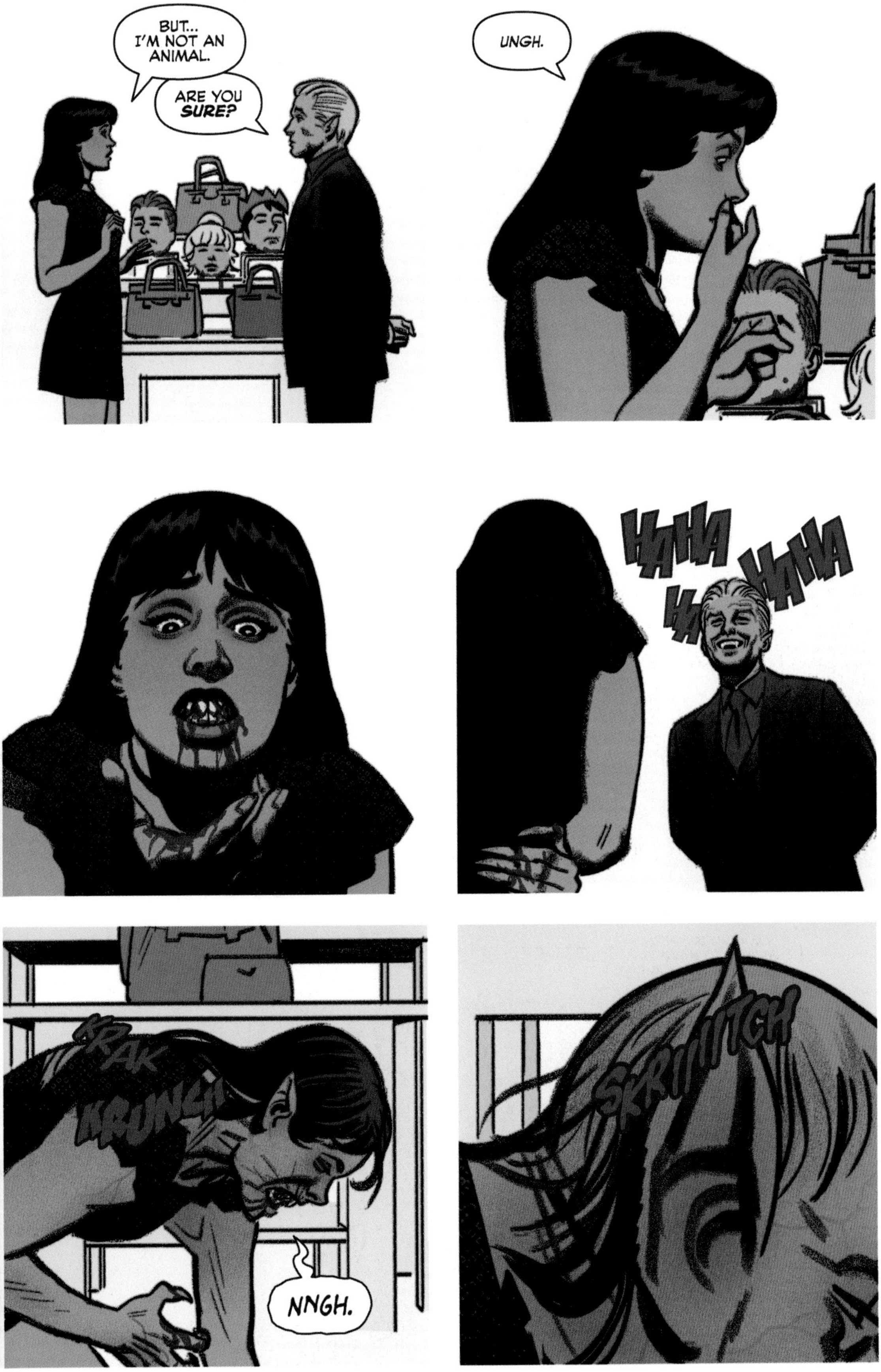
BUT... I'M NOT AN ANIMAL.
ARE YOU SURE?
UNGH.
HAHA
HA
HAHA
KRAK
KRUNCH
NNGH.
SKRIIIITCH

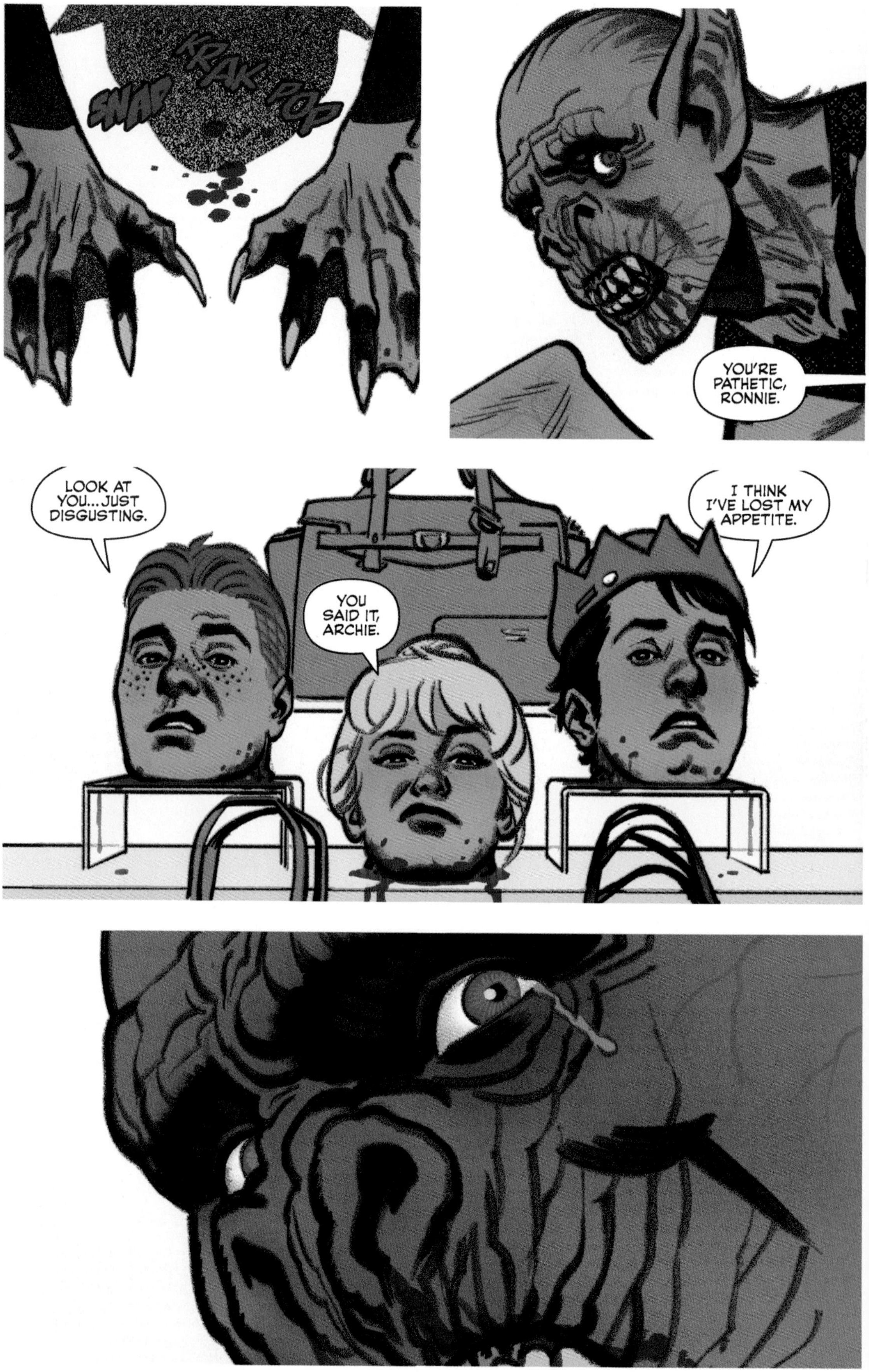
SNAP
KRAK
POP
YOU'RE PATHETIC, RONNIE.
LOOK AT YOU...JUST DISGUSTING.
YOU SAID IT, ARCHIE.
I THINK I'VE LOST MY APPETITE.

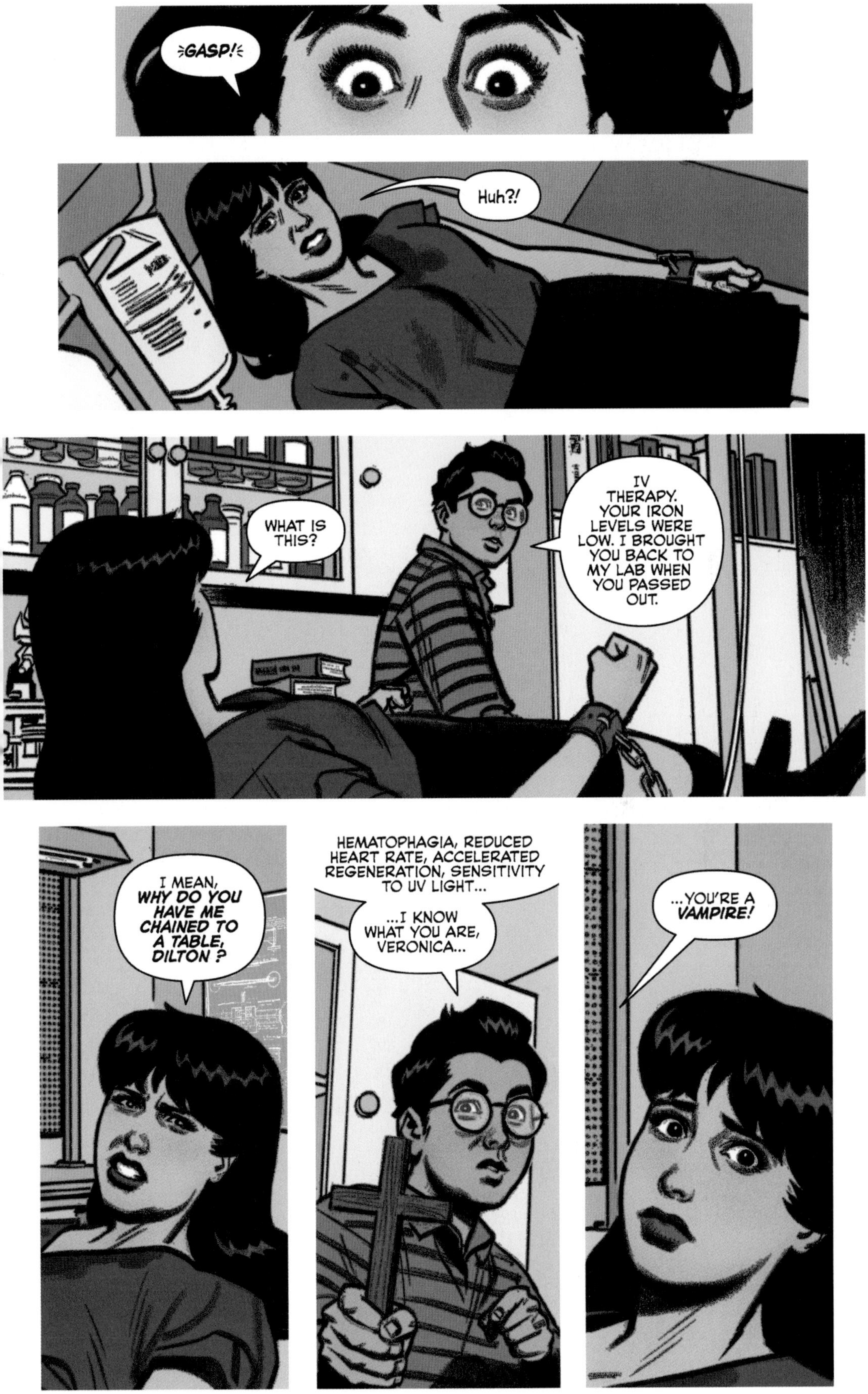
GASP!
Huh?!
WHAT IS THIS?
IV THERAPY. YOUR IRON LEVELS WERE LOW. I BROUGHT YOU BACK TO MY LAB WHEN YOU PASSED OUT.
I MEAN, WHY DO YOU HAVE ME CHAINED TO A TABLE, DILTON ?
HEMATOPHAGIA, REDUCED HEART RATE, ACCELERATED REGENERATION, SENSITIVITY TO UV LIGHT...
...I KNOW WHAT YOU ARE, VERONICA...
...YOU'RE A VAMPIRE!

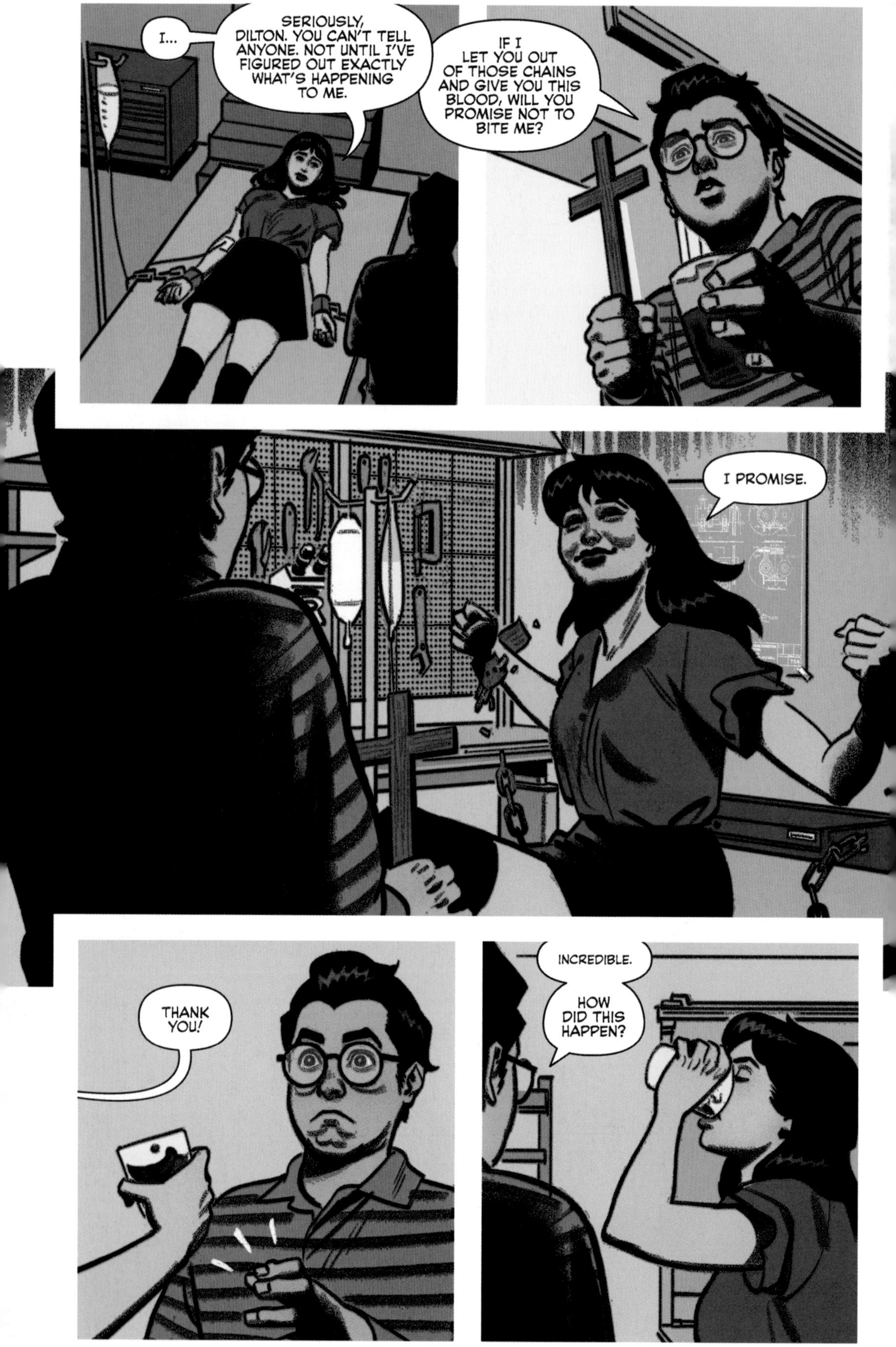
I...
SERIOUSLY, DILTON. YOU CAN'T TELL ANYONE. NOT UNTIL I'VE FIGURED OUT EXACTLY WHAT'S HAPPENING TO ME.
IF I LET YOU OUT OF THOSE CHAINS AND GIVE YOU THIS BLOOD, WILL YOU PROMISE NOT TO BITE ME?
I PROMISE.
THANK YOU!
INCREDIBLE.
HOW DID THIS HAPPEN?

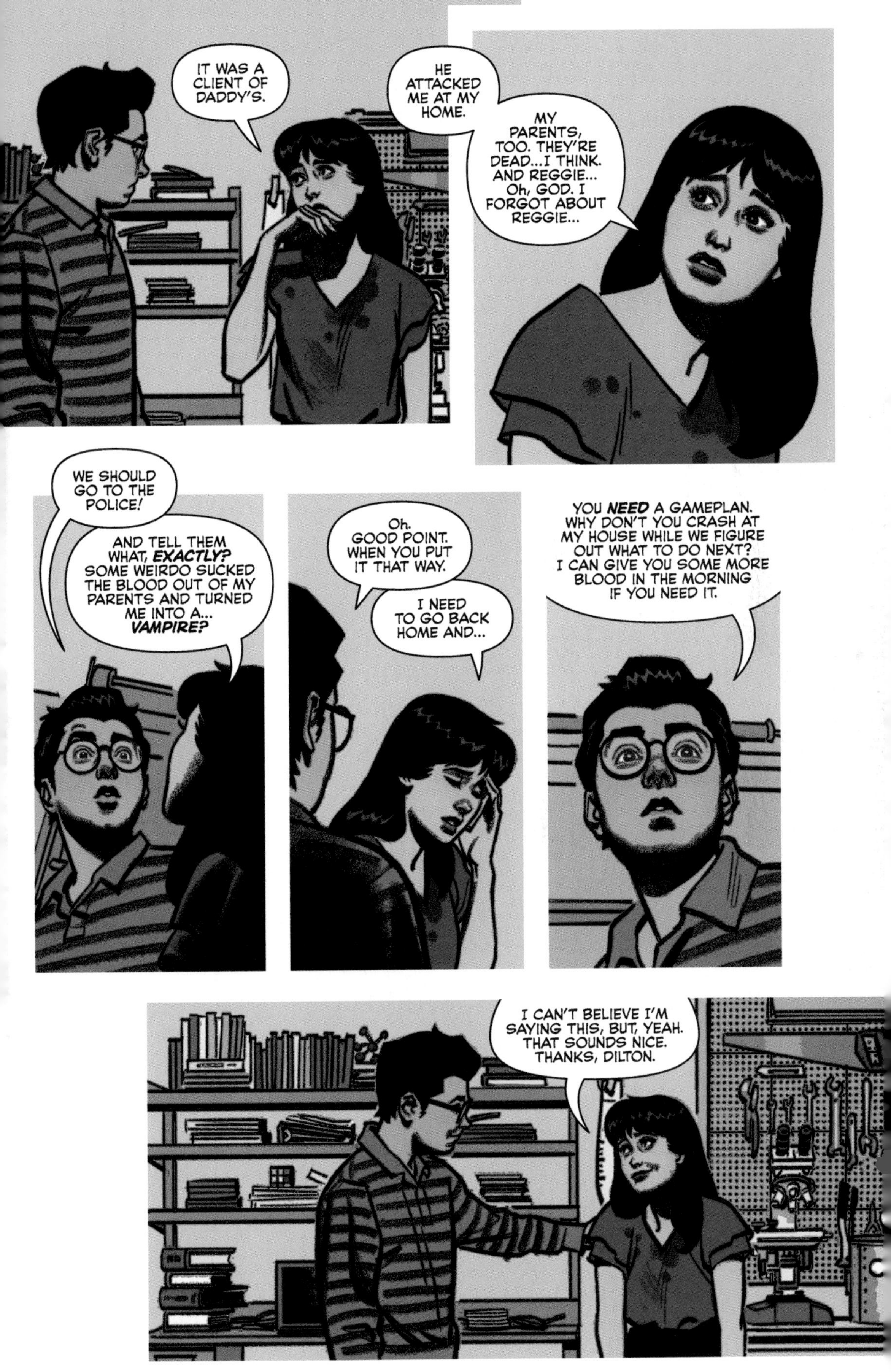
IT WAS A CLIENT OF DADDY'S.
HE ATTACKED ME AT MY HOME.
MY PARENTS, TOO. THEY'RE DEAD...I THINK. AND REGGIE... Oh, GOD. I FORGOT ABOUT REGGIE...
WE SHOULD GO TO THE POLICE!
AND TELL THEM WHAT, EXACTLY? SOME WEIRDO SUCKED THE BLOOD OUT OF MY PARENTS AND TURNED ME INTO A... VAMPIRE?
Oh. GOOD POINT. WHEN YOU PUT IT THAT WAY.
I NEED TO GO BACK HOME AND...
YOU NEED A GAMEPLAN. WHY DON'T YOU CRASH AT MY HOUSE WHILE WE FIGURE OUT WHAT TO DO NEXT? I CAN GIVE YOU SOME MORE BLOOD IN THE MORNING IF YOU NEED IT.
I CAN'T BELIEVE I'M SAYING THIS, BUT, YEAH. THAT SOUNDS NICE. THANKS, DILTON.

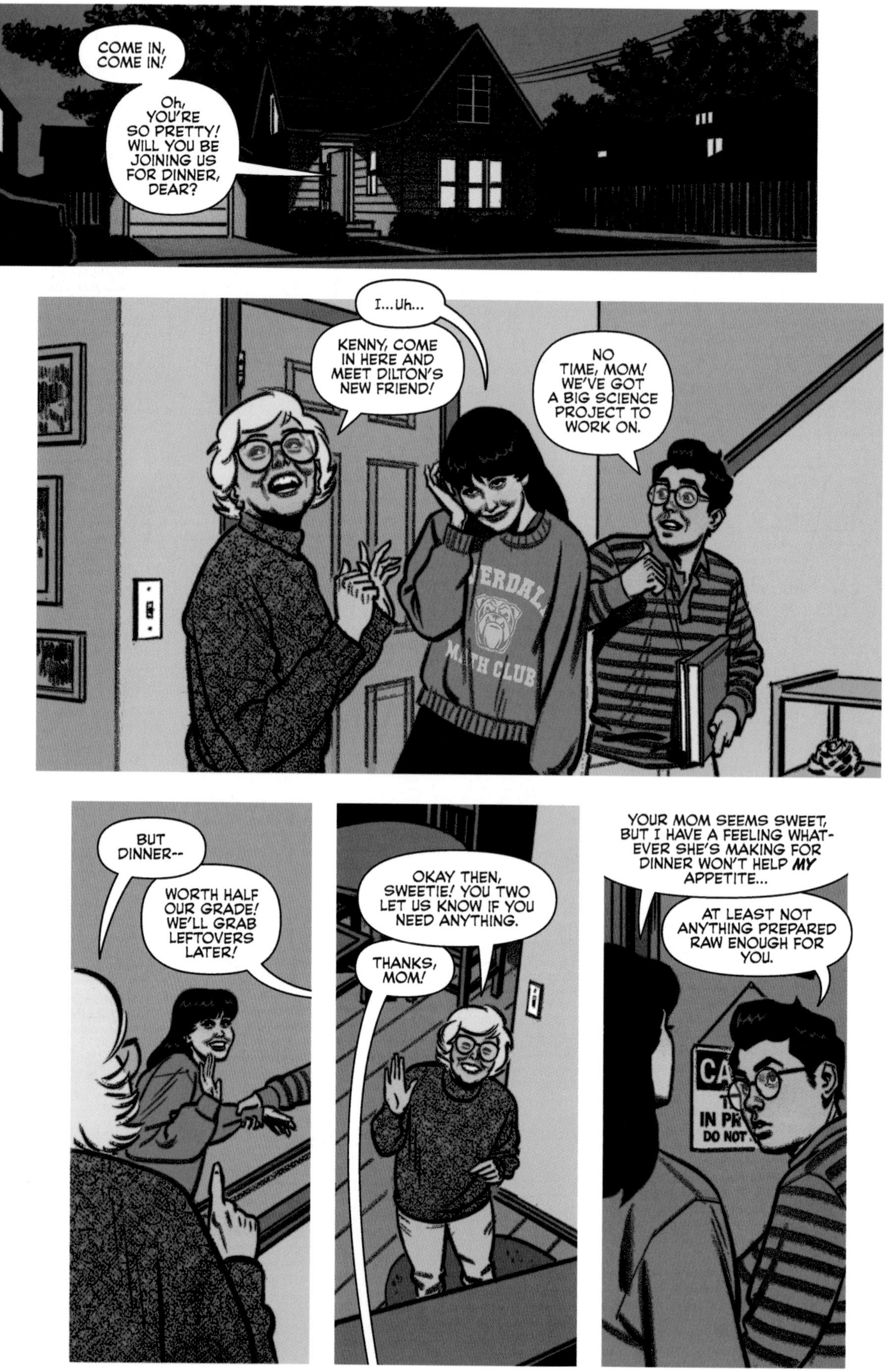
COME IN, COME IN!
Oh, YOU'RE SO PRETTY! WILL YOU BE JOINING US FOR DINNER, DEAR?
I...Uh...
KENNY, COME IN HERE AND MEET DILTON'S NEW FRIEND!
NO TIME, MOM! WE'VE GOT A BIG SCIENCE PROJECT TO WORK ON.
BUT DINNER--
WORTH HALF OUR GRADE! WE'LL GRAB LEFTOVERS LATER!
OKAY THEN, SWEETIE! YOU TWO LET US KNOW IF YOU NEED ANYTHING.
THANKS, MOM!
YOUR MOM SEEMS SWEET, BUT I HAVE A FEELING WHAT-EVER SHE'S MAKING FOR DINNER WON'T HELP *MY* APPETITE...
AT LEAST NOT ANYTHING PREPARED RAW ENOUGH FOR YOU.

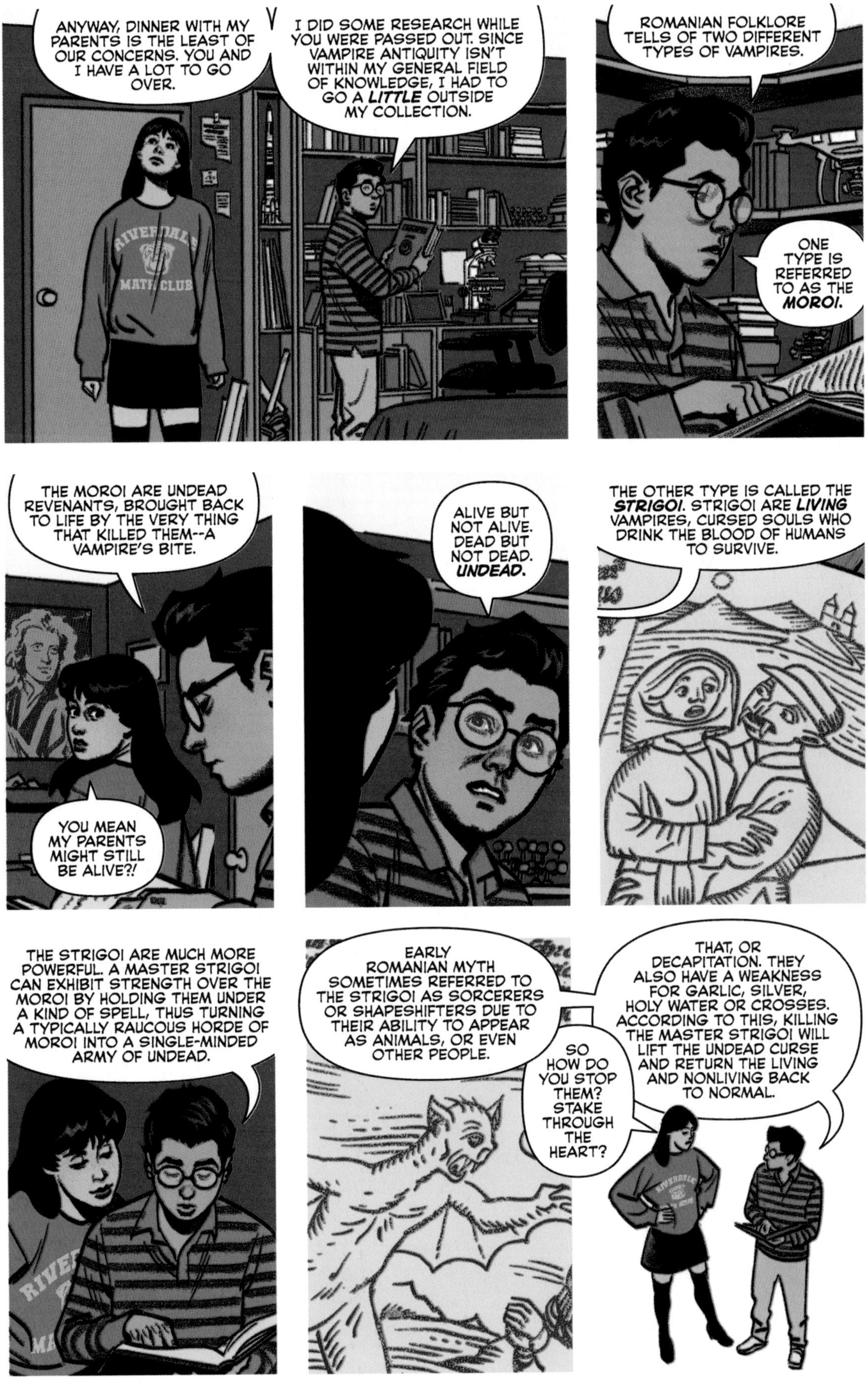

ANYWAY, DINNER WITH MY PARENTS IS THE LEAST OF OUR CONCERNS. YOU AND I HAVE A LOT TO GO OVER.
I DID SOME RESEARCH WHILE YOU WERE PASSED OUT. SINCE VAMPIRE ANTIQUITY ISN'T WITHIN MY GENERAL FIELD OF KNOWLEDGE, I HAD TO GO A *LITTLE* OUTSIDE MY COLLECTION.
RIVERDALE MATH CLUB
ROMANIAN FOLKLORE TELLS OF TWO DIFFERENT TYPES OF VAMPIRES.
ONE TYPE IS REFERRED TO AS THE *MOROI.*
THE MOROI ARE UNDEAD REVENANTS, BROUGHT BACK TO LIFE BY THE VERY THING THAT KILLED THEM--A VAMPIRE'S BITE.
YOU MEAN MY PARENTS MIGHT STILL BE ALIVE?!
ALIVE BUT NOT ALIVE. DEAD BUT NOT DEAD. *UNDEAD.*
THE OTHER TYPE IS CALLED THE *STRIGOI.* STRIGOI ARE *LIVING* VAMPIRES, CURSED SOULS WHO DRINK THE BLOOD OF HUMANS TO SURVIVE.
THE STRIGOI ARE MUCH MORE POWERFUL. A MASTER STRIGOI CAN EXHIBIT STRENGTH OVER THE MOROI BY HOLDING THEM UNDER A KIND OF SPELL, THUS TURNING A TYPICALLY RAUCOUS HORDE OF MOROI INTO A SINGLE-MINDED ARMY OF UNDEAD.
EARLY ROMANIAN MYTH SOMETIMES REFERRED TO THE STRIGOI AS SORCERERS OR SHAPESHIFTERS DUE TO THEIR ABILITY TO APPEAR AS ANIMALS, OR EVEN OTHER PEOPLE.
SO HOW DO YOU STOP THEM? STAKE THROUGH THE HEART?
THAT, OR DECAPITATION. THEY ALSO HAVE A WEAKNESS FOR GARLIC, SILVER, HOLY WATER OR CROSSES. ACCORDING TO THIS, KILLING THE MASTER STRIGOI WILL LIFT THE UNDEAD CURSE AND RETURN THE LIVING AND NONLIVING BACK TO NORMAL.

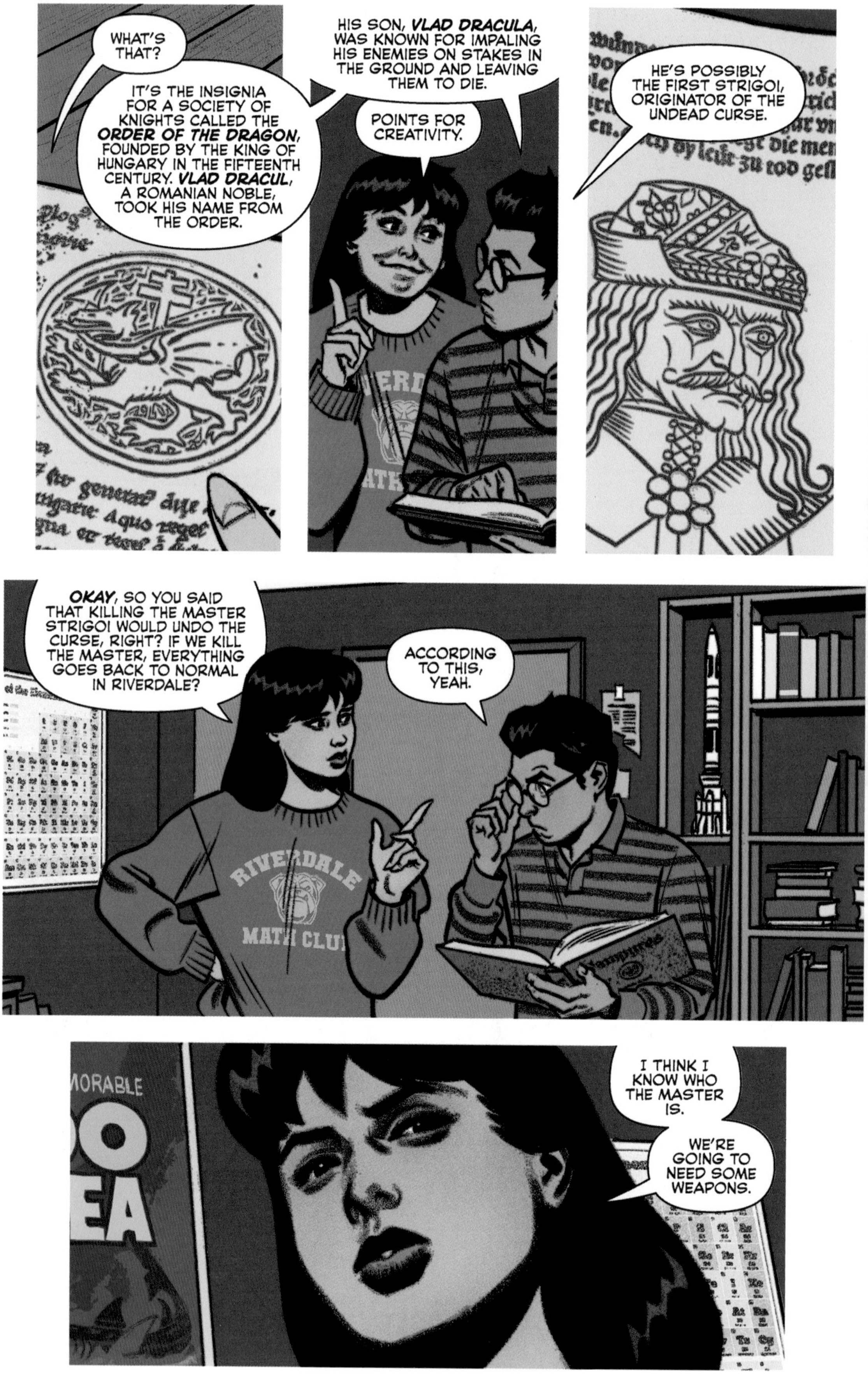
WHAT'S THAT?
IT'S THE INSIGNIA FOR A SOCIETY OF KNIGHTS CALLED THE ORDER OF THE DRAGON, FOUNDED BY THE KING OF HUNGARY IN THE FIFTEENTH CENTURY. VLAD DRACUL, A ROMANIAN NOBLE, TOOK HIS NAME FROM THE ORDER.
HIS SON, VLAD DRACULA, WAS KNOWN FOR IMPALING HIS ENEMIES ON STAKES IN THE GROUND AND LEAVING THEM TO DIE.
POINTS FOR CREATIVITY.
HE'S POSSIBLY THE FIRST STRIGOI, ORIGINATOR OF THE UNDEAD CURSE.
OKAY, SO YOU SAID THAT KILLING THE MASTER STRIGOI WOULD UNDO THE CURSE, RIGHT? IF WE KILL THE MASTER, EVERYTHING GOES BACK TO NORMAL IN RIVERDALE?
ACCORDING TO THIS, YEAH.
RIVERDALE
MATH CLUB
I THINK I KNOW WHO THE MASTER IS.
WE'RE GOING TO NEED SOME WEAPONS.

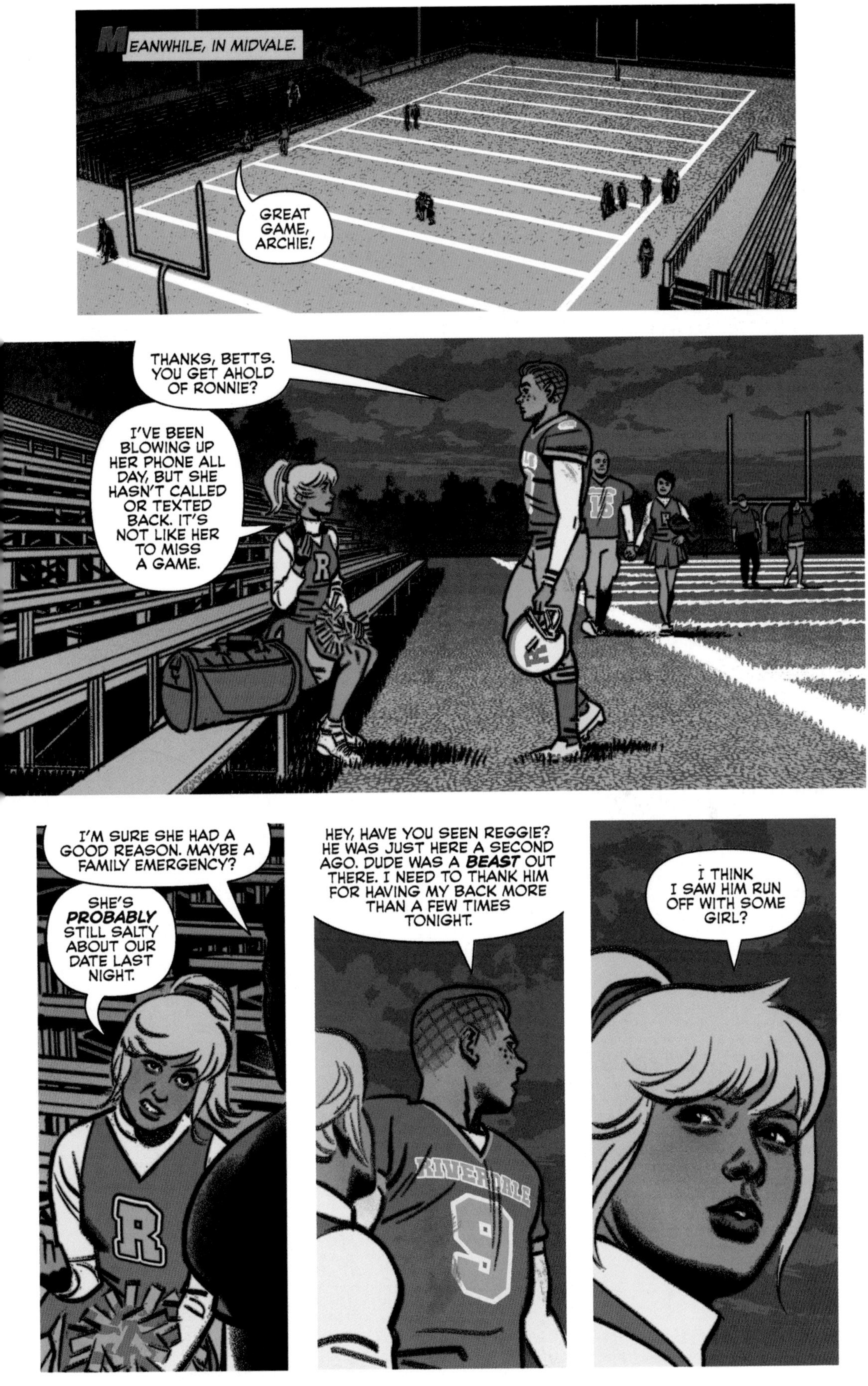
MEANWHILE, IN MIDVALE.
GREAT GAME, ARCHIE!
THANKS, BETTS. YOU GET AHOLD OF RONNIE?
I'VE BEEN BLOWING UP HER PHONE ALL DAY, BUT SHE HASN'T CALLED OR TEXTED BACK. IT'S NOT LIKE HER TO MISS A GAME.
I'M SURE SHE HAD A GOOD REASON. MAYBE A FAMILY EMERGENCY?
SHE'S PROBABLY STILL SALTY ABOUT OUR DATE LAST NIGHT.
HEY, HAVE YOU SEEN REGGIE? HE WAS JUST HERE A SECOND AGO. DUDE WAS A BEAST OUT THERE. I NEED TO THANK HIM FOR HAVING MY BACK MORE THAN A FEW TIMES TONIGHT.
I THINK I SAW HIM RUN OFF WITH SOME GIRL?

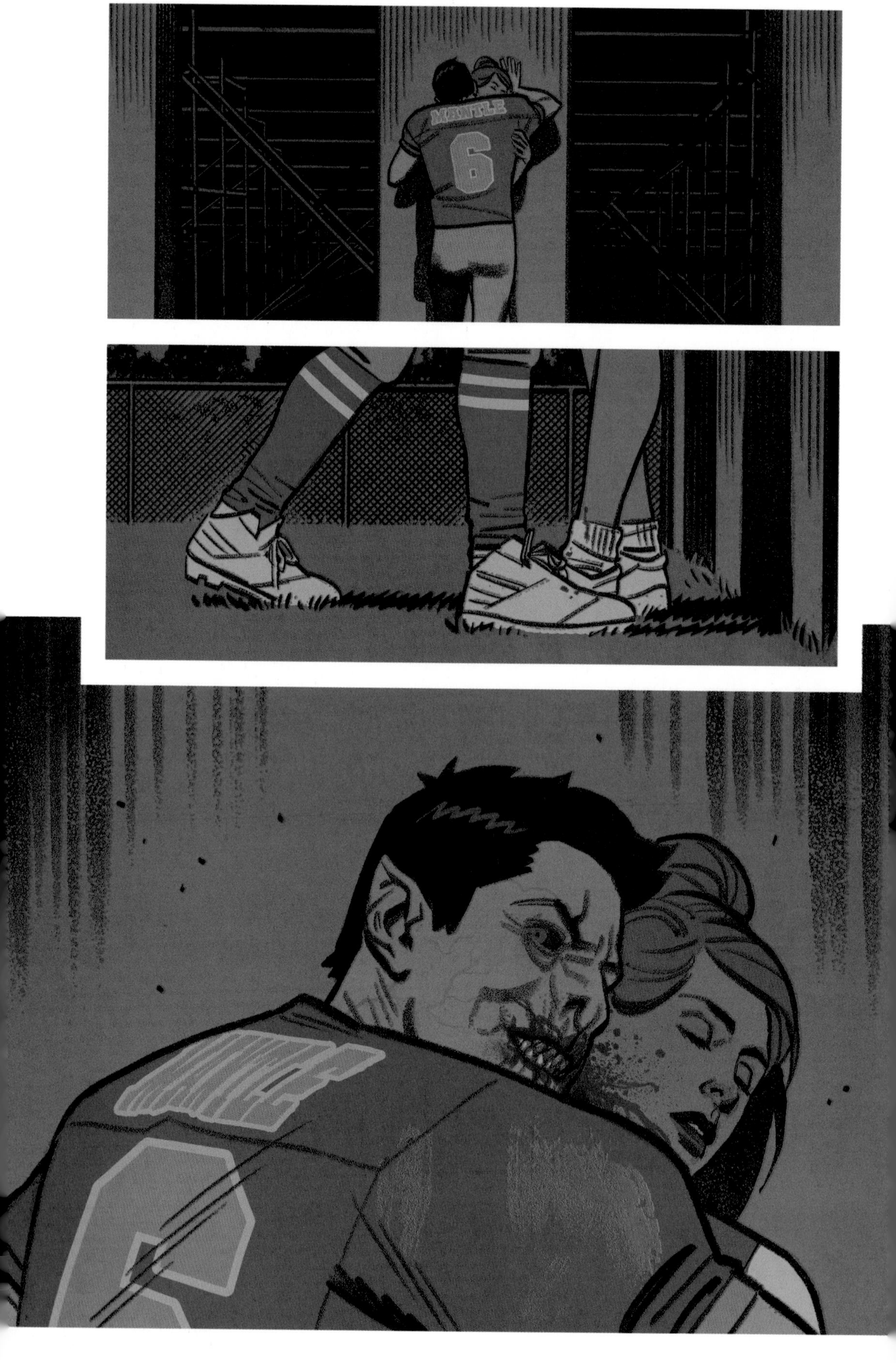
MANTLE
6

TO BE
CONTINUED

CHAPTER THREE

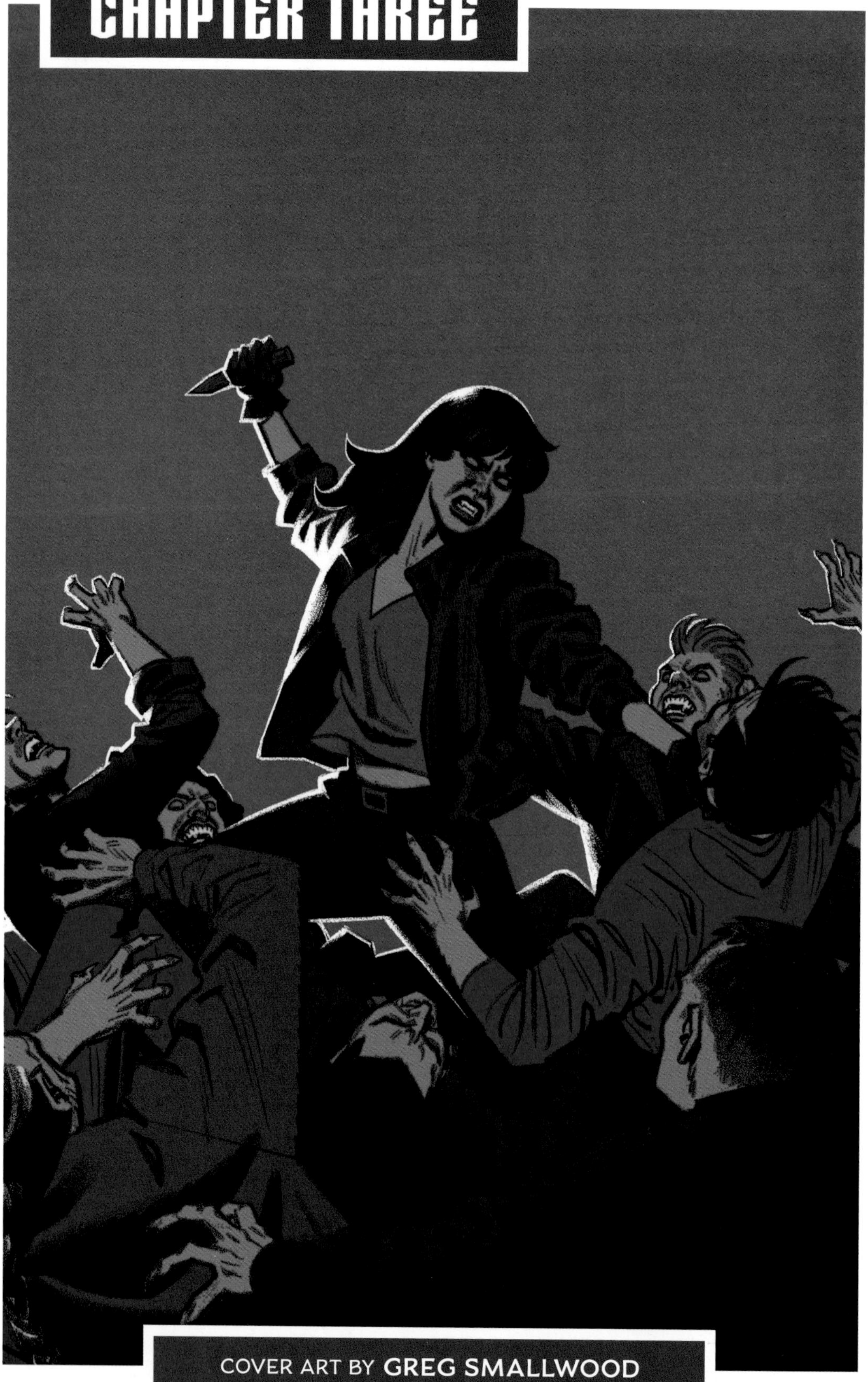

COVER ART BY **GREG SMALLWOOD**

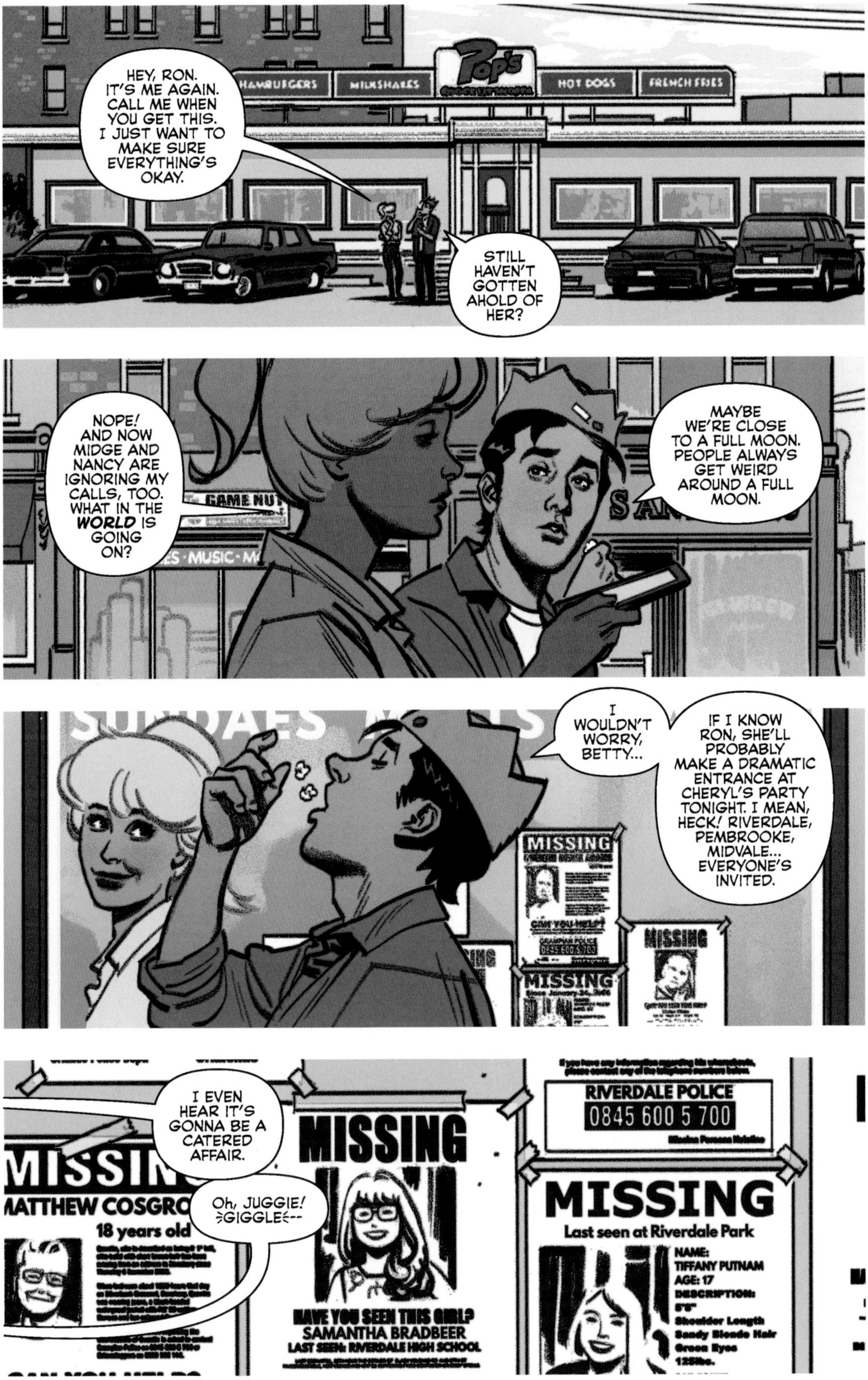

Pop's
HAMBURGERS
MILKSHAKES
HOT DOGS
FRENCH FRIES
HEY, RON. IT'S ME AGAIN. CALL ME WHEN YOU GET THIS. I JUST WANT TO MAKE SURE EVERYTHING'S OKAY.
STILL HAVEN'T GOTTEN AHOLD OF HER?
NOPE! AND NOW MIDGE AND NANCY ARE IGNORING MY CALLS, TOO. WHAT IN THE **WORLD** IS GOING ON?
MAYBE WE'RE CLOSE TO A FULL MOON. PEOPLE ALWAYS GET WEIRD AROUND A FULL MOON.
I WOULDN'T WORRY, BETTY...
IF I KNOW RON, SHE'LL PROBABLY MAKE A DRAMATIC ENTRANCE AT CHERYL'S PARTY TONIGHT. I MEAN, HECK! RIVERDALE, PEMBROOKE, MIDVALE... EVERYONE'S INVITED.
MISSING
MISSING
MISSING
I EVEN HEAR IT'S GONNA BE A CATERED AFFAIR.
Oh, JUGGIE! ⋟GIGGLE⋞--
MATTHEW COSGRO
18 years old
MISSING
HAVE YOU SEEN THIS GIRL?
SAMANTHA BRADBEER
LAST SEEN: RIVERDALE HIGH SCHOOL
RIVERDALE POLICE
0845 600 5 700
MISSING
Last seen at Riverdale Park
NAME: TIFFANY PUTNAM
AGE: 17
DESCRIPTION:
5'8"
Shoulder Length
Sandy Blonde Hair
Green Eyes
125lbs.

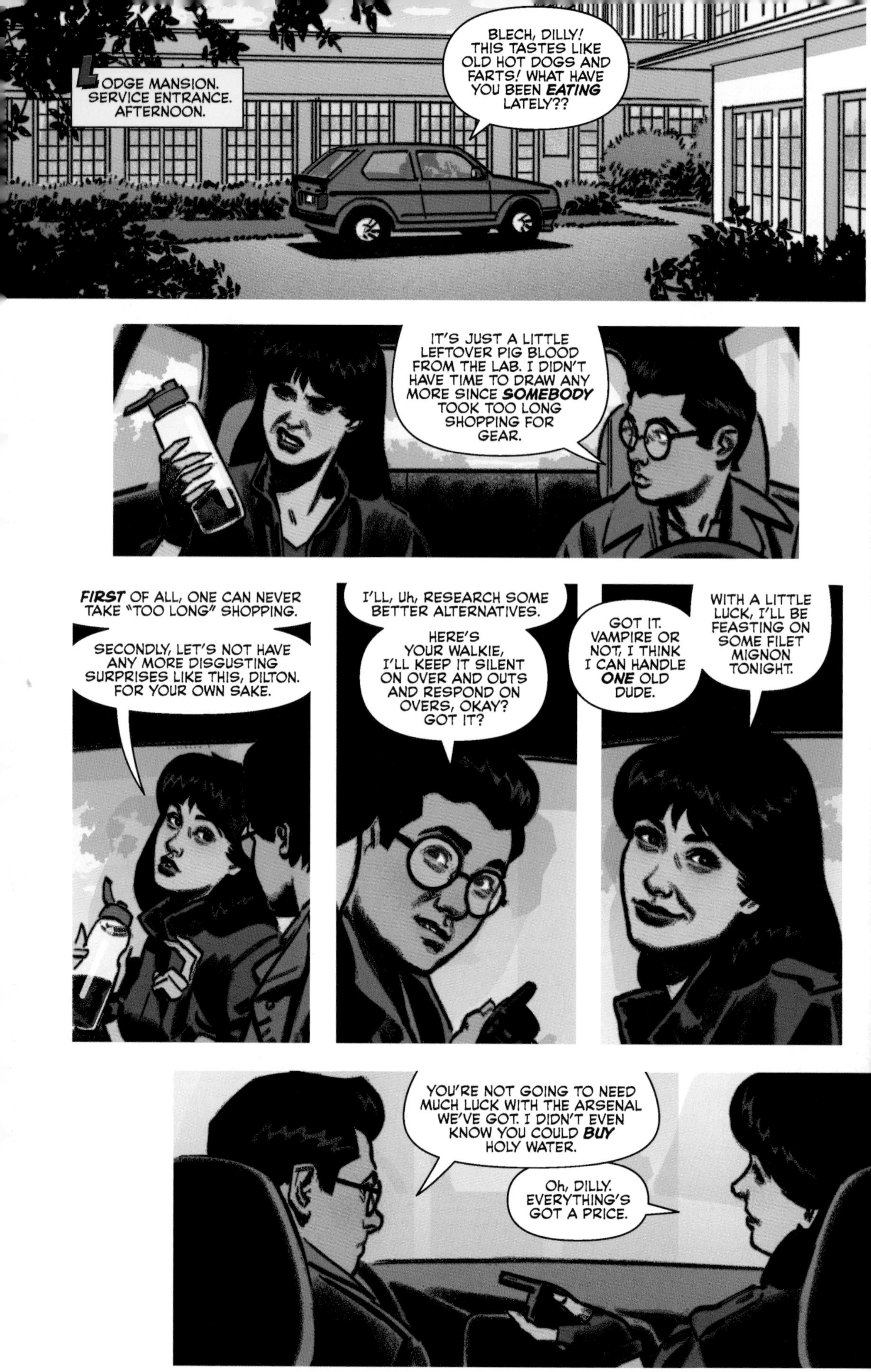
LODGE MANSION. SERVICE ENTRANCE. AFTERNOON.
BLECH, DILLY! THIS TASTES LIKE OLD HOT DOGS AND FARTS! WHAT HAVE YOU BEEN EATING LATELY??
IT'S JUST A LITTLE LEFTOVER PIG BLOOD FROM THE LAB. I DIDN'T HAVE TIME TO DRAW ANY MORE SINCE SOMEBODY TOOK TOO LONG SHOPPING FOR GEAR.
FIRST OF ALL, ONE CAN NEVER TAKE "TOO LONG" SHOPPING.
SECONDLY, LET'S NOT HAVE ANY MORE DISGUSTING SURPRISES LIKE THIS, DILTON. FOR YOUR OWN SAKE.
I'LL, Uh, RESEARCH SOME BETTER ALTERNATIVES.
HERE'S YOUR WALKIE, I'LL KEEP IT SILENT ON OVER AND OUTS AND RESPOND ON OVERS, OKAY? GOT IT?
GOT IT. VAMPIRE OR NOT, I THINK I CAN HANDLE ONE OLD DUDE.
WITH A LITTLE LUCK, I'LL BE FEASTING ON SOME FILET MIGNON TONIGHT.
YOU'RE NOT GOING TO NEED MUCH LUCK WITH THE ARSENAL WE'VE GOT. I DIDN'T EVEN KNOW YOU COULD BUY HOLY WATER.
Oh, DILLY. EVERYTHING'S GOT A PRICE.

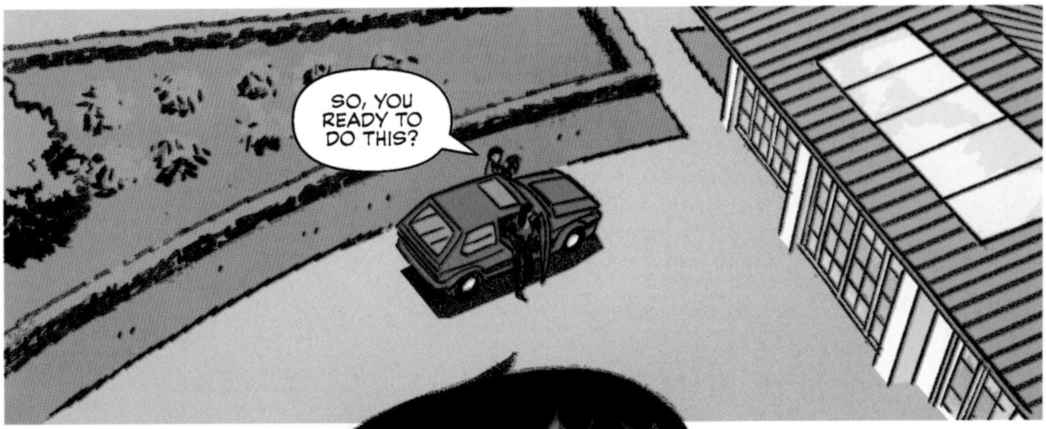
SO, YOU READY TO DO THIS?

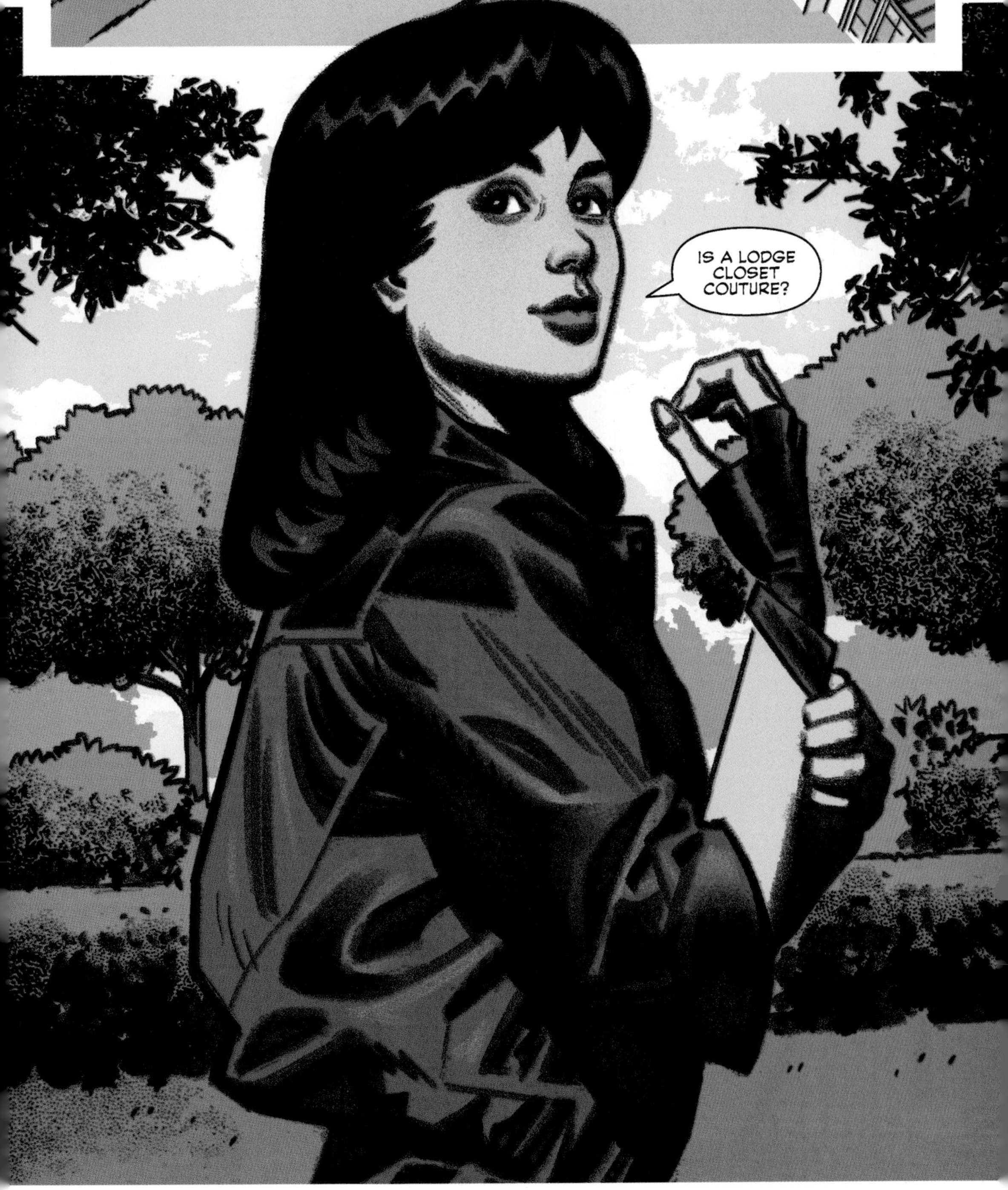
IS A LODGE CLOSET COUTURE?

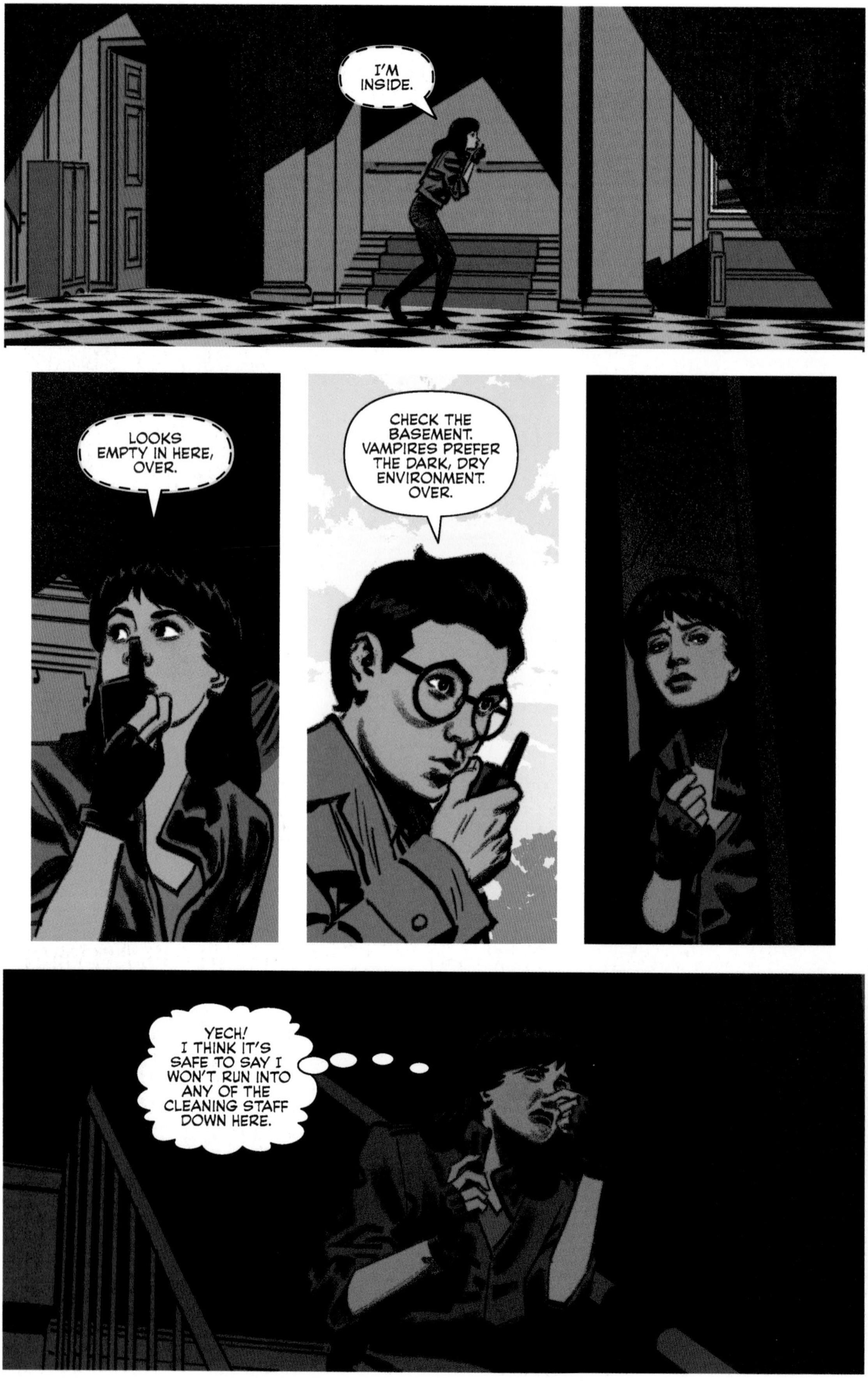
I'M INSIDE.
LOOKS EMPTY IN HERE, OVER.
CHECK THE BASEMENT. VAMPIRES PREFER THE DARK, DRY ENVIRONMENT. OVER.
YECH! I THINK IT'S SAFE TO SAY I WON'T RUN INTO ANY OF THE CLEANING STAFF DOWN HERE.

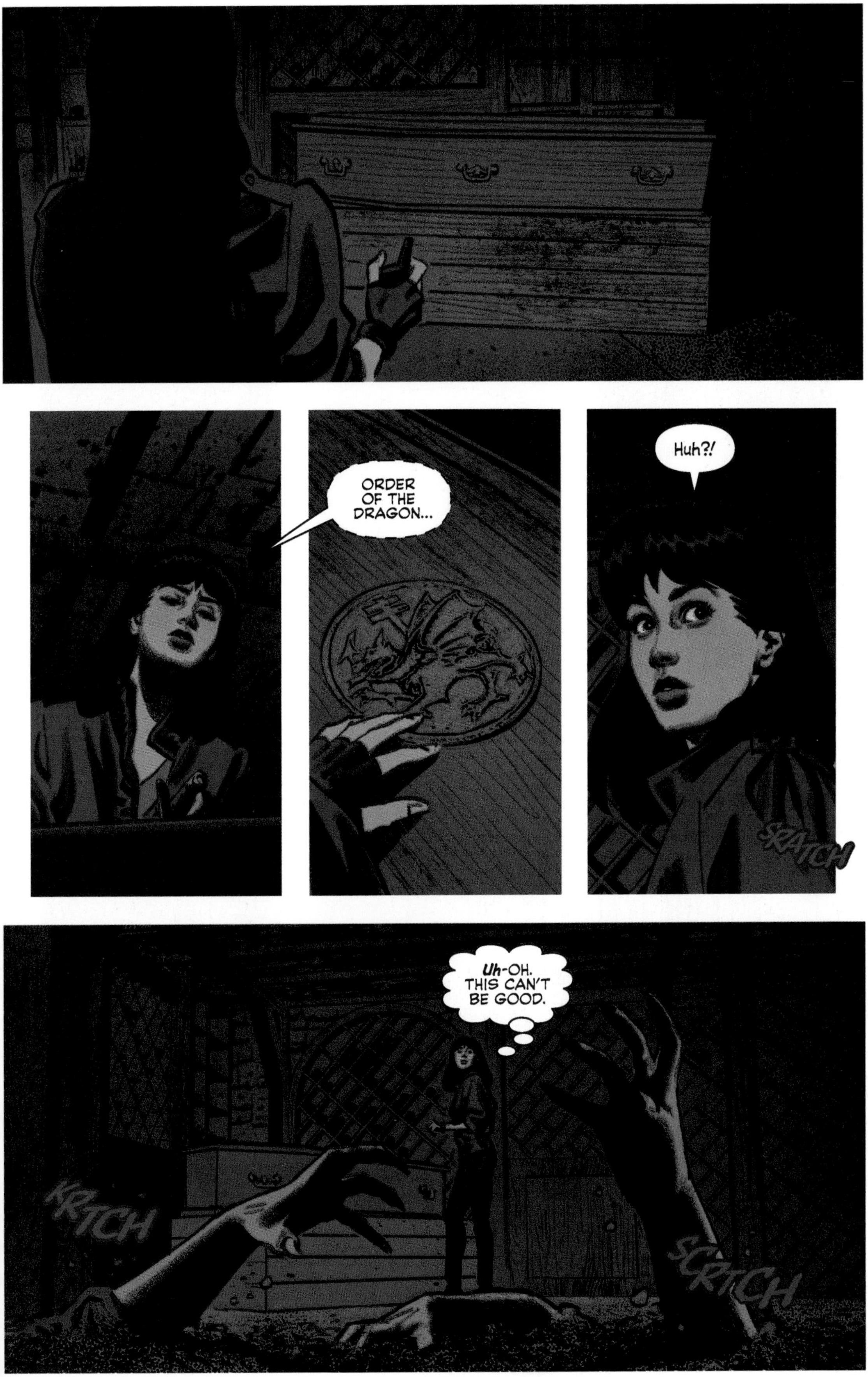
ORDER OF THE DRAGON...
Huh?!
SRATCH
Uh-OH. THIS CAN'T BE GOOD.
KRTCH
SCRTCH

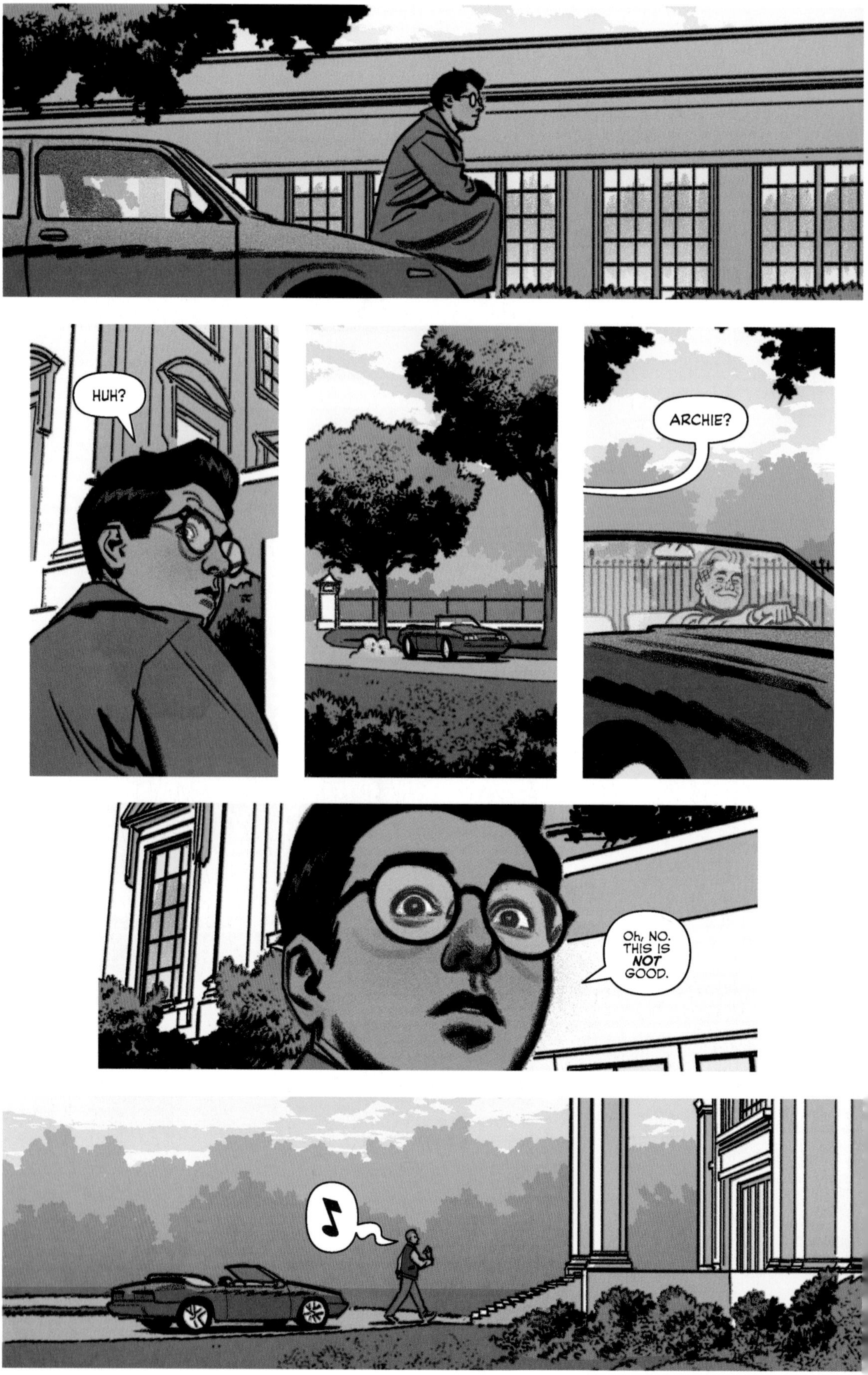
HUH?
ARCHIE?
Oh, NO.
THIS IS
NOT
GOOD.
♪

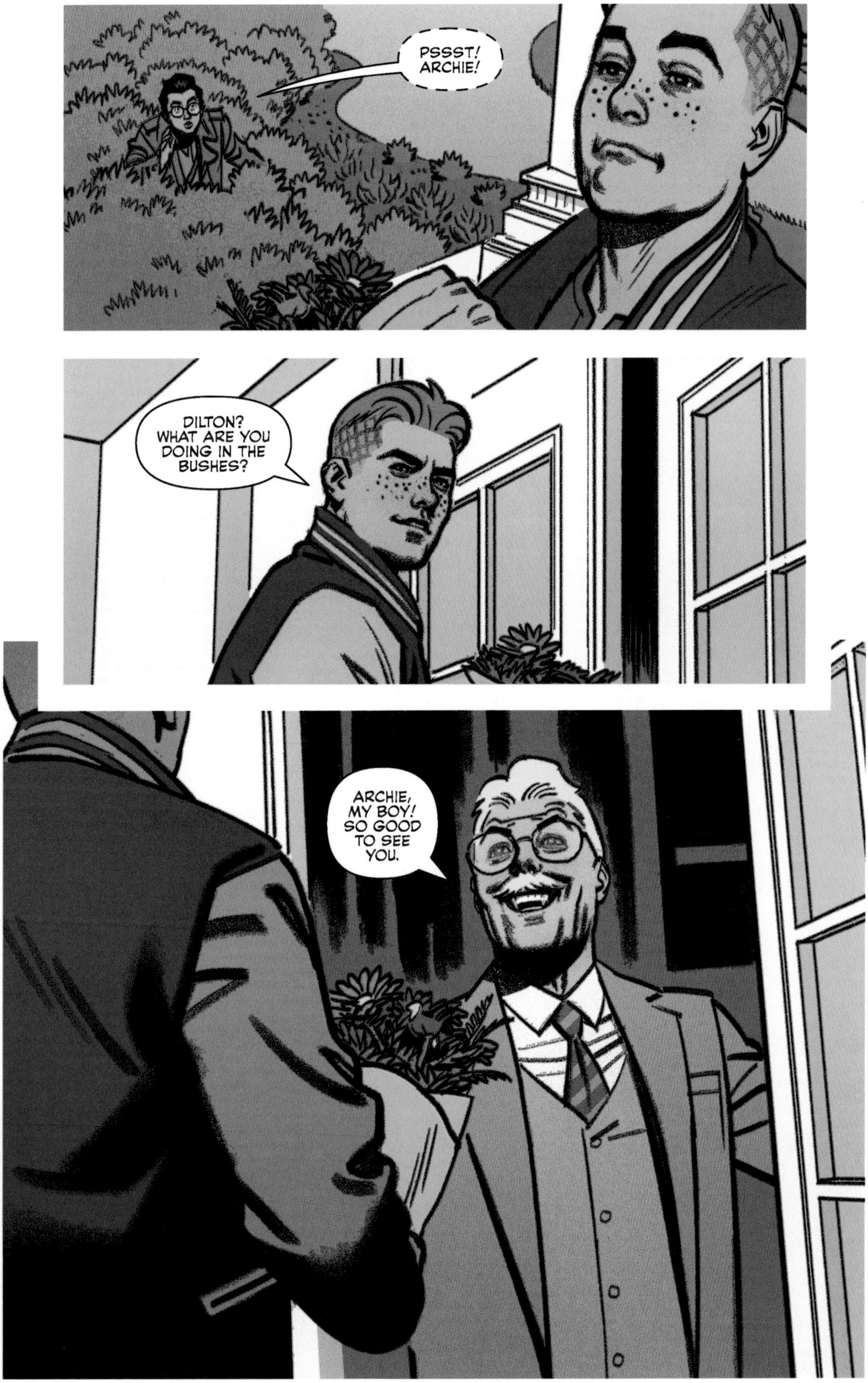
PSSST! ARCHIE!
DILTON? WHAT ARE YOU DOING IN THE BUSHES?
ARCHIE, MY BOY! SO GOOD TO SEE YOU.

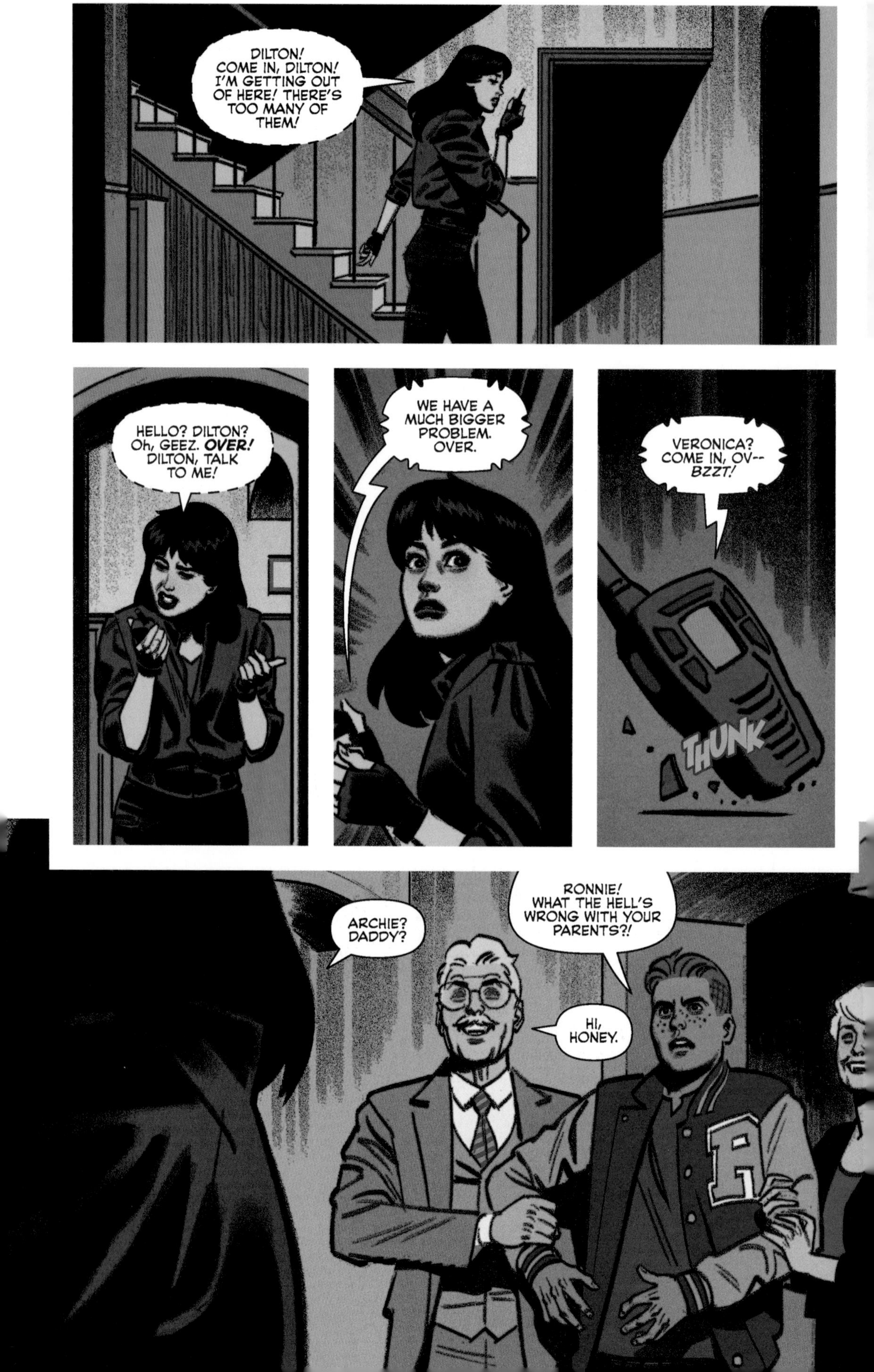
DILTON! COME IN, DILTON! I'M GETTING OUT OF HERE! THERE'S TOO MANY OF THEM!
HELLO? DILTON? Oh, GEEZ. OVER! DILTON, TALK TO ME!
WE HAVE A MUCH BIGGER PROBLEM. OVER.
VERONICA? COME IN, OV-- BZZT!
THUNK
ARCHIE? DADDY?
RONNIE! WHAT THE HELL'S WRONG WITH YOUR PARENTS?!
HI, HONEY.

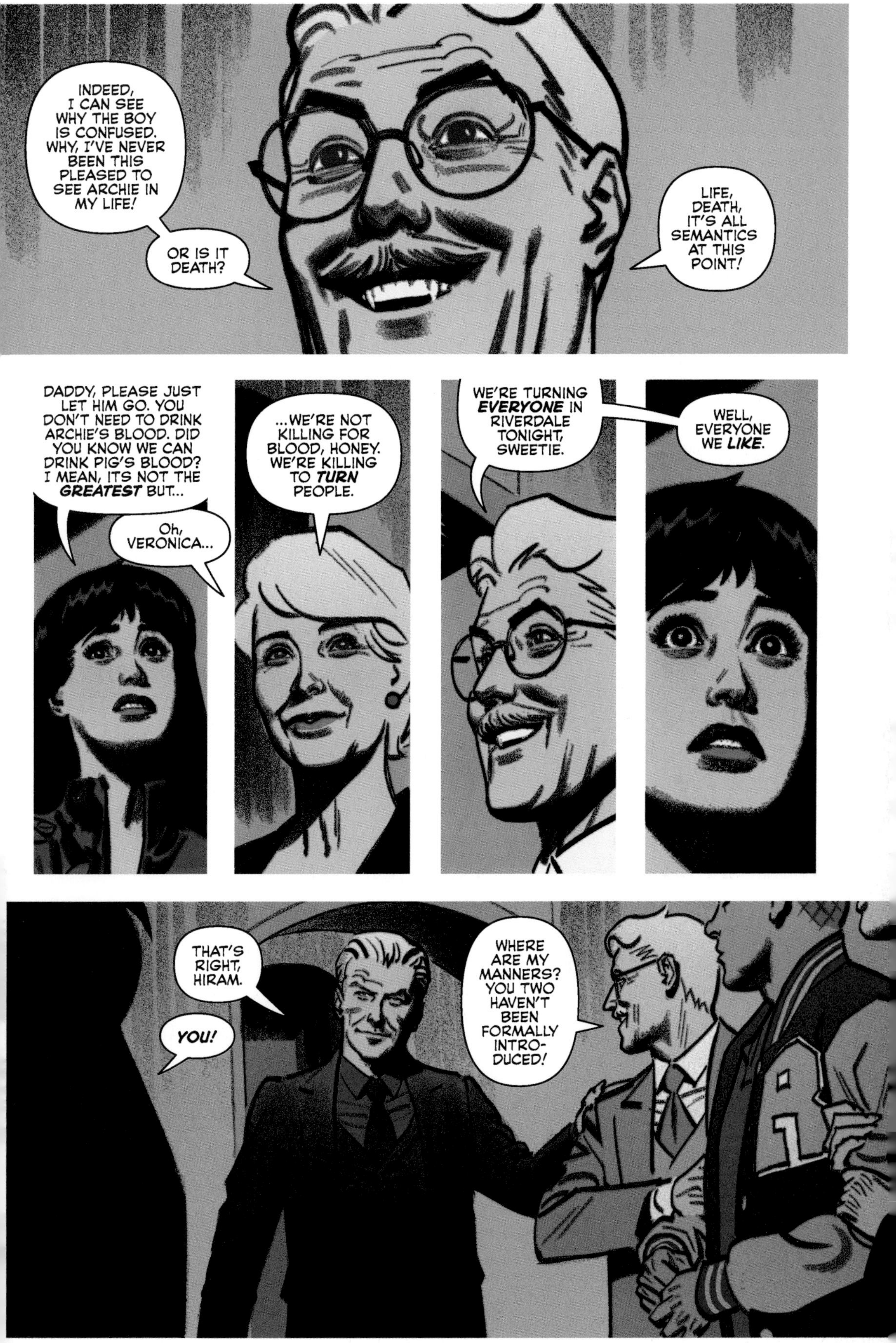
INDEED, I CAN SEE WHY THE BOY IS CONFUSED. WHY, I'VE NEVER BEEN THIS PLEASED TO SEE ARCHIE IN MY LIFE!
OR IS IT DEATH?
LIFE, DEATH, IT'S ALL SEMANTICS AT THIS POINT!
DADDY, PLEASE JUST LET HIM GO. YOU DON'T NEED TO DRINK ARCHIE'S BLOOD. DID YOU KNOW WE CAN DRINK PIG'S BLOOD? I MEAN, ITS NOT THE ***GREATEST*** BUT...
Oh, VERONICA...
...WE'RE NOT KILLING FOR BLOOD, HONEY. WE'RE KILLING TO ***TURN*** PEOPLE.
WE'RE TURNING ***EVERYONE*** IN RIVERDALE TONIGHT, SWEETIE.
WELL, EVERYONE WE ***LIKE***.
THAT'S RIGHT, HIRAM.
YOU!
WHERE ARE MY MANNERS? YOU TWO HAVEN'T BEEN FORMALLY INTRO-DUCED!

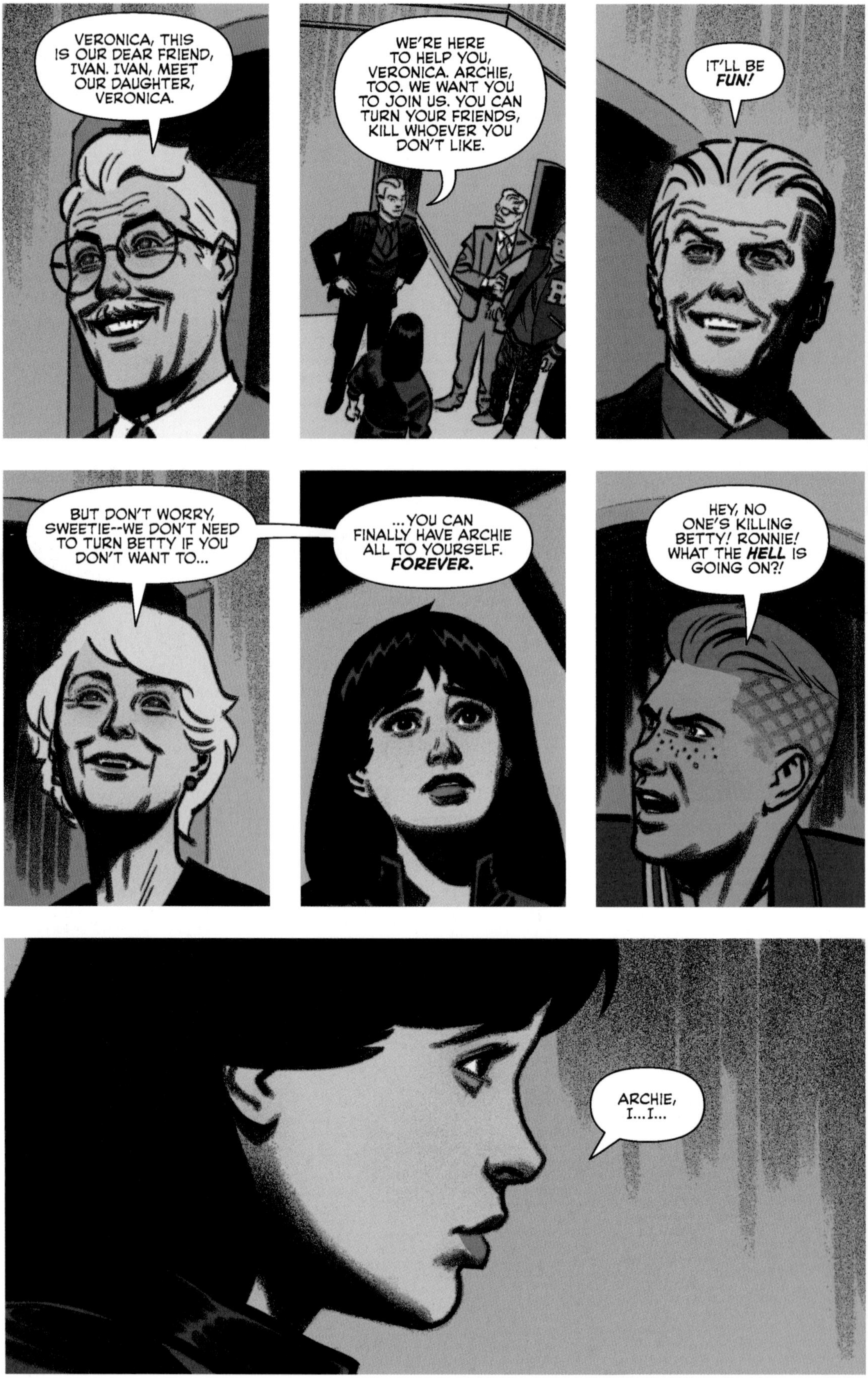
VERONICA, THIS IS OUR DEAR FRIEND, IVAN. IVAN, MEET OUR DAUGHTER, VERONICA.
WE'RE HERE TO HELP YOU, VERONICA. ARCHIE, TOO. WE WANT YOU TO JOIN US. YOU CAN TURN YOUR FRIENDS, KILL WHOEVER YOU DON'T LIKE.
IT'LL BE *FUN!*
BUT DON'T WORRY, SWEETIE--WE DON'T NEED TO TURN BETTY IF YOU DON'T WANT TO...
...YOU CAN FINALLY HAVE ARCHIE ALL TO YOURSELF. ***FOREVER.***
HEY, NO ONE'S KILLING BETTY! RONNIE! WHAT THE ***HELL*** IS GOING ON?!
ARCHIE, I...I...

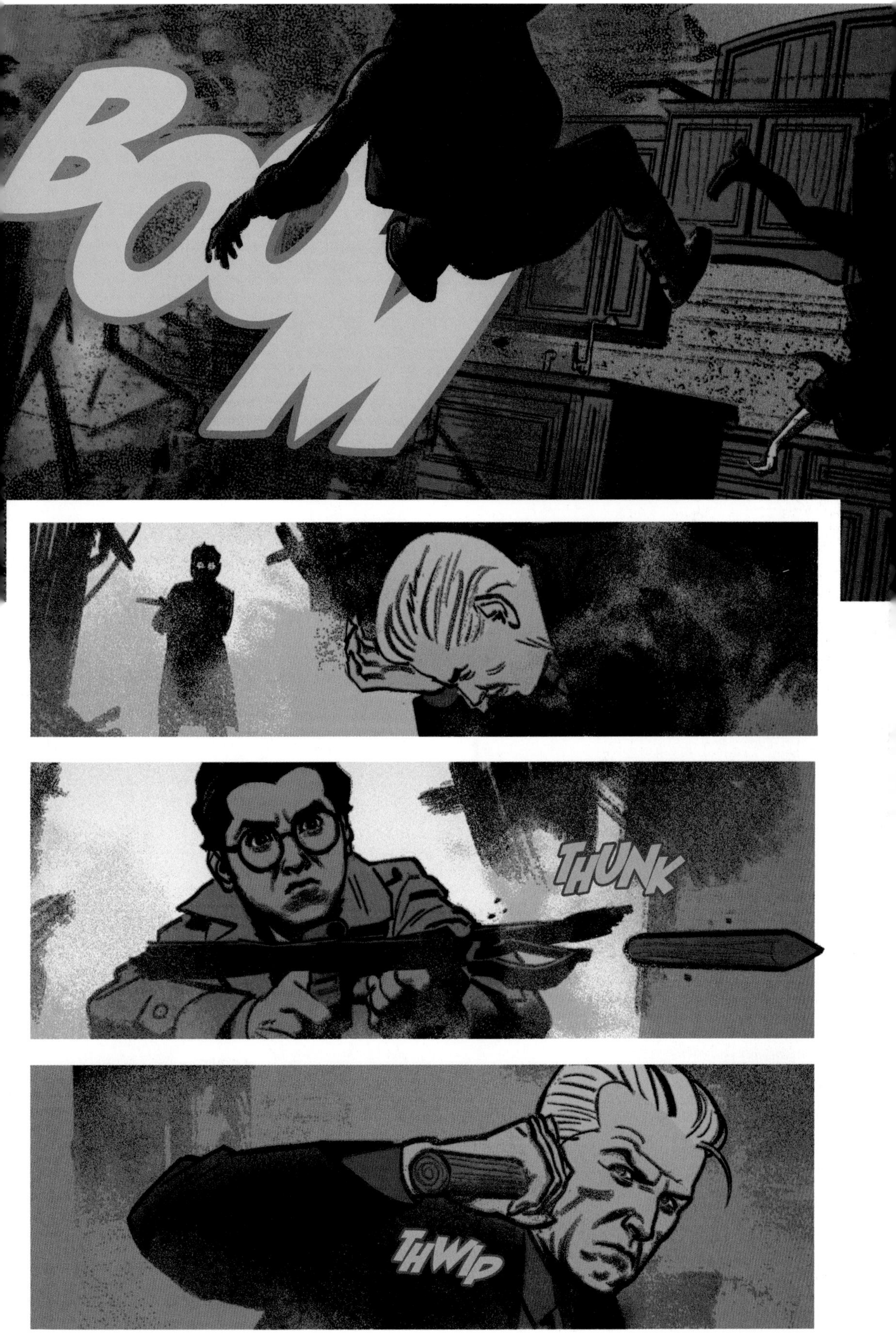
BOOM
THUNK
THWIP

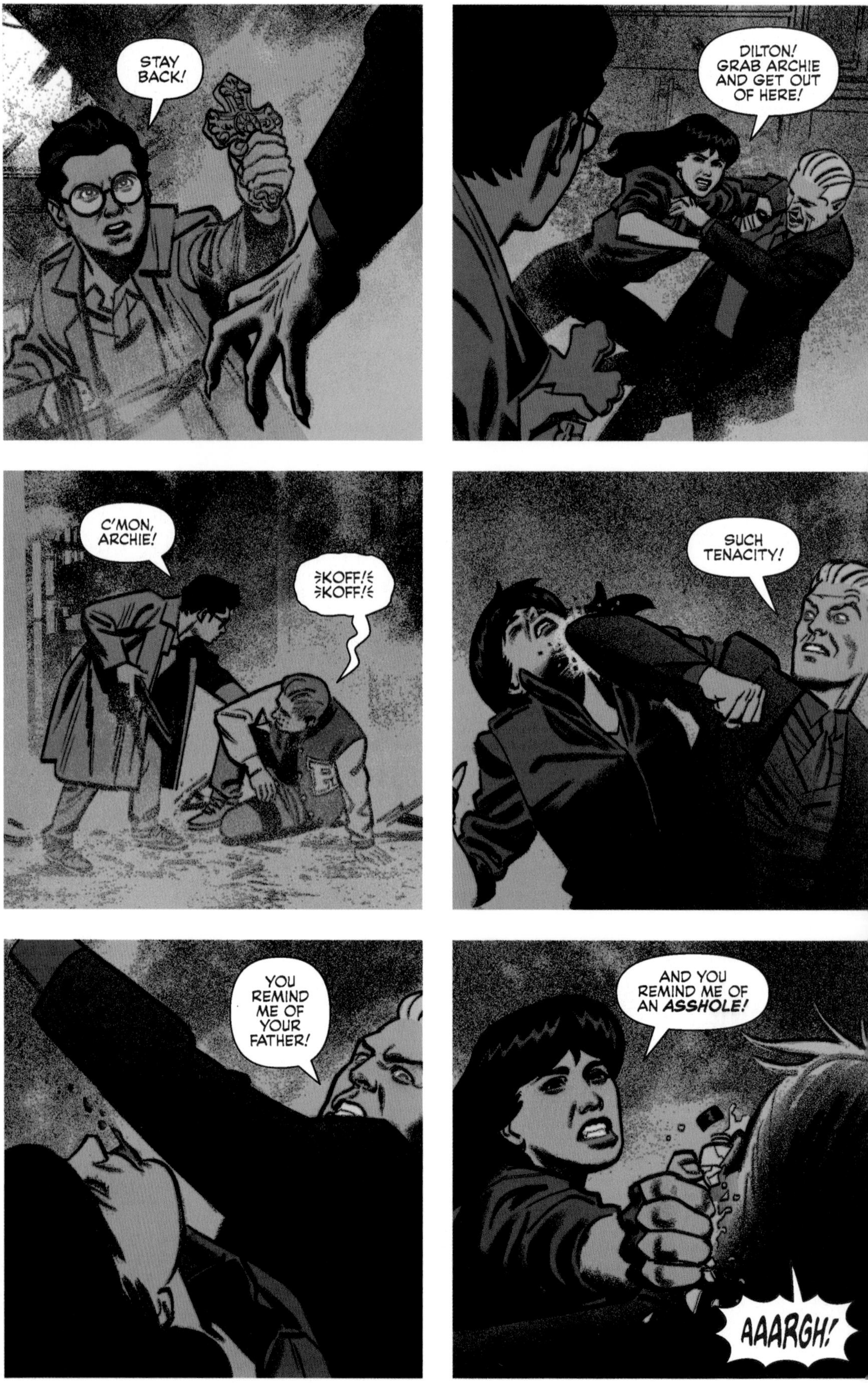
STAY BACK!
DILTON! GRAB ARCHIE AND GET OUT OF HERE!
C'MON, ARCHIE!
KOFF! KOFF!
SUCH TENACITY!
YOU REMIND ME OF YOUR FATHER!
AND YOU REMIND ME OF AN ASSHOLE!
AAARGH!

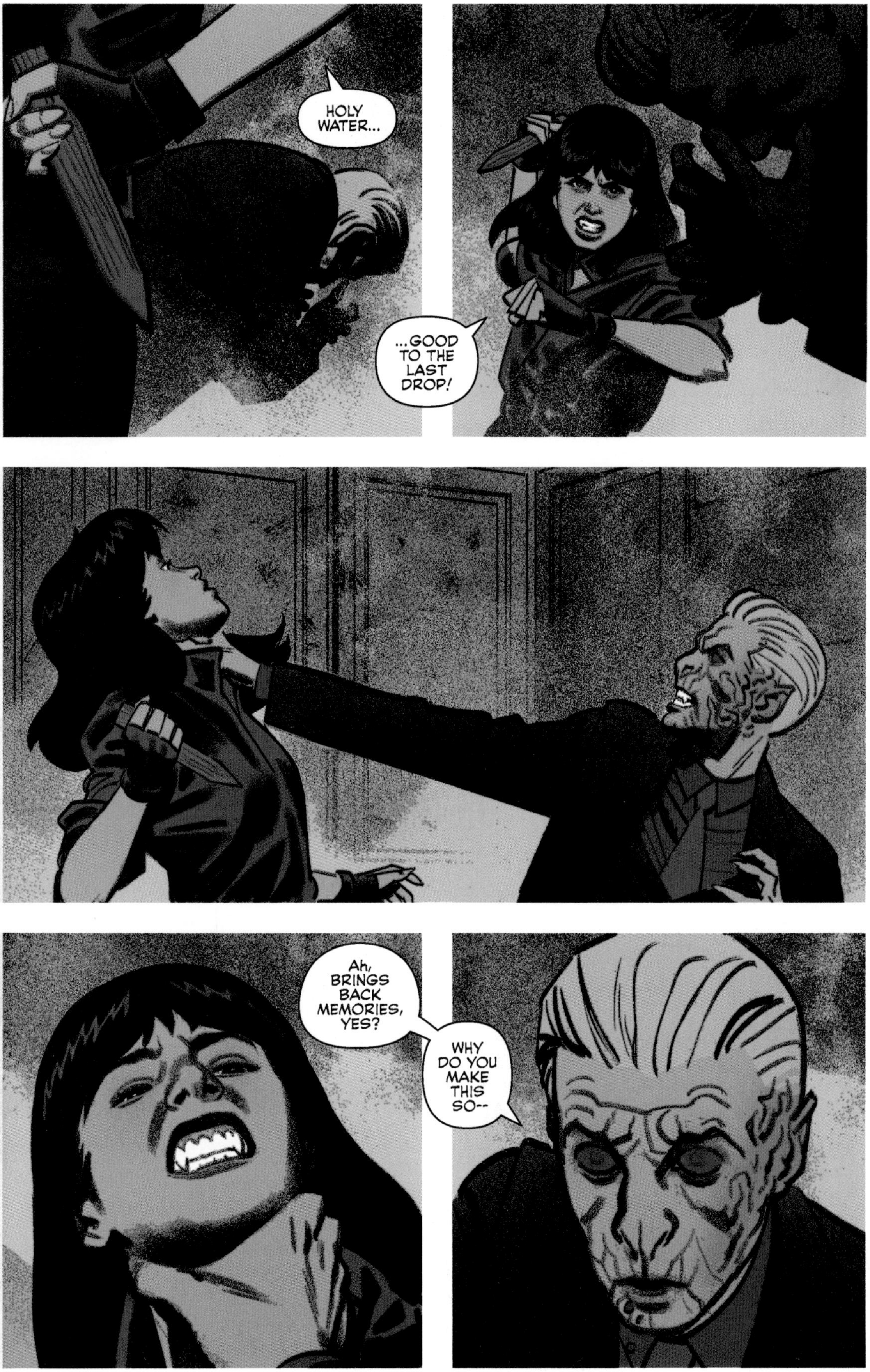
HOLY WATER...
...GOOD TO THE LAST DROP!
Ah, BRINGS BACK MEMORIES, YES?
WHY DO YOU MAKE THIS SO--

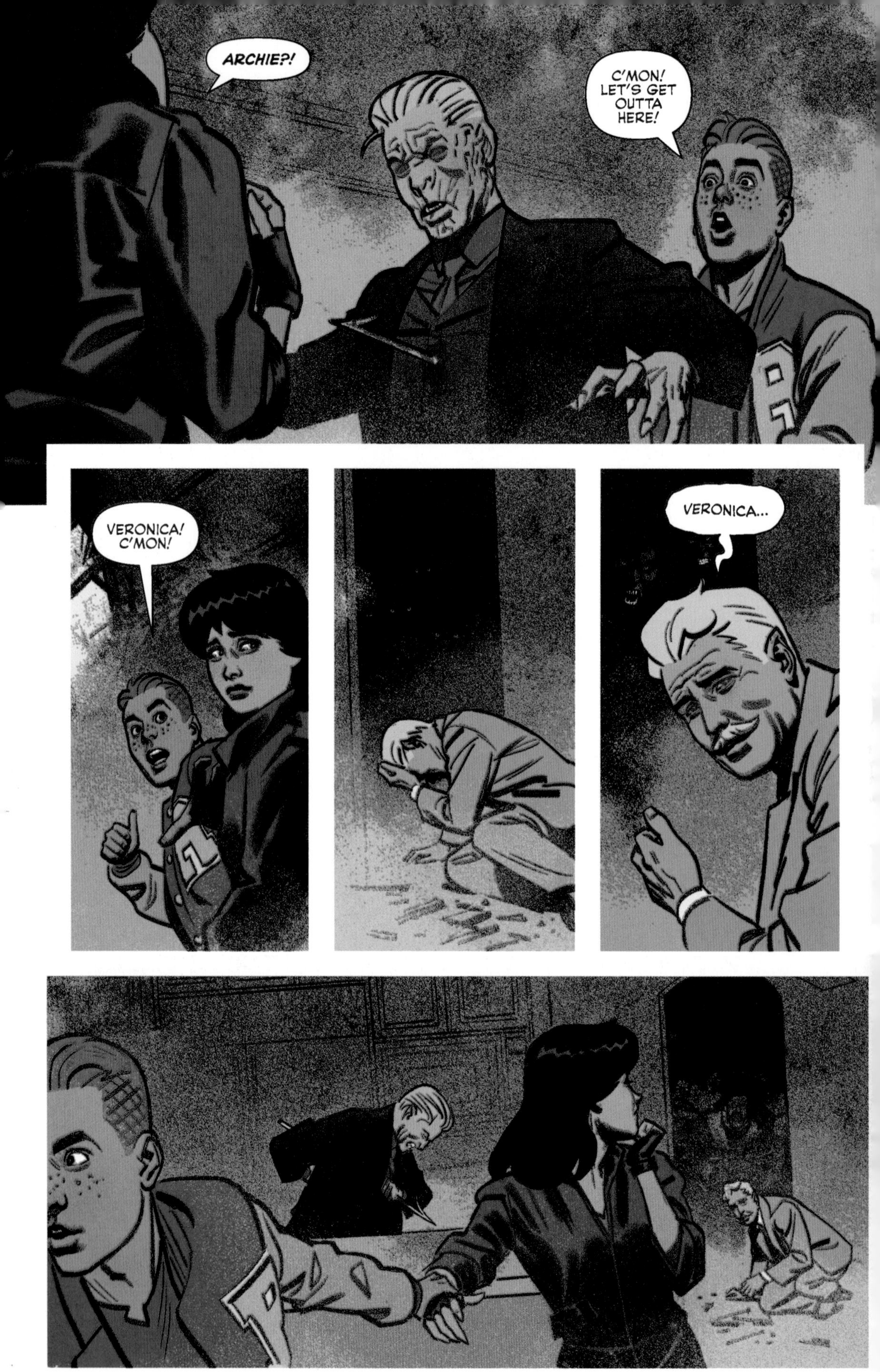
ARCHIE?!
C'MON! LET'S GET OUTTA HERE!
VERONICA! C'MON!
VERONICA...

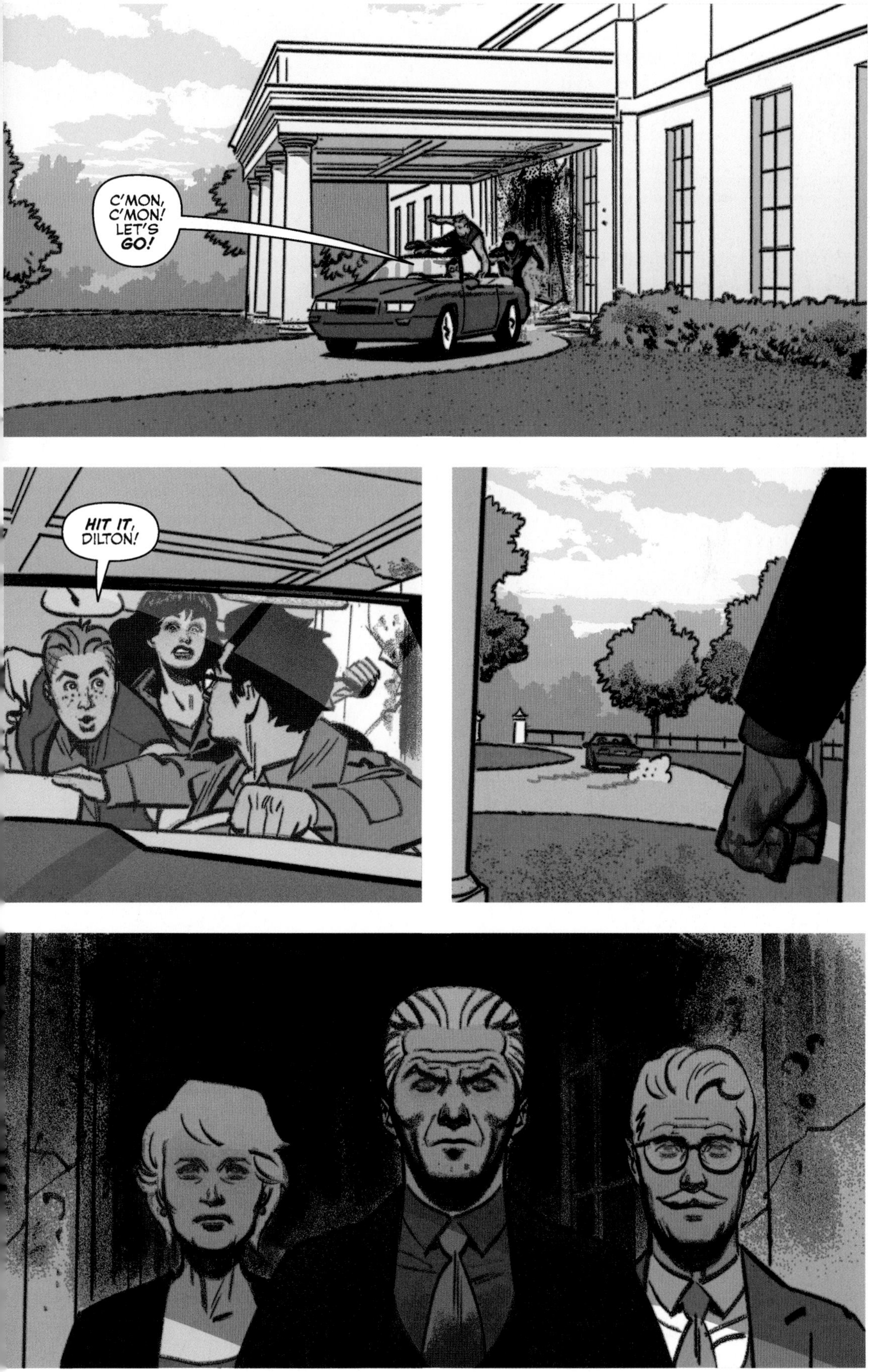
C'MON, C'MON! LET'S GO!
HIT IT, DILTON!

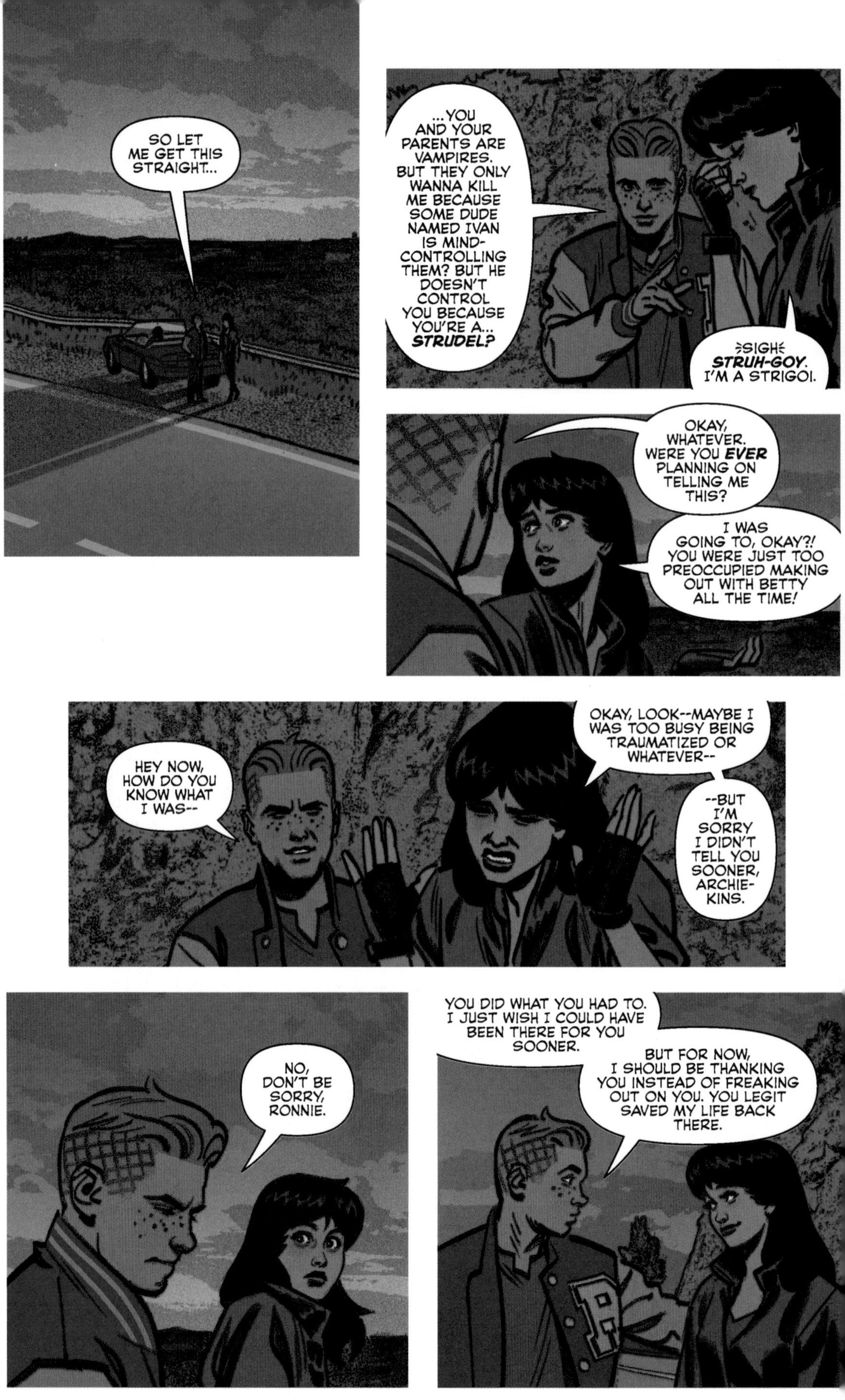
SO LET ME GET THIS STRAIGHT...
...YOU AND YOUR PARENTS ARE VAMPIRES. BUT THEY ONLY WANNA KILL ME BECAUSE SOME DUDE NAMED IVAN IS MIND-CONTROLLING THEM? BUT HE DOESN'T CONTROL YOU BECAUSE YOU'RE A... STRUDEL?
SIGH STRUH-GOY. I'M A STRIGOI.
OKAY, WHATEVER. WERE YOU EVER PLANNING ON TELLING ME THIS?
I WAS GOING TO, OKAY?! YOU WERE JUST TOO PREOCCUPIED MAKING OUT WITH BETTY ALL THE TIME!
HEY NOW, HOW DO YOU KNOW WHAT I WAS--
OKAY, LOOK--MAYBE I WAS TOO BUSY BEING TRAUMATIZED OR WHATEVER--
--BUT I'M SORRY I DIDN'T TELL YOU SOONER, ARCHIE-KINS.
NO, DON'T BE SORRY, RONNIE.
YOU DID WHAT YOU HAD TO. I JUST WISH I COULD HAVE BEEN THERE FOR YOU SOONER.
BUT FOR NOW, I SHOULD BE THANKING YOU INSTEAD OF FREAKING OUT ON YOU. YOU LEGIT SAVED MY LIFE BACK THERE.

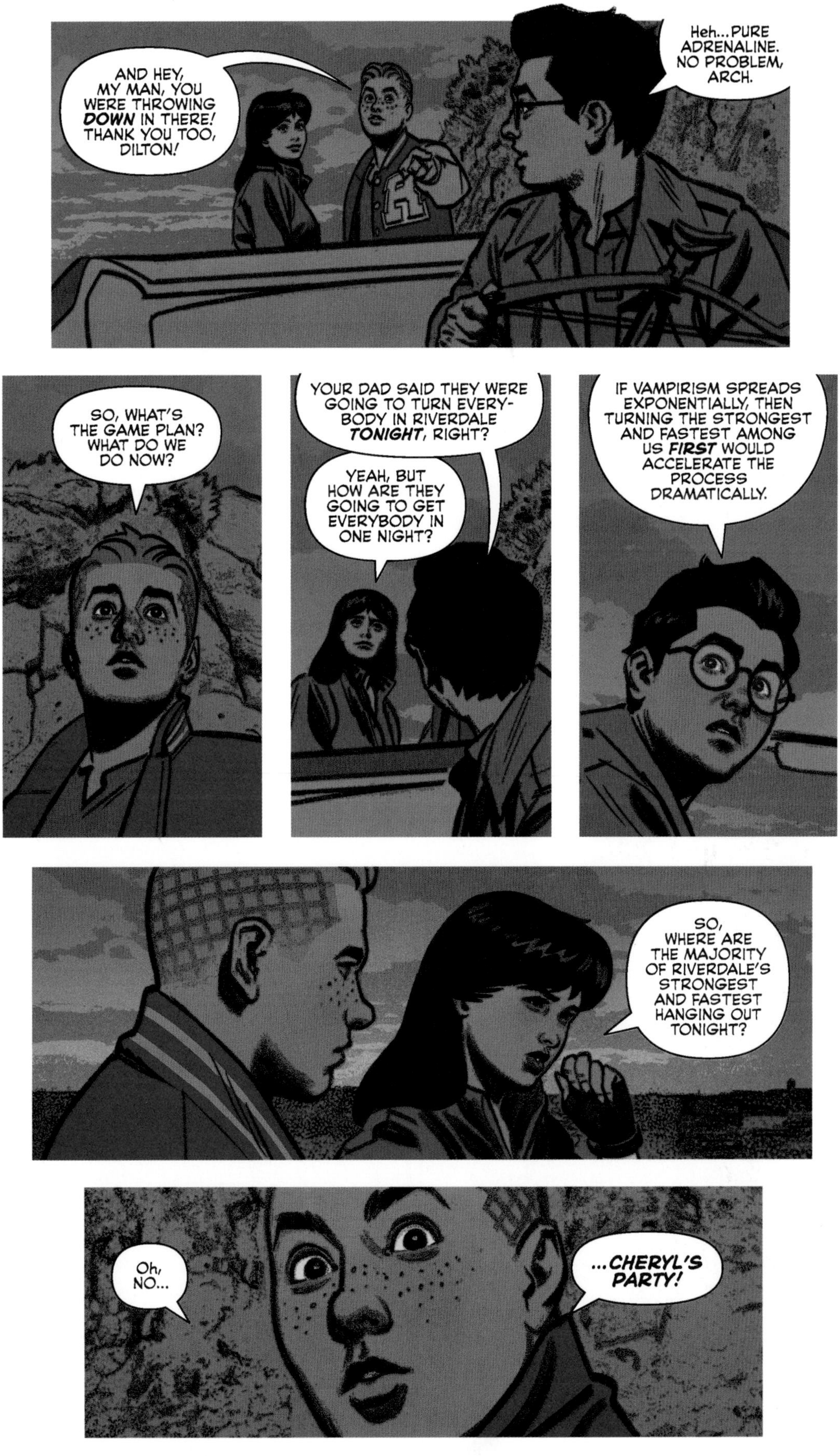
AND HEY, MY MAN, YOU WERE THROWING DOWN IN THERE! THANK YOU TOO, DILTON!
Heh... PURE ADRENALINE. NO PROBLEM, ARCH.
SO, WHAT'S THE GAME PLAN? WHAT DO WE DO NOW?
YOUR DAD SAID THEY WERE GOING TO TURN EVERY-BODY IN RIVERDALE TONIGHT, RIGHT?
YEAH, BUT HOW ARE THEY GOING TO GET EVERYBODY IN ONE NIGHT?
IF VAMPIRISM SPREADS EXPONENTIALLY, THEN TURNING THE STRONGEST AND FASTEST AMONG US FIRST WOULD ACCELERATE THE PROCESS DRAMATICALLY.
SO, WHERE ARE THE MAJORITY OF RIVERDALE'S STRONGEST AND FASTEST HANGING OUT TONIGHT?
Oh, NO...
...CHERYL'S PARTY!

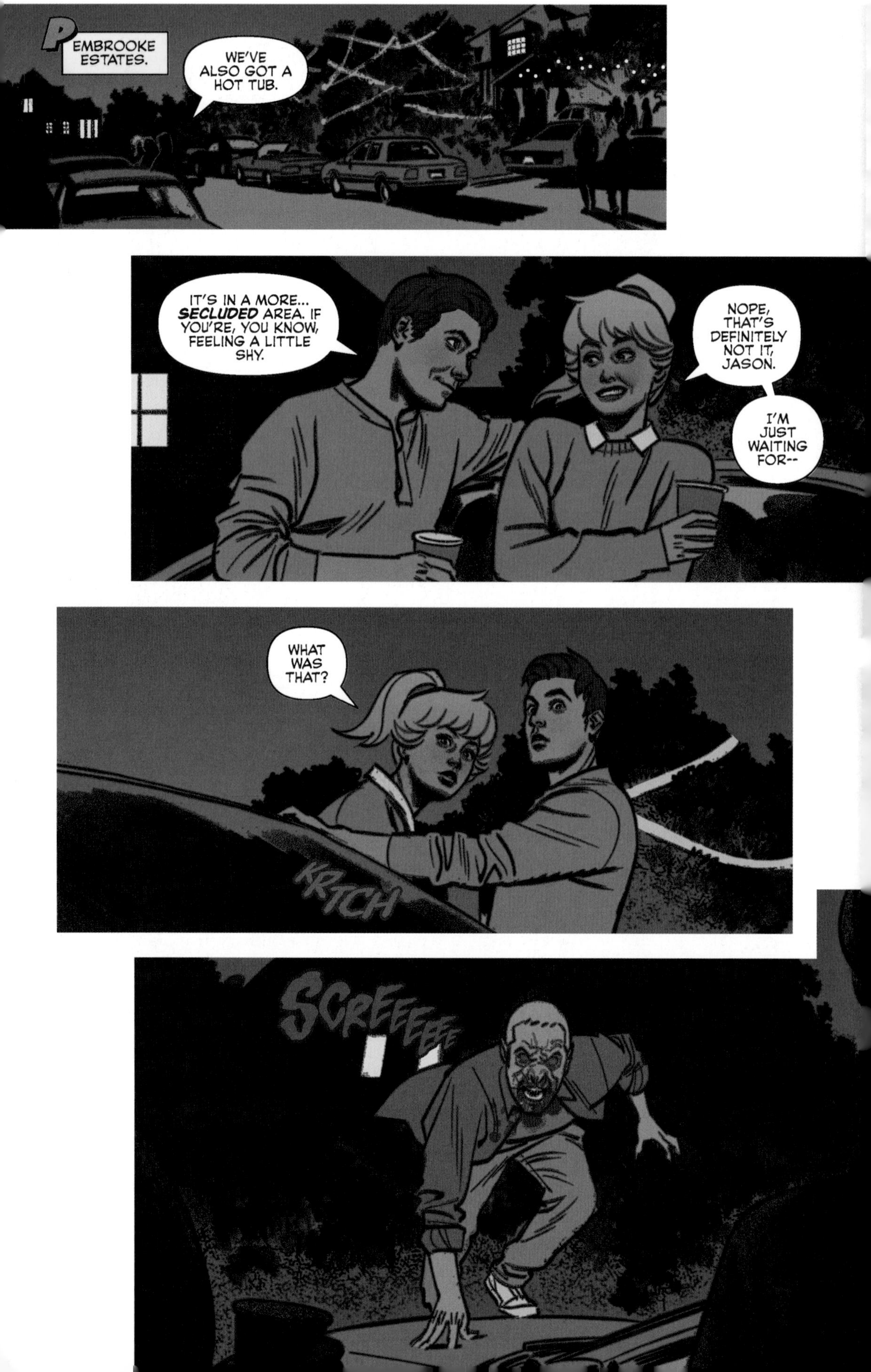

PEMBROOKE ESTATES.
WE'VE ALSO GOT A HOT TUB.
IT'S IN A MORE... ***SECLUDED*** AREA. IF YOU'RE, YOU KNOW, FEELING A LITTLE SHY.
NOPE, THAT'S DEFINITELY NOT IT, JASON.
I'M JUST WAITING FOR--
WHAT WAS THAT?
KRTCH
SCREEEEEE

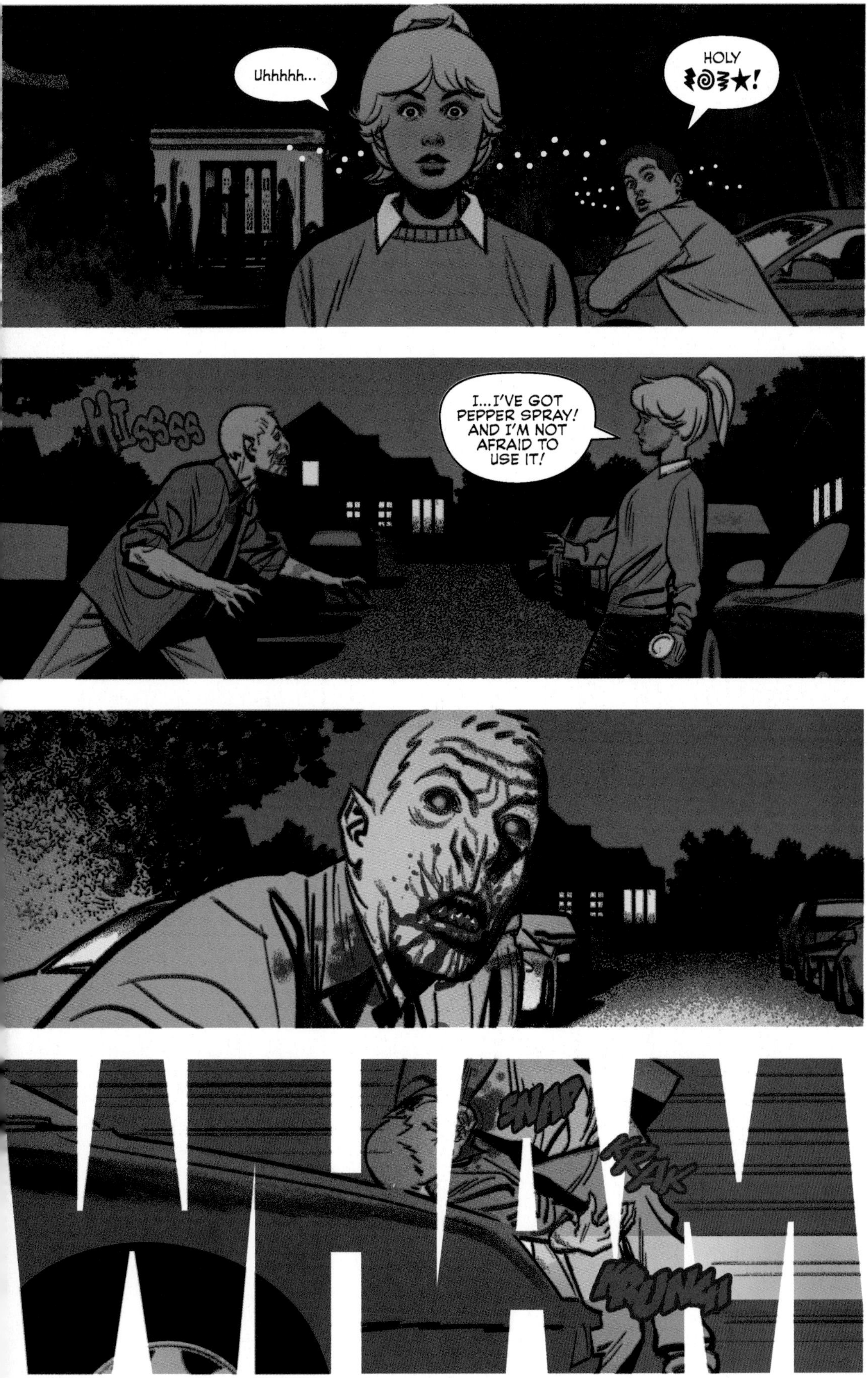
Uhhhhh...
HOLY
HISSSS
I...I'VE GOT PEPPER SPRAY! AND I'M NOT AFRAID TO USE IT!
WHAM
SNAP
KRAK
KRUNK

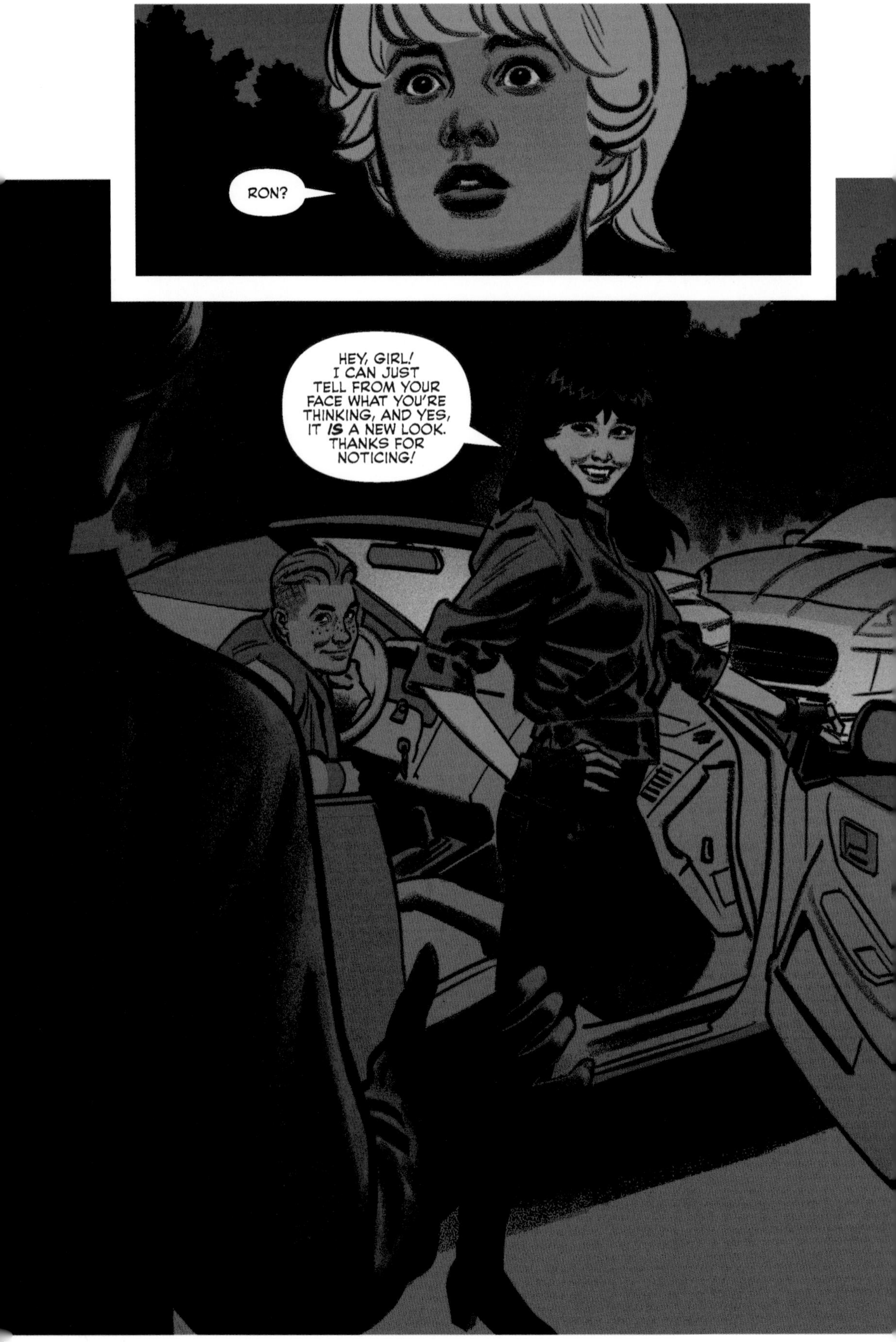
RON?
HEY, GIRL! I CAN JUST TELL FROM YOUR FACE WHAT YOU'RE THINKING, AND YES, IT IS A NEW LOOK. THANKS FOR NOTICING!

TO BE
CONTINUED

CHAPTER FOUR

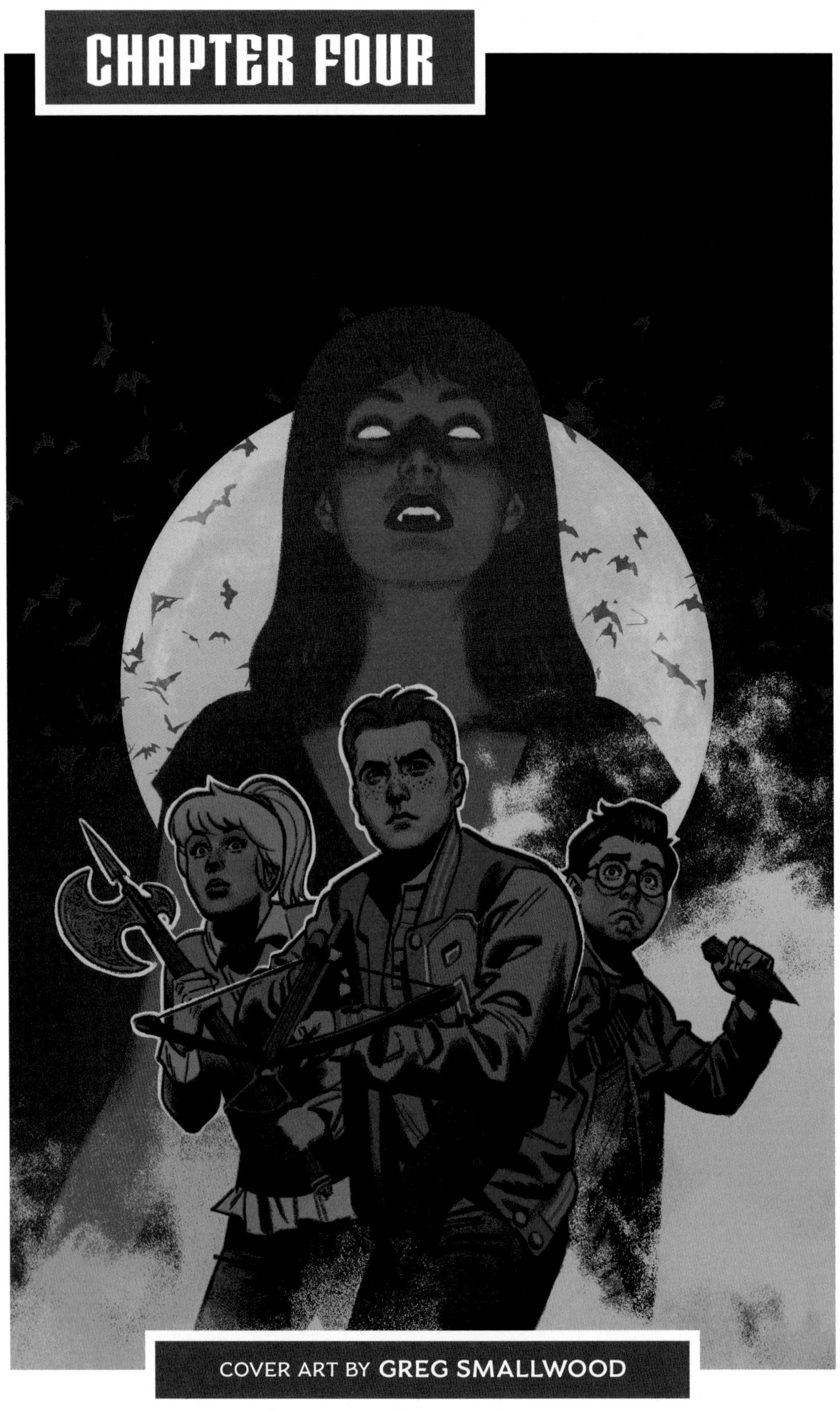

COVER ART BY **GREG SMALLWOOD**

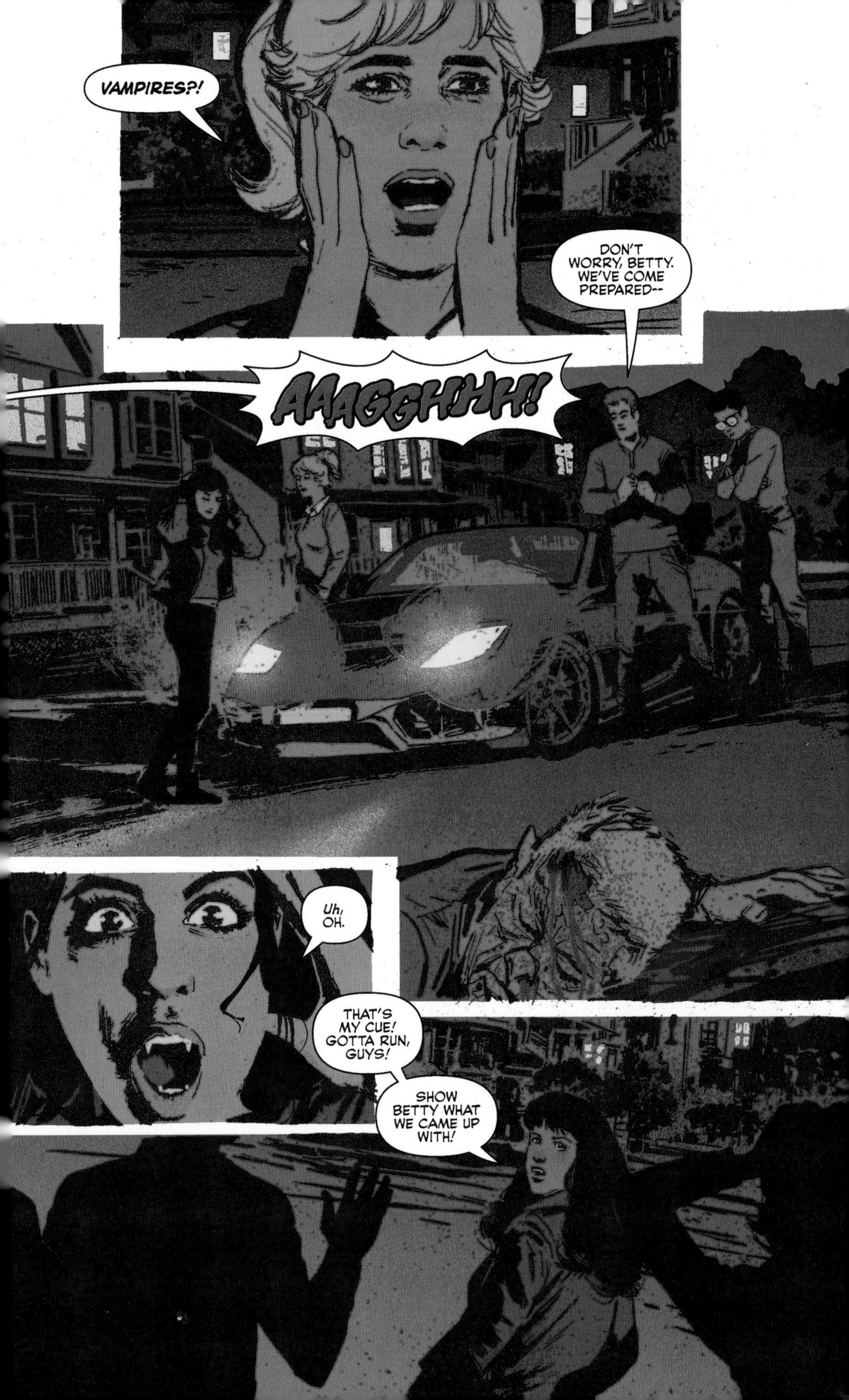
VAMPIRES?!
DON'T WORRY, BETTY. WE'VE COME PREPARED--
AAAGGHHH!
Uh, OH.
THAT'S MY CUE! GOTTA RUN, GUYS!
SHOW BETTY WHAT WE CAME UP WITH!

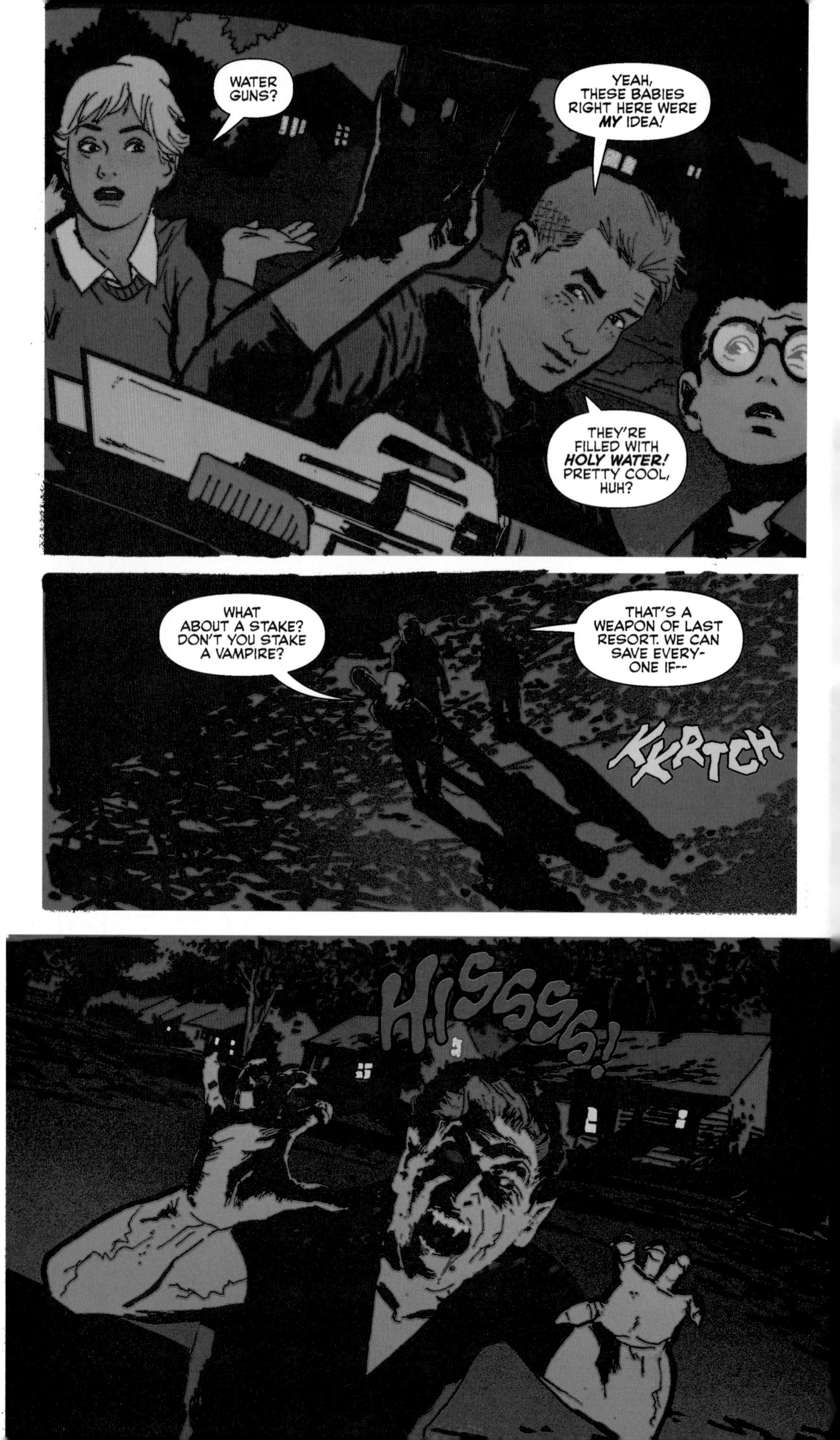
WATER GUNS?
YEAH, THESE BABIES RIGHT HERE WERE MY IDEA!
THEY'RE FILLED WITH HOLY WATER! PRETTY COOL, HUH?
WHAT ABOUT A STAKE? DON'T YOU STAKE A VAMPIRE?
THAT'S A WEAPON OF LAST RESORT. WE CAN SAVE EVERY-ONE IF--
KKRTCH
HISSSSS!

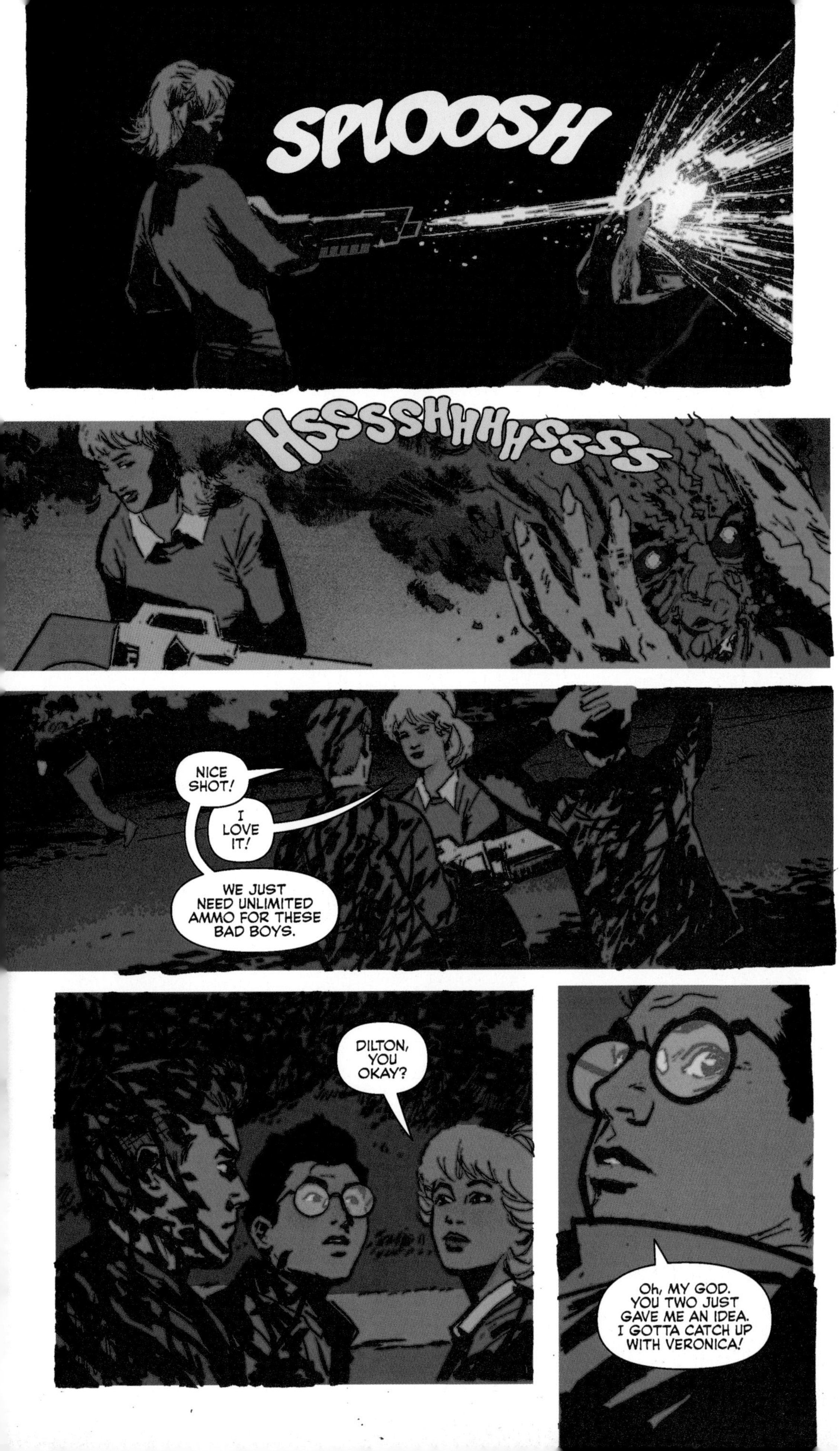
SPLOOSH
HSSSSHHHHSSSS
NICE SHOT!
I LOVE IT!
WE JUST NEED UNLIMITED AMMO FOR THESE BAD BOYS.
DILTON, YOU OKAY?
Oh, MY GOD. YOU TWO JUST GAVE ME AN IDEA. I GOTTA CATCH UP WITH VERONICA!

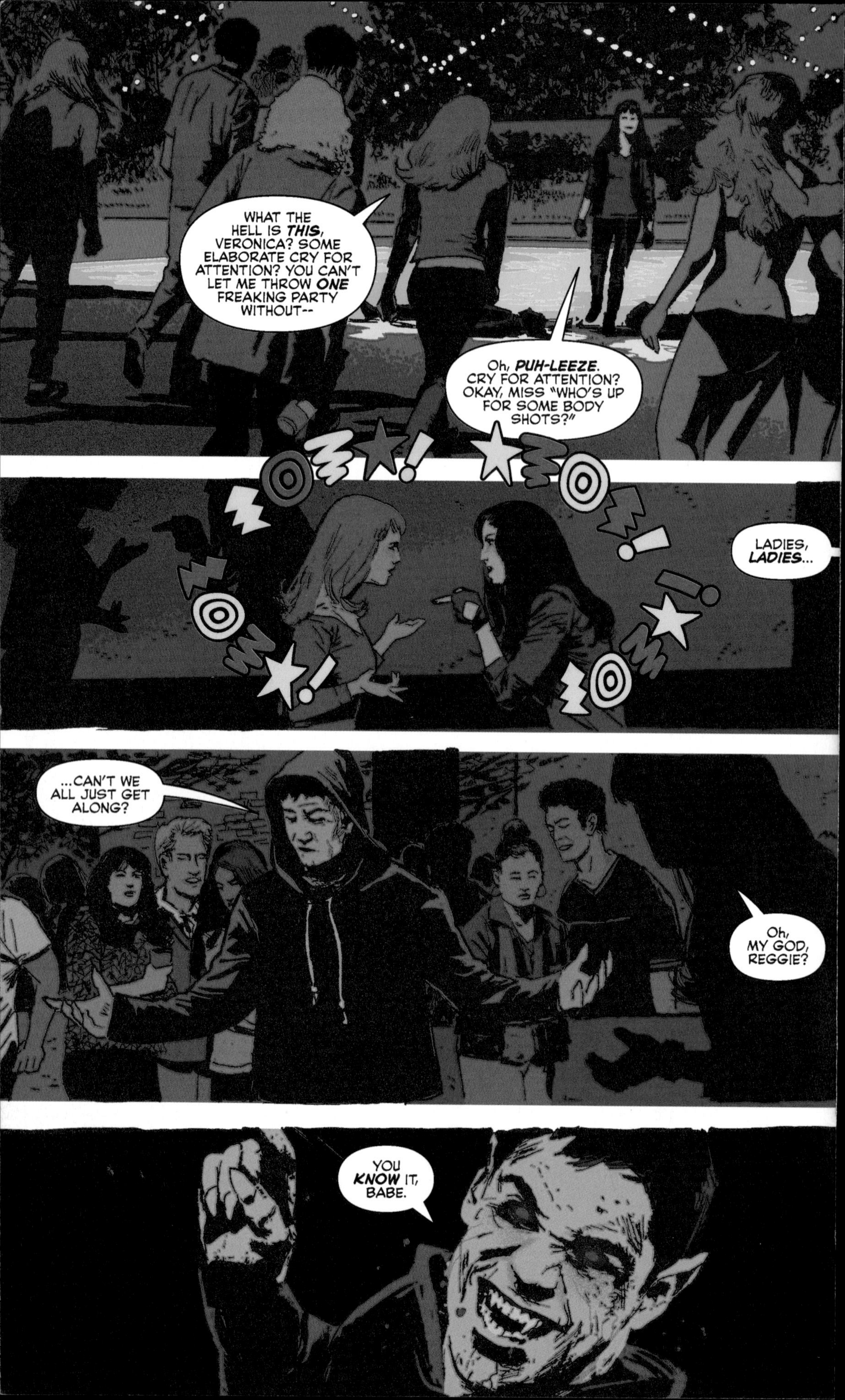
WHAT THE HELL IS THIS, VERONICA? SOME ELABORATE CRY FOR ATTENTION? YOU CAN'T LET ME THROW ONE FREAKING PARTY WITHOUT--
Oh, PUH-LEEZE. CRY FOR ATTENTION? OKAY, MISS "WHO'S UP FOR SOME BODY SHOTS?"
LADIES, LADIES...
...CAN'T WE ALL JUST GET ALONG?
Oh, MY GOD, REGGIE?
YOU KNOW IT, BABE.

TELL ME, RONNIE...

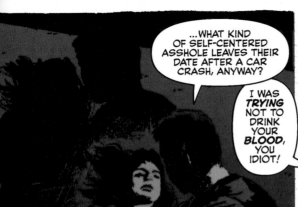

...WHAT KIND OF SELF-CENTERED ASSHOLE LEAVES THEIR DATE AFTER A CAR CRASH, ANYWAY?

I WAS *TRYING* NOT TO DRINK YOUR *BLOOD*, YOU IDIOT!

SORRY, NOT SORRY!

KRAK

Heh.

STORY OF YOUR *LIFE*, YOU--

THOK

Oh, SHUDDUP!

I DIDN'T WANT TO GO OUT WITH YOU *ANYWAY*!

VERONICA! I'VE GOT AN IDEA...

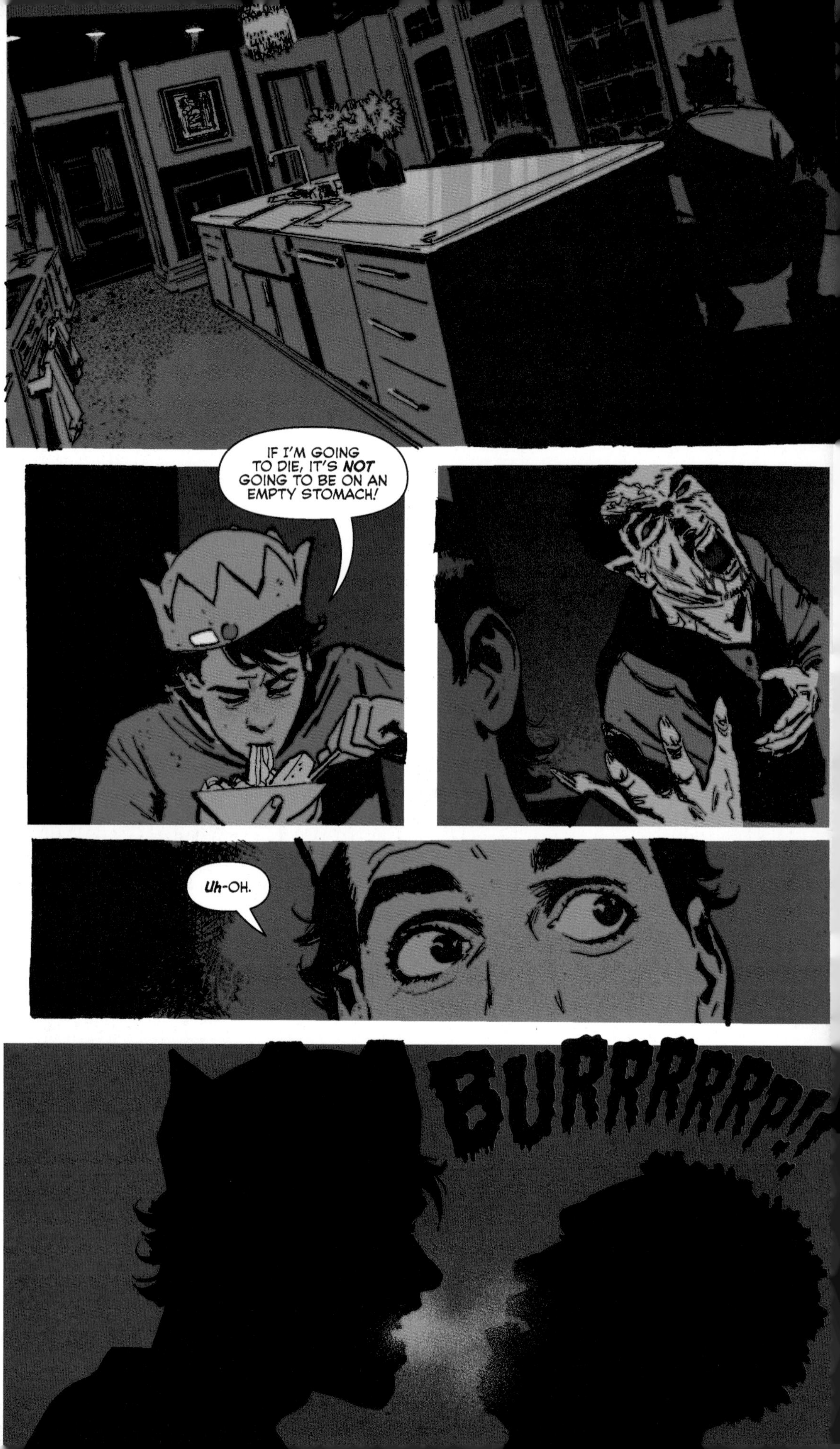
IF I'M GOING TO DIE, IT'S NOT GOING TO BE ON AN EMPTY STOMACH!
Uh-OH.
BURRRRRP!!

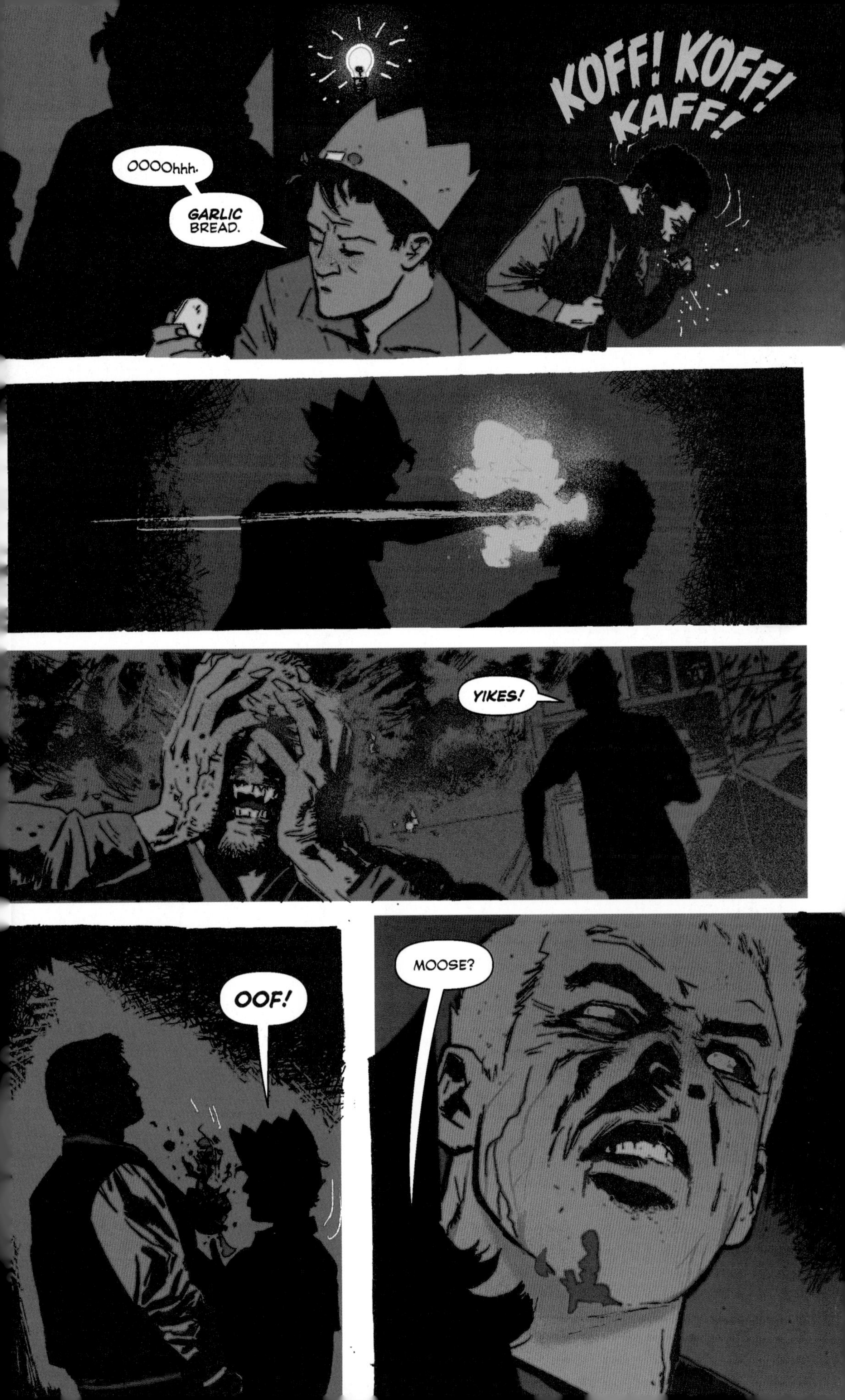
KOFF! KOFF! KAFF!
OOOOhhh.
GARLIC BREAD.
YIKES!
OOF!
MOOSE?

SSSSSSSS

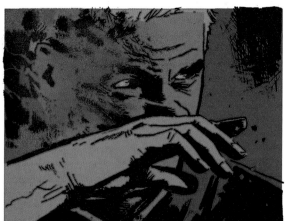

Uh... SORRY?

SKRASH

OOF!

UNGH...

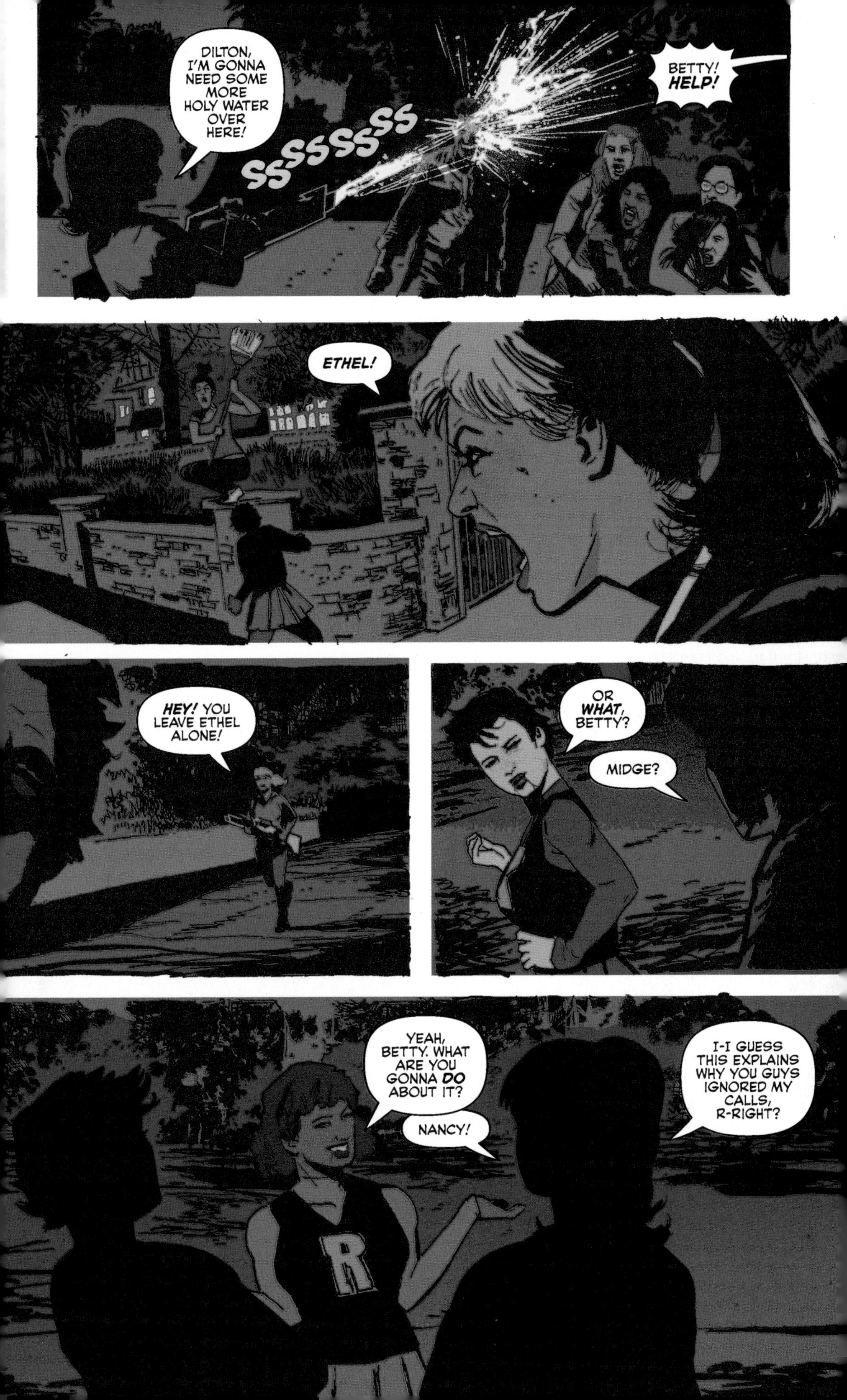
DILTON, I'M GONNA NEED SOME MORE HOLY WATER OVER HERE!
SSSSSSSSS
BETTY! HELP!
ETHEL!
HEY! YOU LEAVE ETHEL ALONE!
OR WHAT, BETTY?
MIDGE?
YEAH, BETTY. WHAT ARE YOU GONNA DO ABOUT IT?
NANCY!
I-I GUESS THIS EXPLAINS WHY YOU GUYS IGNORED MY CALLS, R-RIGHT?

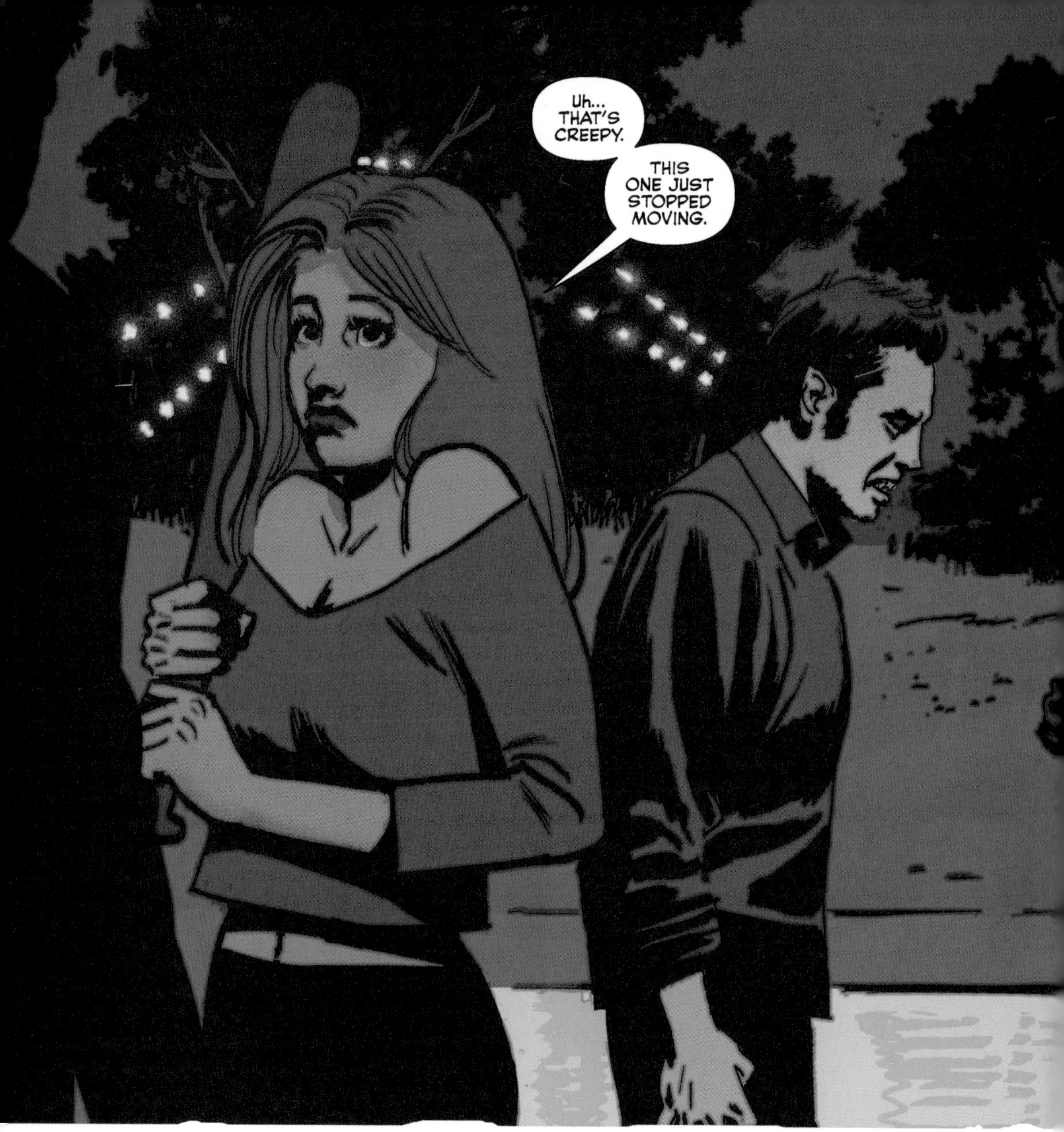
Uh... THAT'S CREEPY.
THIS ONE JUST STOPPED MOVING.

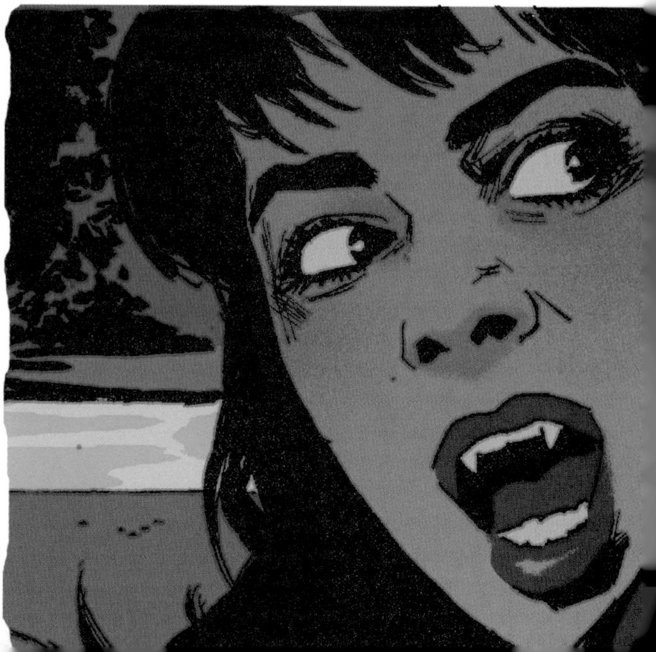

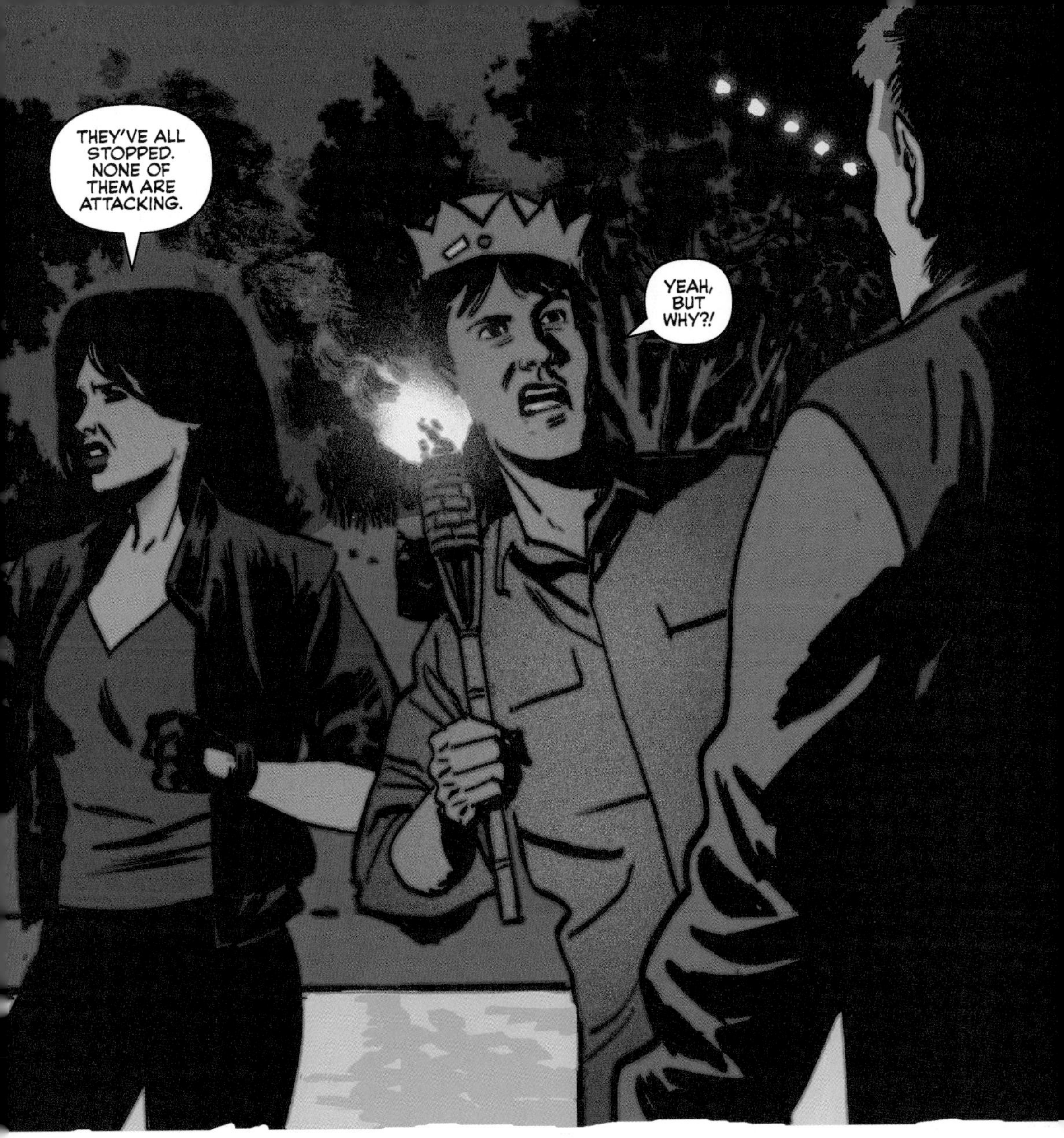
THEY'VE ALL STOPPED. NONE OF THEM ARE ATTACKING.
YEAH, BUT WHY?!

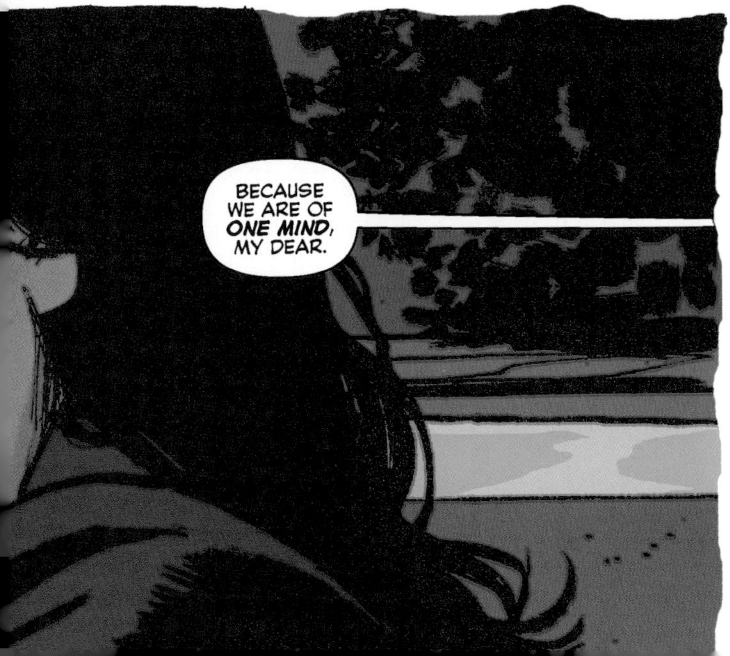
BECAUSE WE ARE OF ***ONE MIND***, MY DEAR.

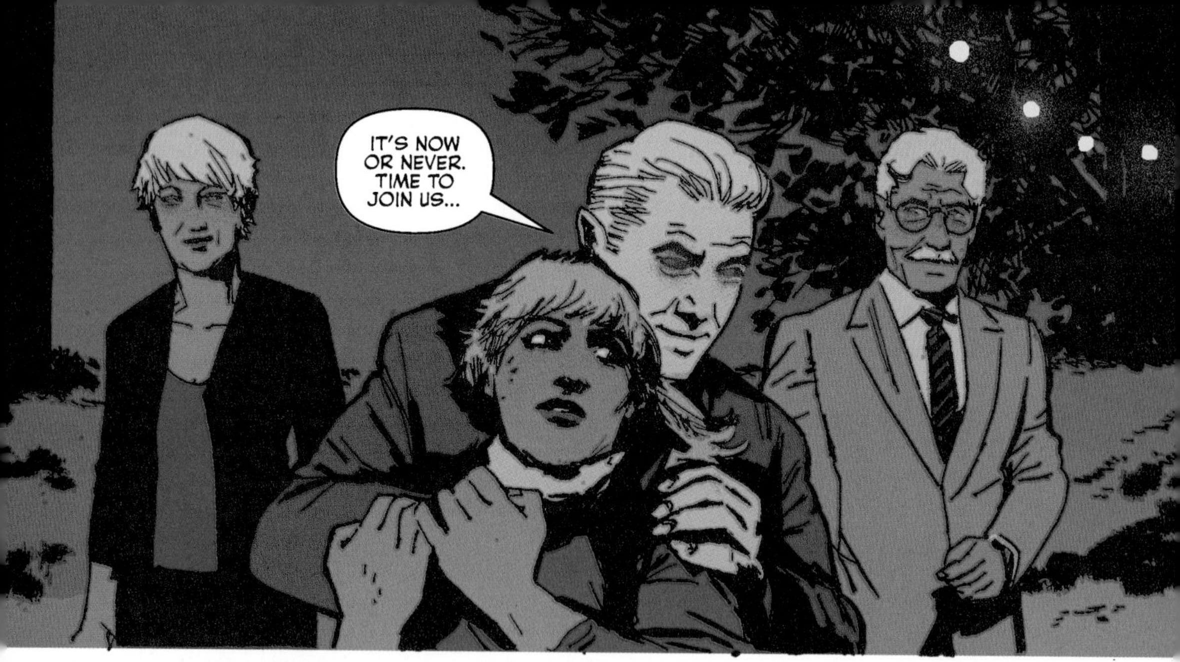
IT'S NOW OR NEVER. TIME TO JOIN US...

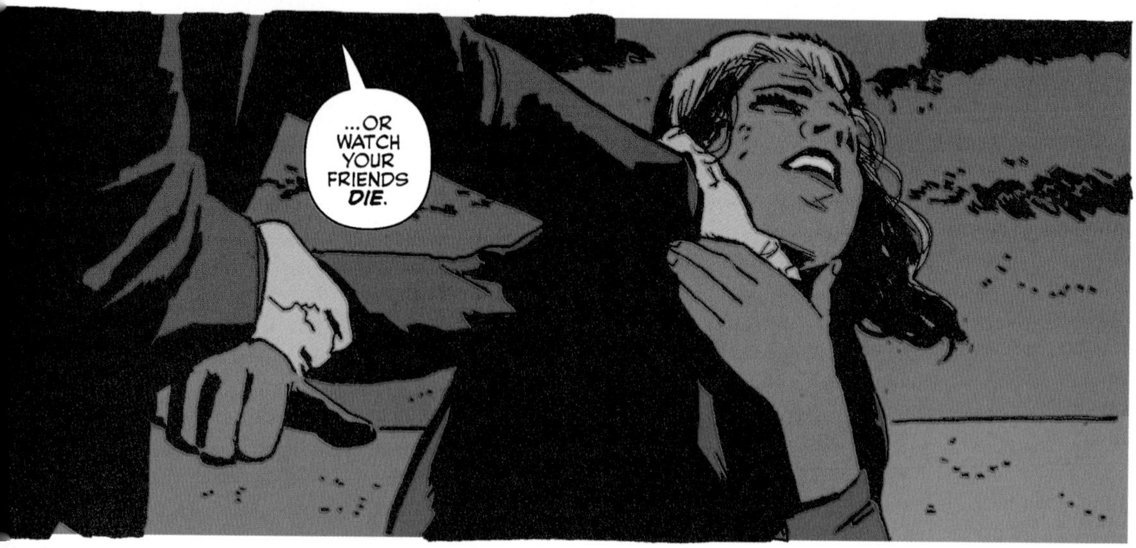
...OR WATCH YOUR FRIENDS *DIE*.

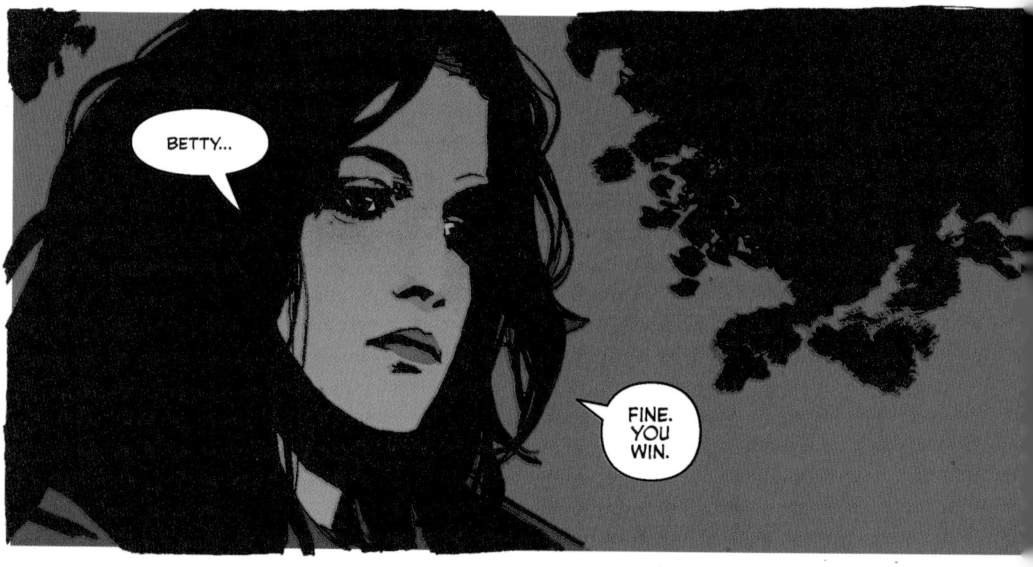
BETTY...
FINE. YOU WIN.

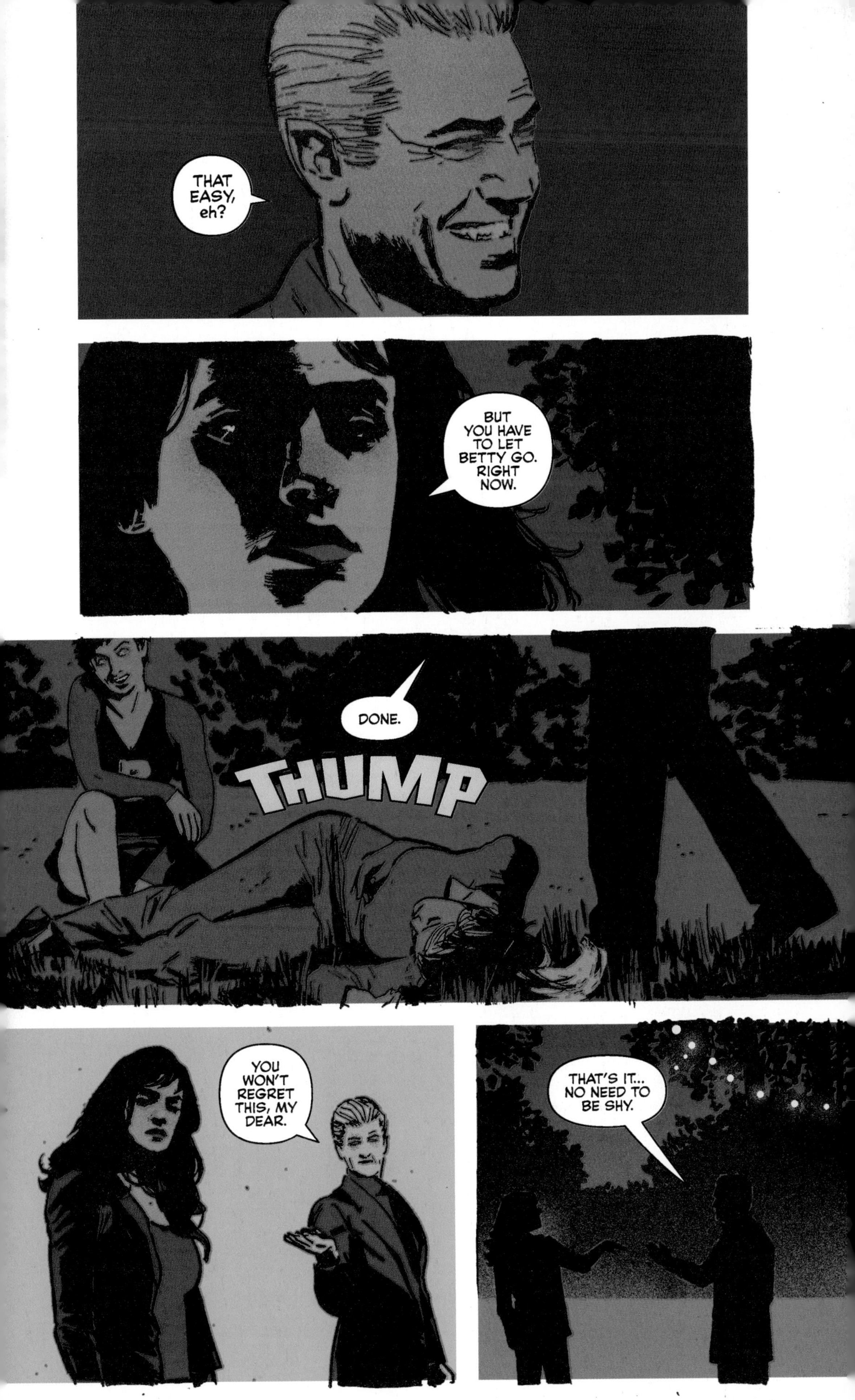
THAT EASY, eh?
BUT YOU HAVE TO LET BETTY GO. RIGHT NOW.
DONE.
THUMP
YOU WON'T REGRET THIS, MY DEAR.
THAT'S IT... NO NEED TO BE SHY.

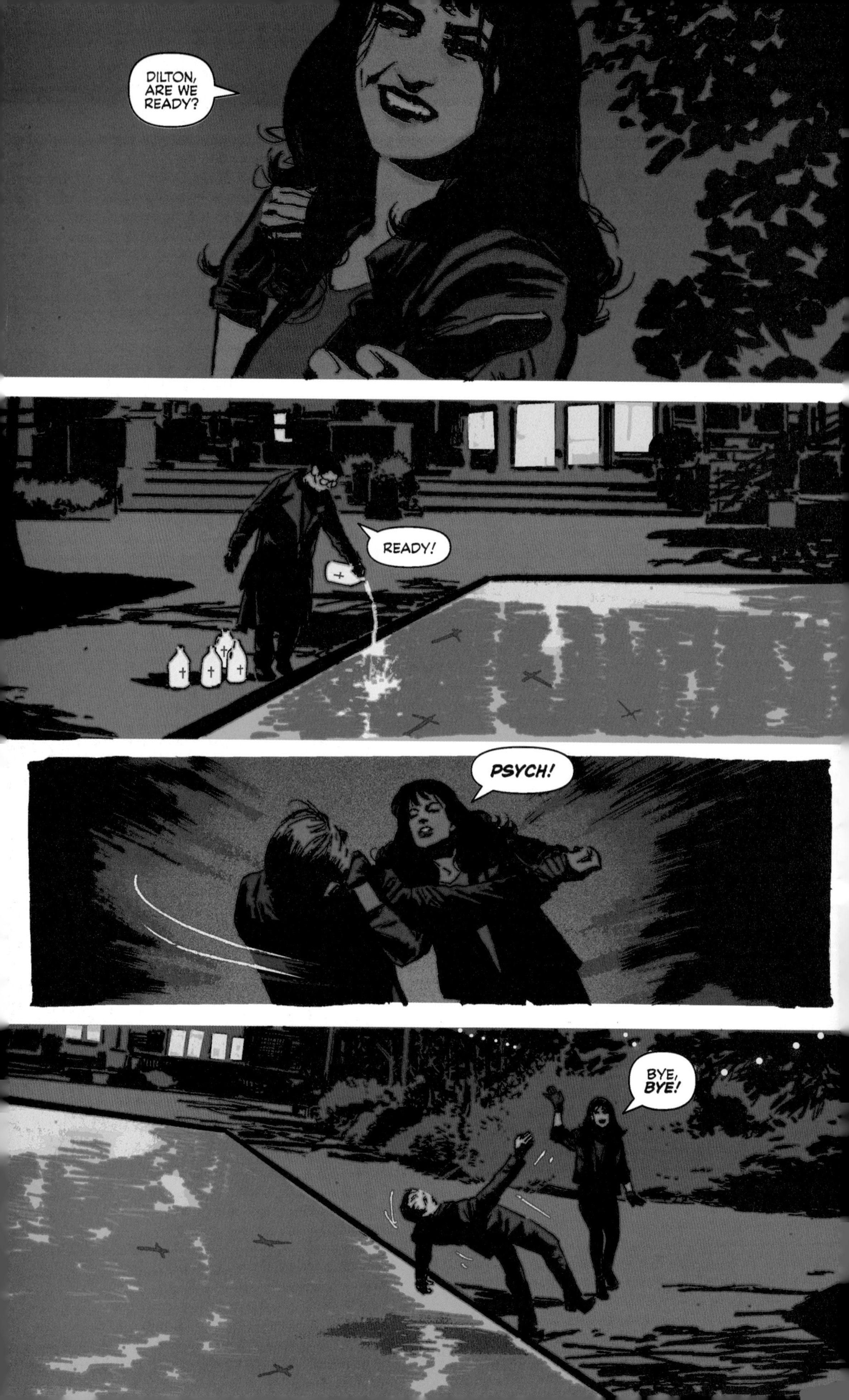
DILTON, ARE WE READY?
READY!
PSYCH!
BYE, BYE!

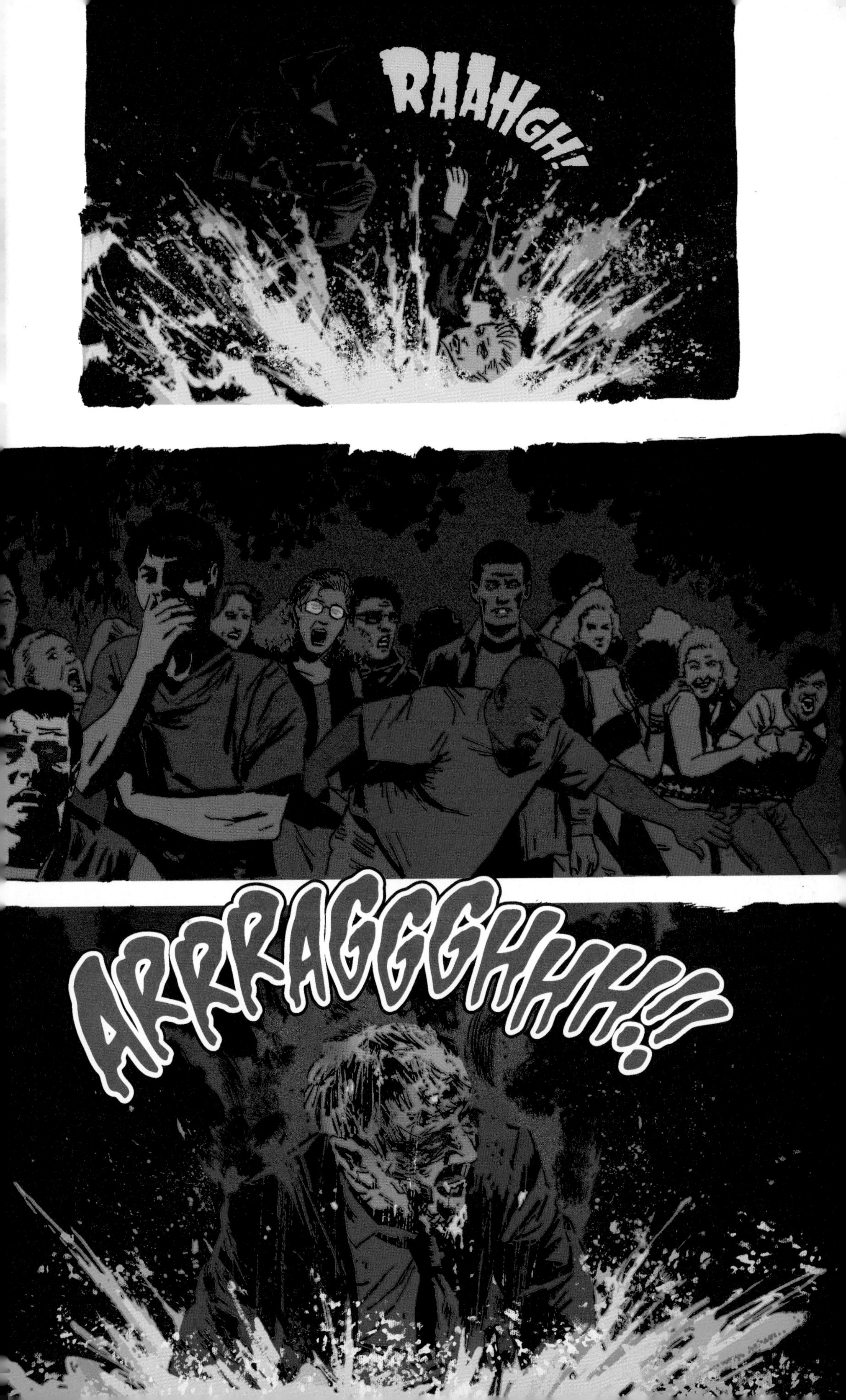
RAAHGH!
ARRRAGGGHHH!!!

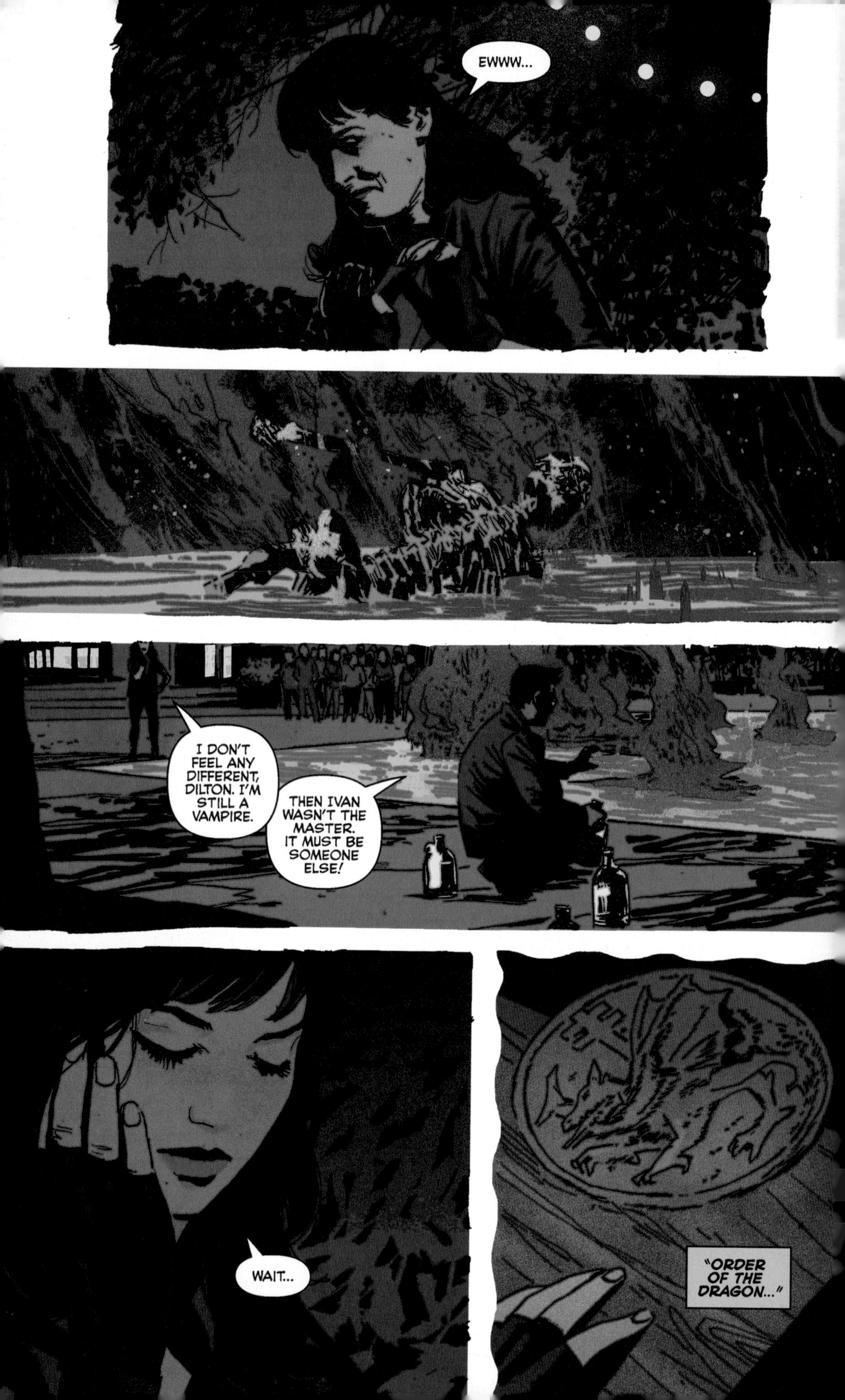
EWWW...
I DON'T FEEL ANY DIFFERENT, DILTON. I'M STILL A VAMPIRE.
THEN IVAN WASN'T THE MASTER. IT MUST BE SOMEONE ELSE!
WAIT...
"ORDER OF THE DRAGON..."

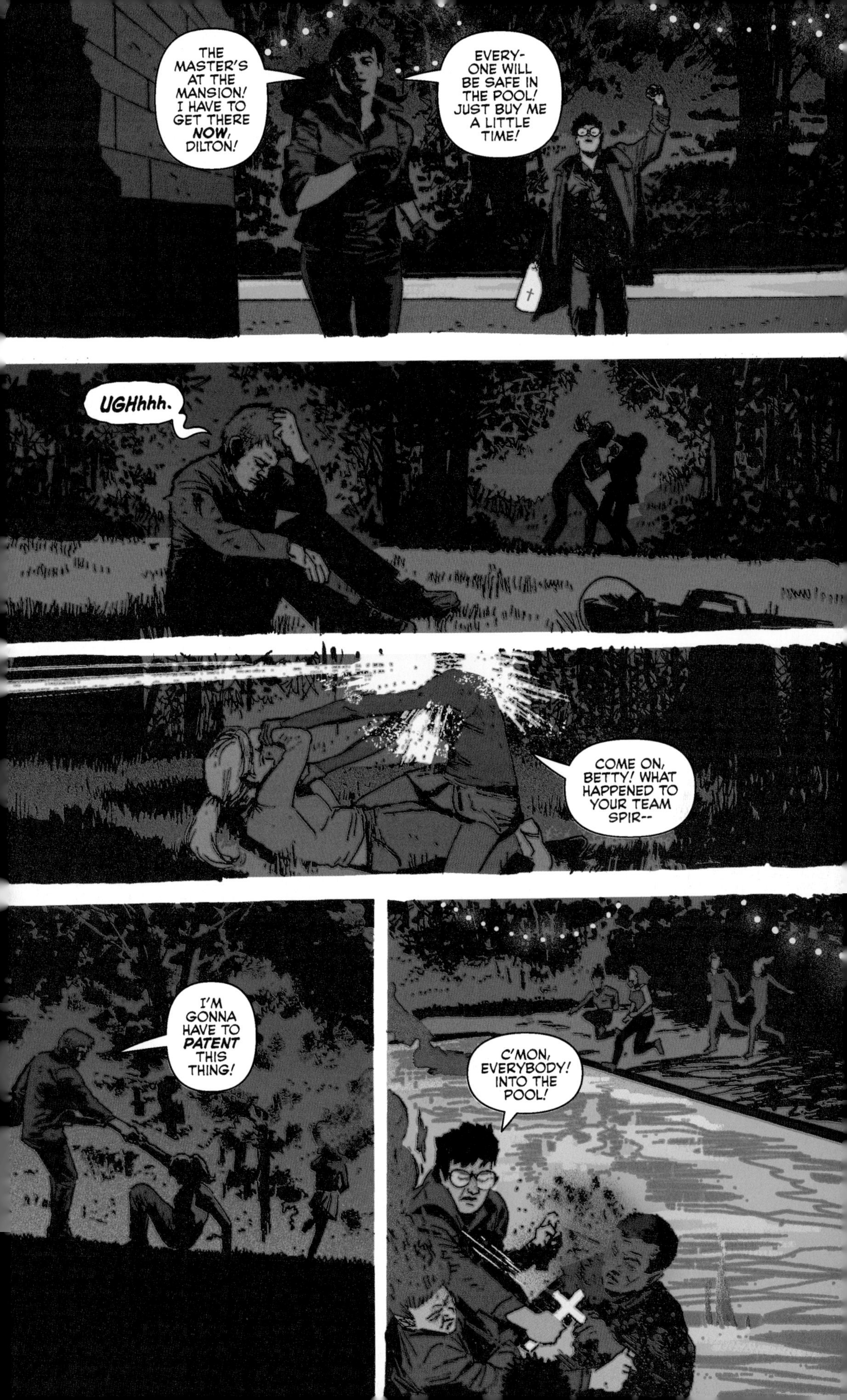
THE MASTER'S AT THE MANSION! I HAVE TO GET THERE NOW, DILTON!
EVERY-ONE WILL BE SAFE IN THE POOL! JUST BUY ME A LITTLE TIME!
UGHhhh.
COME ON, BETTY! WHAT HAPPENED TO YOUR TEAM SPIR--
I'M GONNA HAVE TO PATENT THIS THING!
C'MON, EVERYBODY! INTO THE POOL!

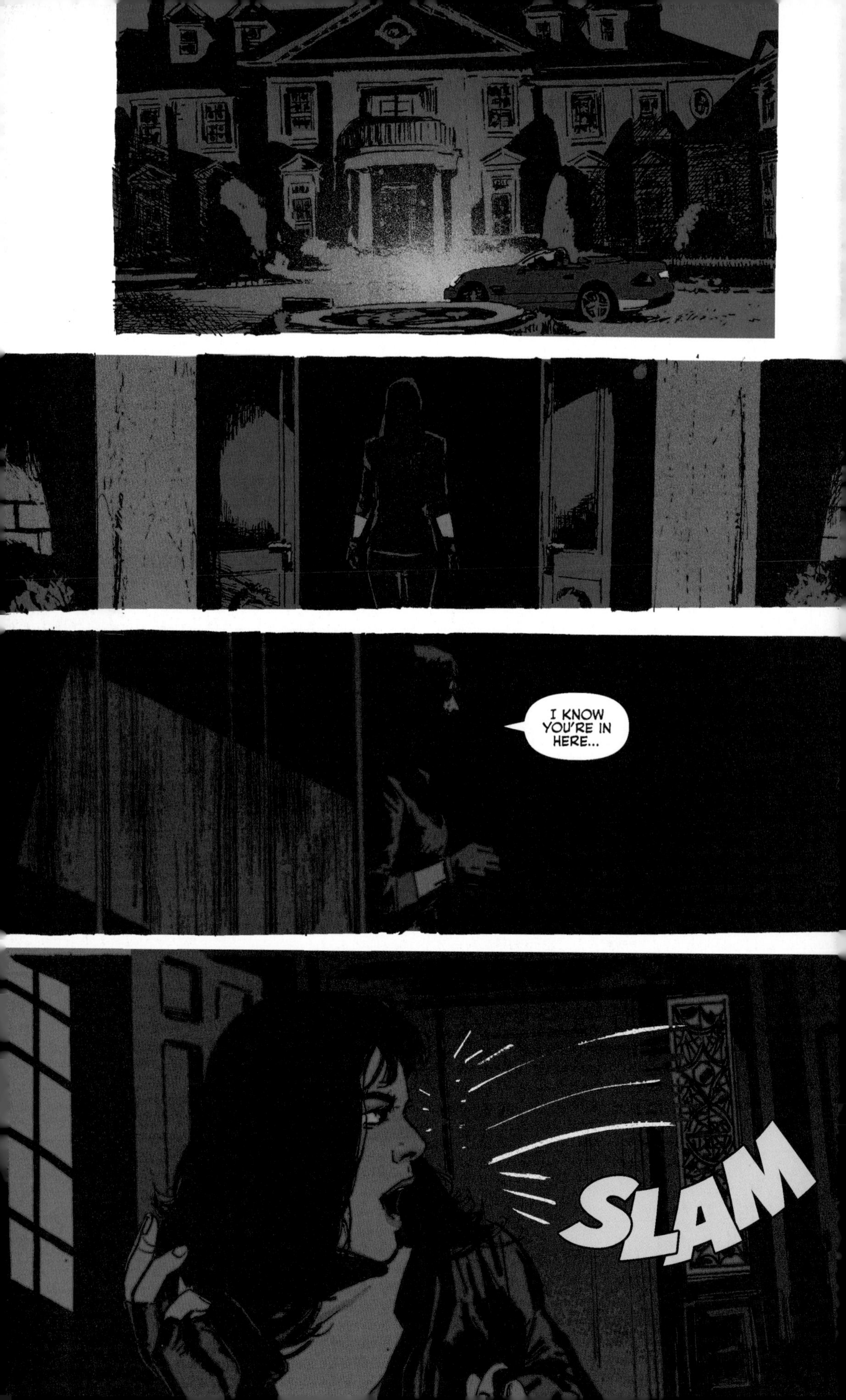
I KNOW YOU'RE IN HERE...
SLAM

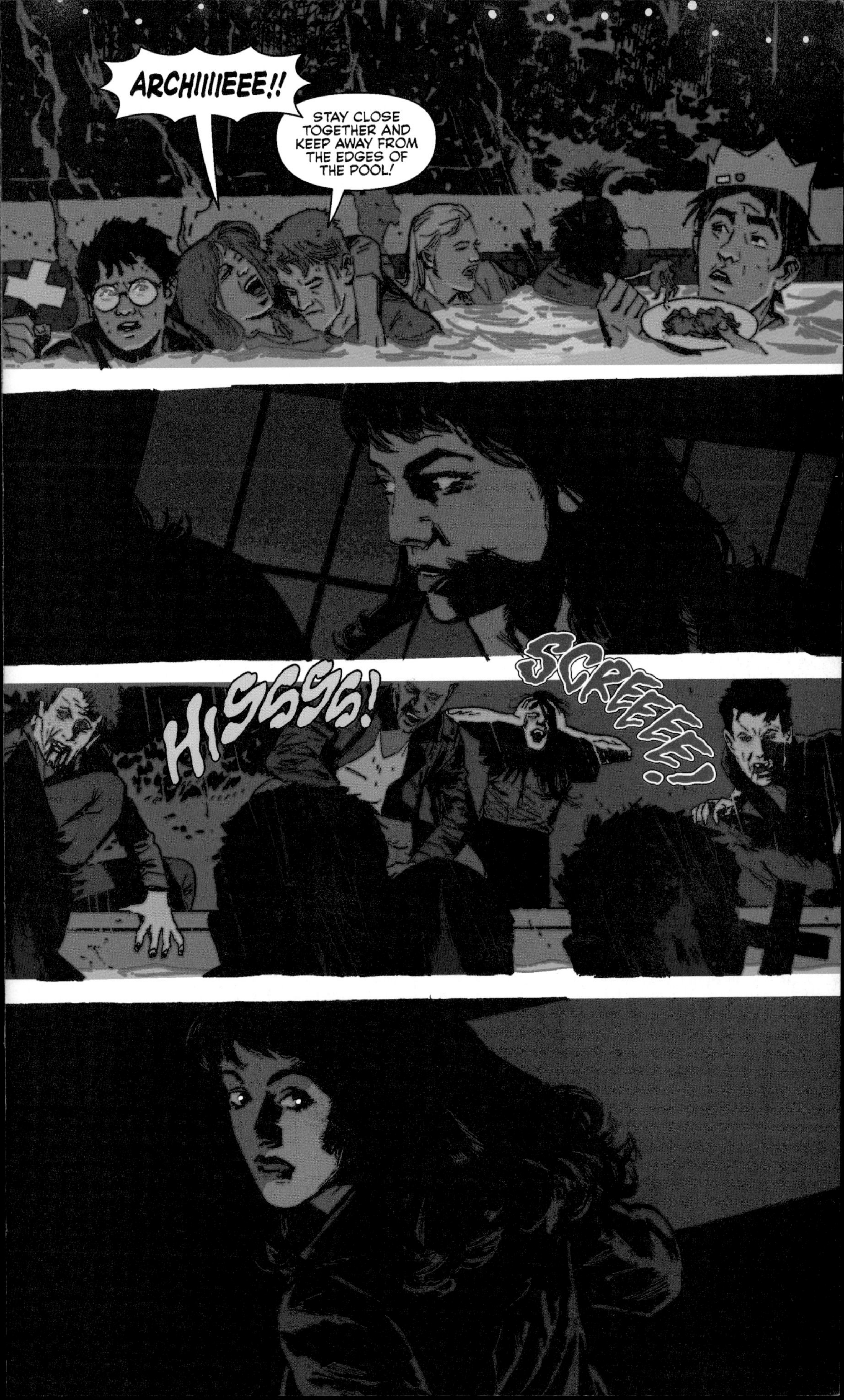
ARCHIIIIEEE!!
STAY CLOSE TOGETHER AND KEEP AWAY FROM THE EDGES OF THE POOL!
HISSSSS!
SCREEEE!

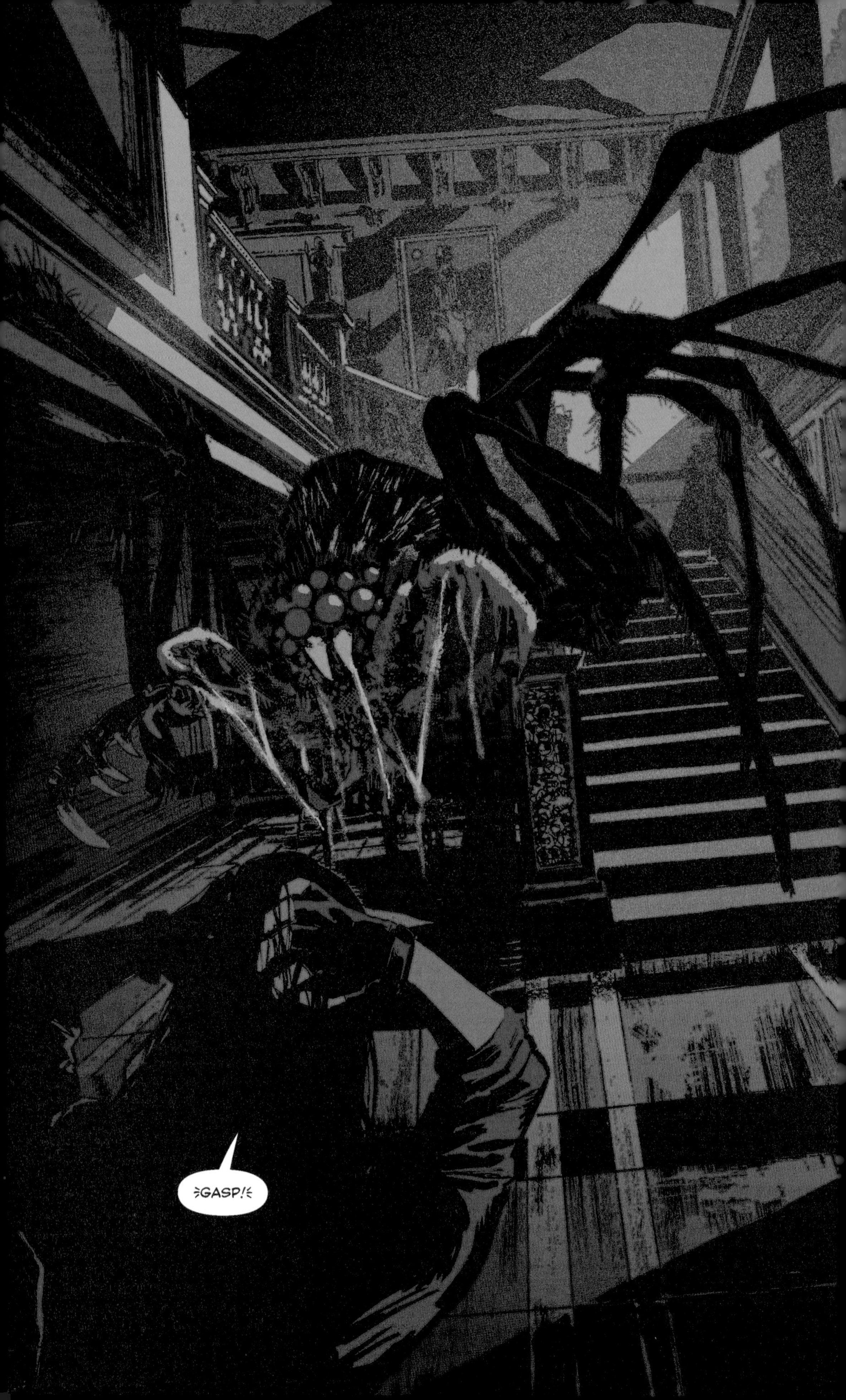
GASP!

TO BE CONTINUED

CHAPTER FIVE

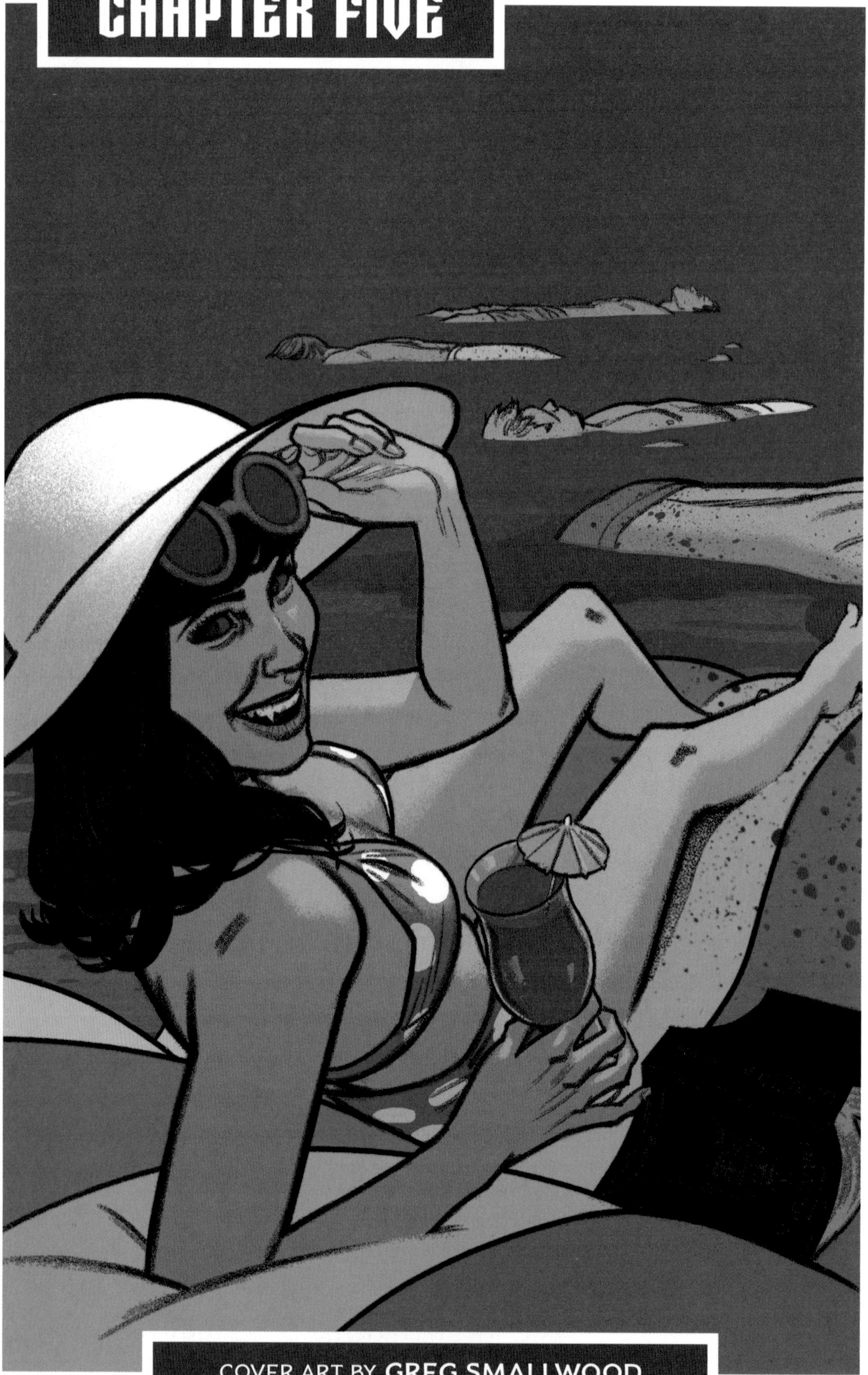

COVER ART BY **GREG SMALLWOOD**

AIEEEEE!!

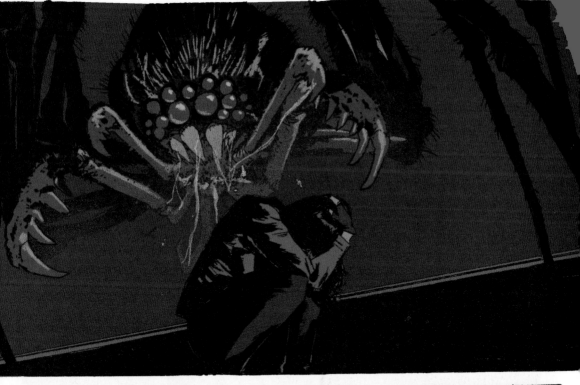

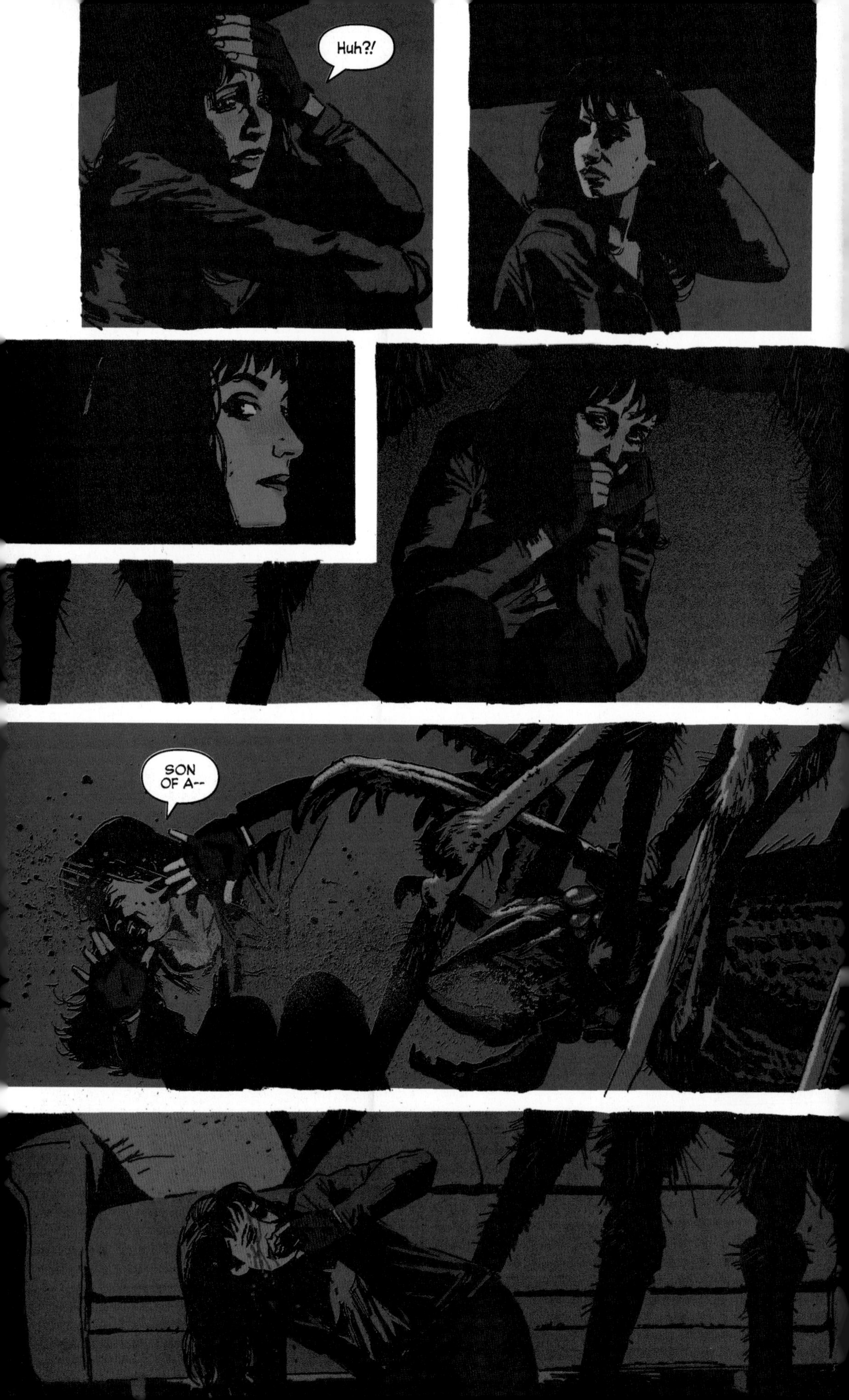
Huh?!
SON OF A--

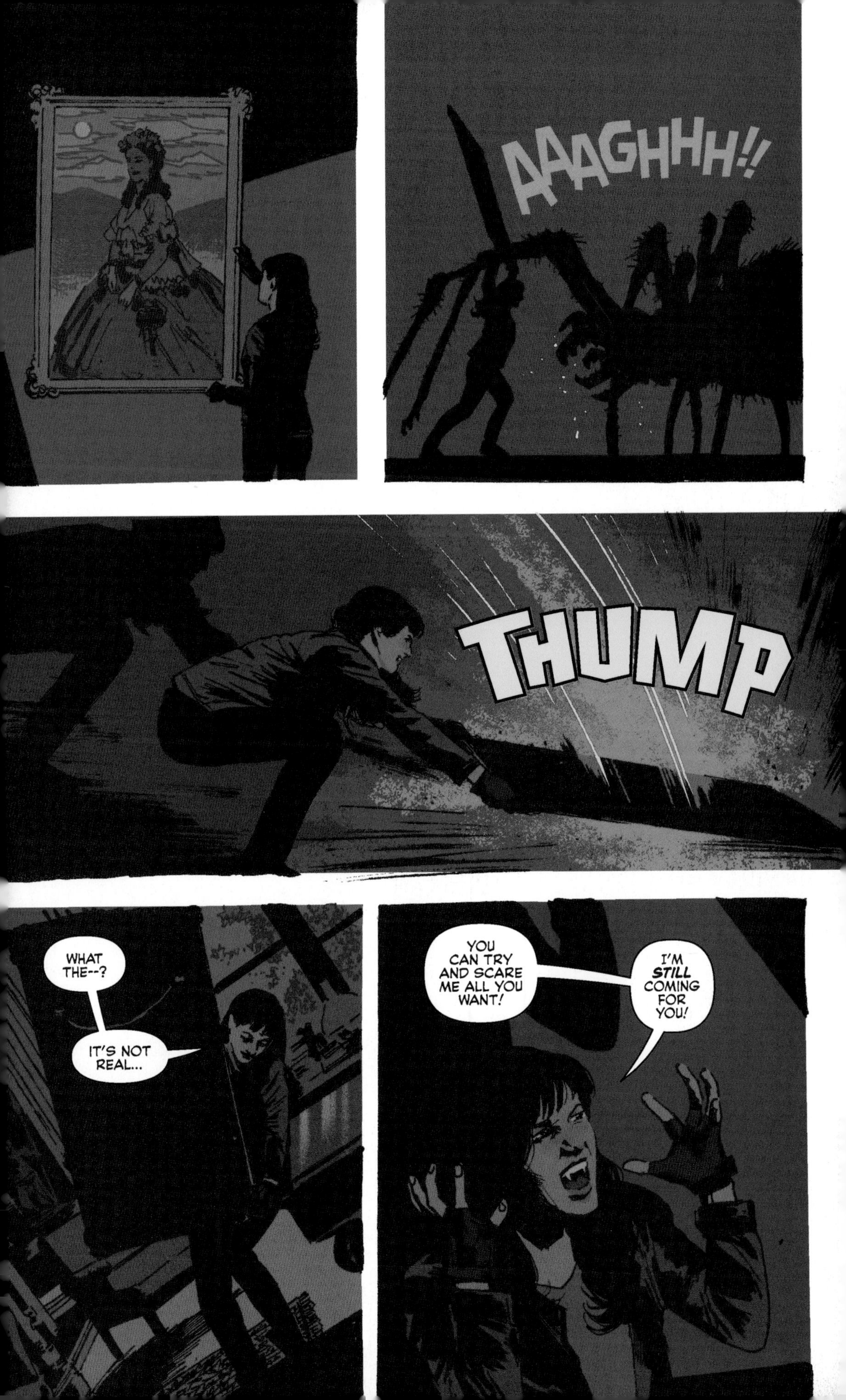
AAAGHHH!!
THUMP
WHAT THE--?
IT'S NOT REAL...
YOU CAN TRY AND SCARE ME ALL YOU WANT!
I'M STILL COMING FOR YOU!

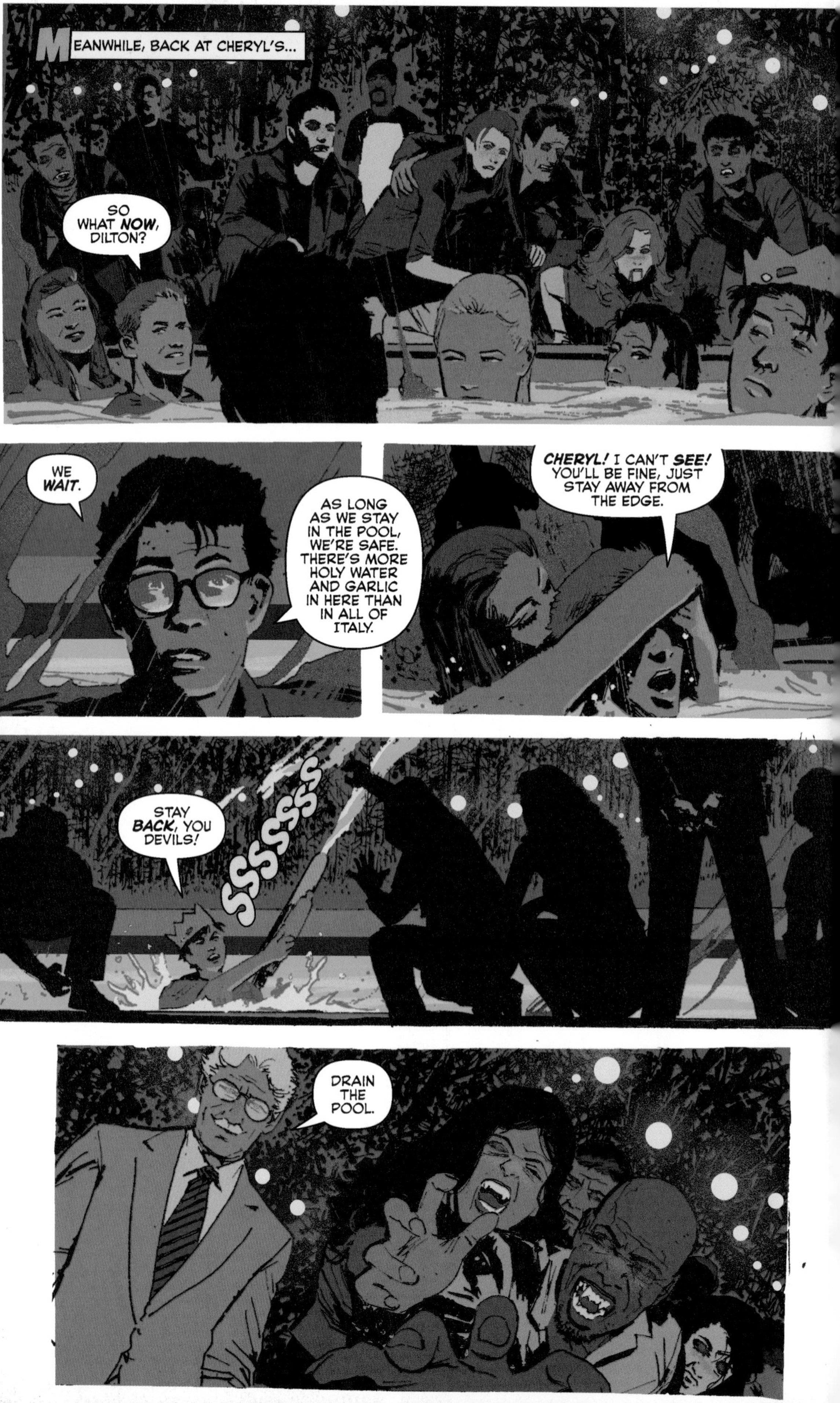
MEANWHILE, BACK AT CHERYL'S...
SO WHAT **NOW**, DILTON?
WE **WAIT**.
AS LONG AS WE STAY IN THE POOL, WE'RE SAFE. THERE'S MORE HOLY WATER AND GARLIC IN HERE THAN IN ALL OF ITALY.
CHERYL! I CAN'T **SEE!**
YOU'LL BE FINE, JUST STAY AWAY FROM THE EDGE.
STAY **BACK**, YOU DEVILS!
SSSSSSS
DRAIN THE POOL.

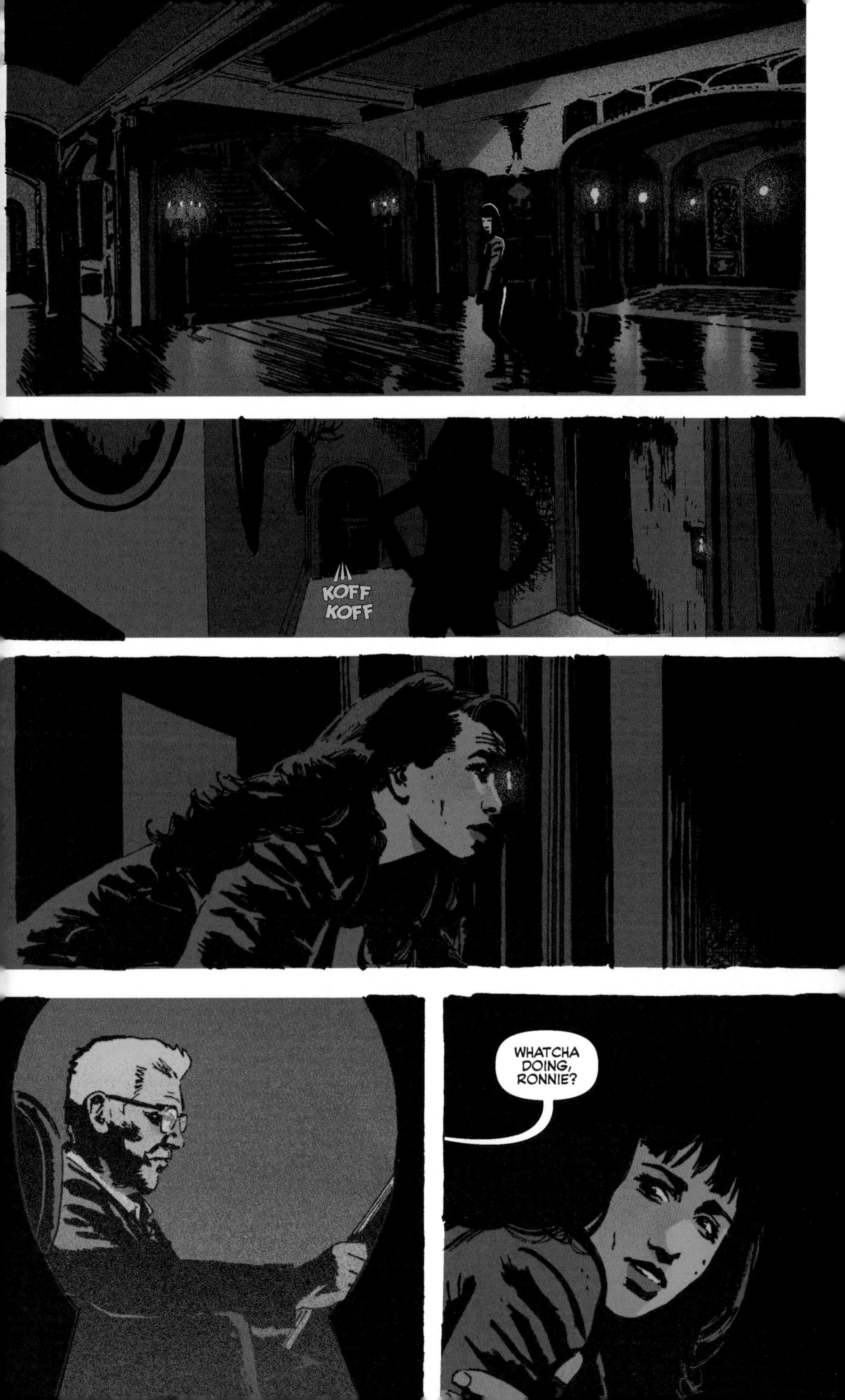
KOFF
KOFF
WHATCHA DOING, RONNIE?

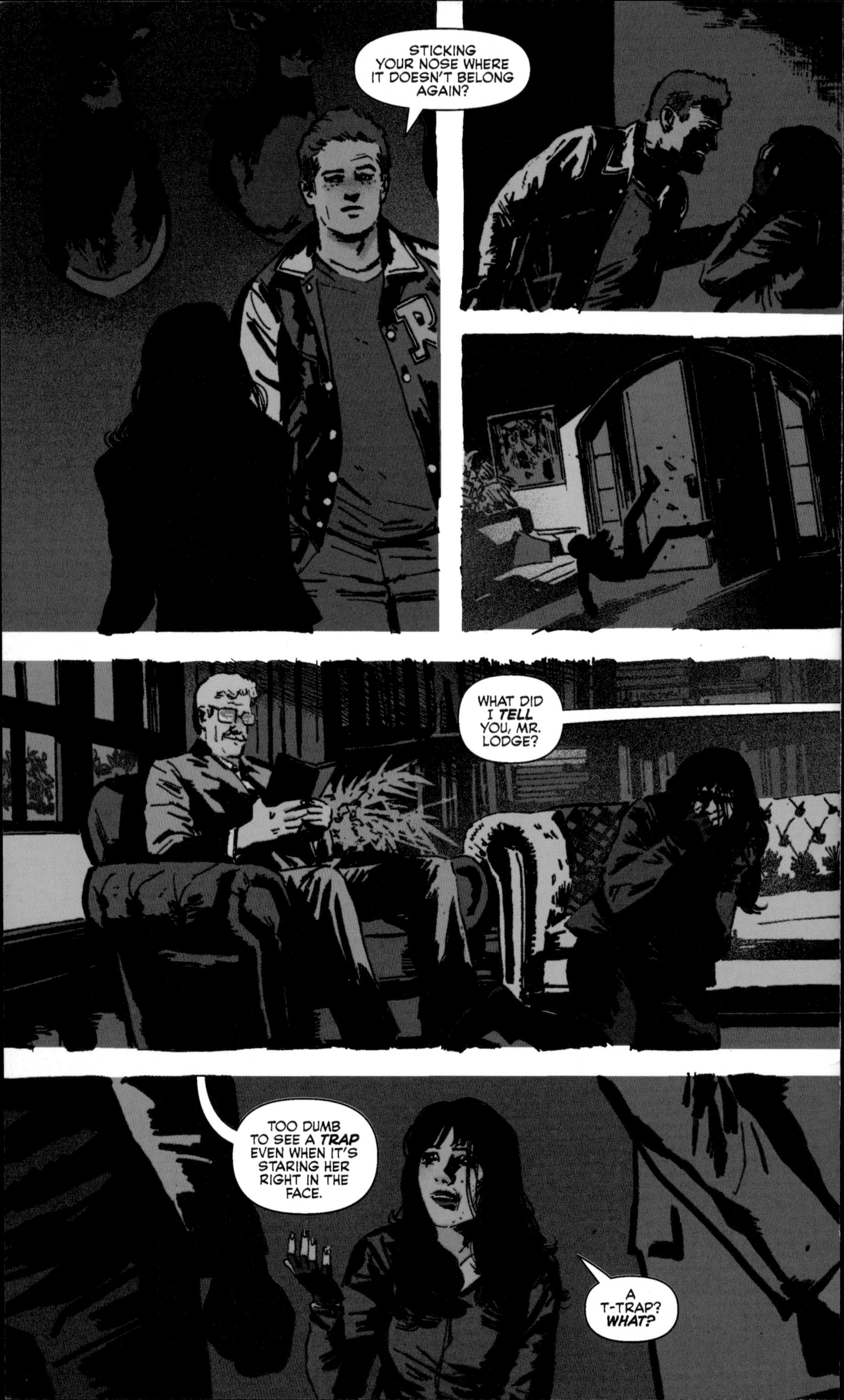
STICKING YOUR NOSE WHERE IT DOESN'T BELONG AGAIN?
WHAT DID I TELL YOU, MR. LODGE?
TOO DUMB TO SEE A TRAP EVEN WHEN IT'S STARING HER RIGHT IN THE FACE.
A T-TRAP? WHAT?

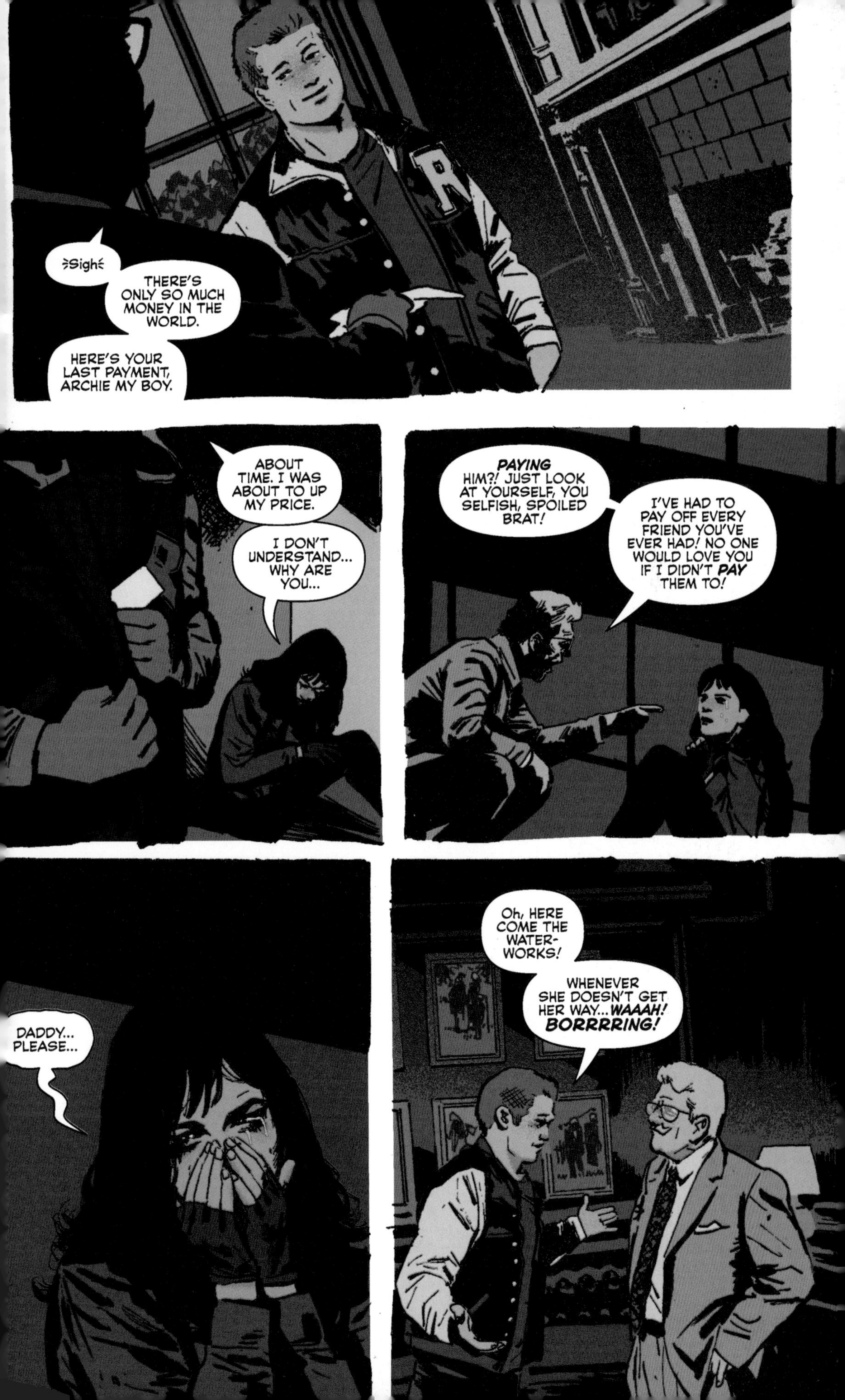
Sigh
THERE'S ONLY SO MUCH MONEY IN THE WORLD.
HERE'S YOUR LAST PAYMENT, ARCHIE MY BOY.
ABOUT TIME. I WAS ABOUT TO UP MY PRICE.
I DON'T UNDERSTAND... WHY ARE YOU...
PAYING HIM?! JUST LOOK AT YOURSELF, YOU SELFISH, SPOILED BRAT!
I'VE HAD TO PAY OFF EVERY FRIEND YOU'VE EVER HAD! NO ONE WOULD LOVE YOU IF I DIDN'T PAY THEM TO!
DADDY... PLEASE...
Oh, HERE COME THE WATER-WORKS!
WHENEVER SHE DOESN'T GET HER WAY...WAAAH! BORRRRING!

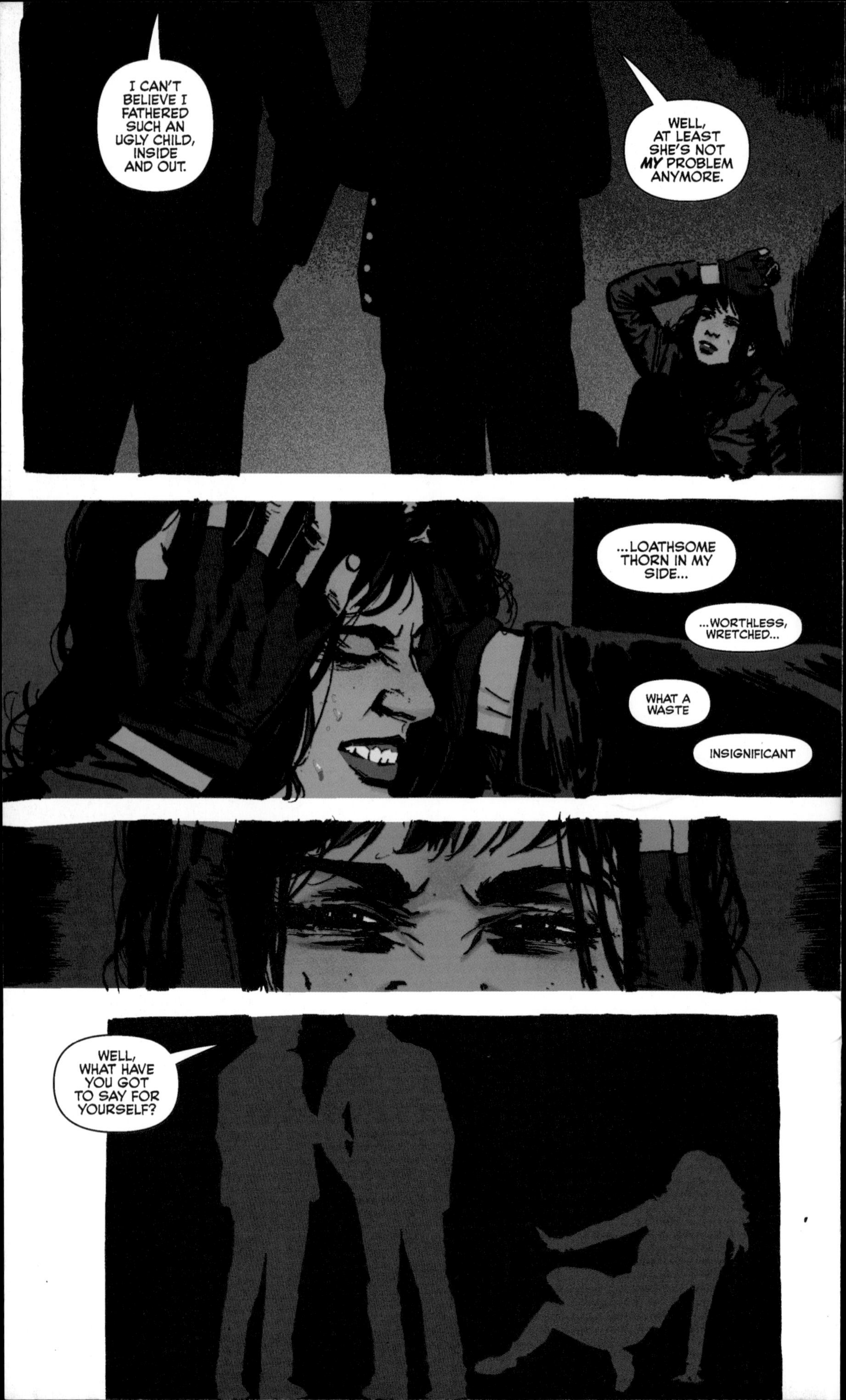
I CAN'T BELIEVE I FATHERED SUCH AN UGLY CHILD, INSIDE AND OUT.
WELL, AT LEAST SHE'S NOT MY PROBLEM ANYMORE.
...LOATHSOME THORN IN MY SIDE...
...WORTHLESS, WRETCHED...
WHAT A WASTE
INSIGNIFICANT
WELL, WHAT HAVE YOU GOT TO SAY FOR YOURSELF?

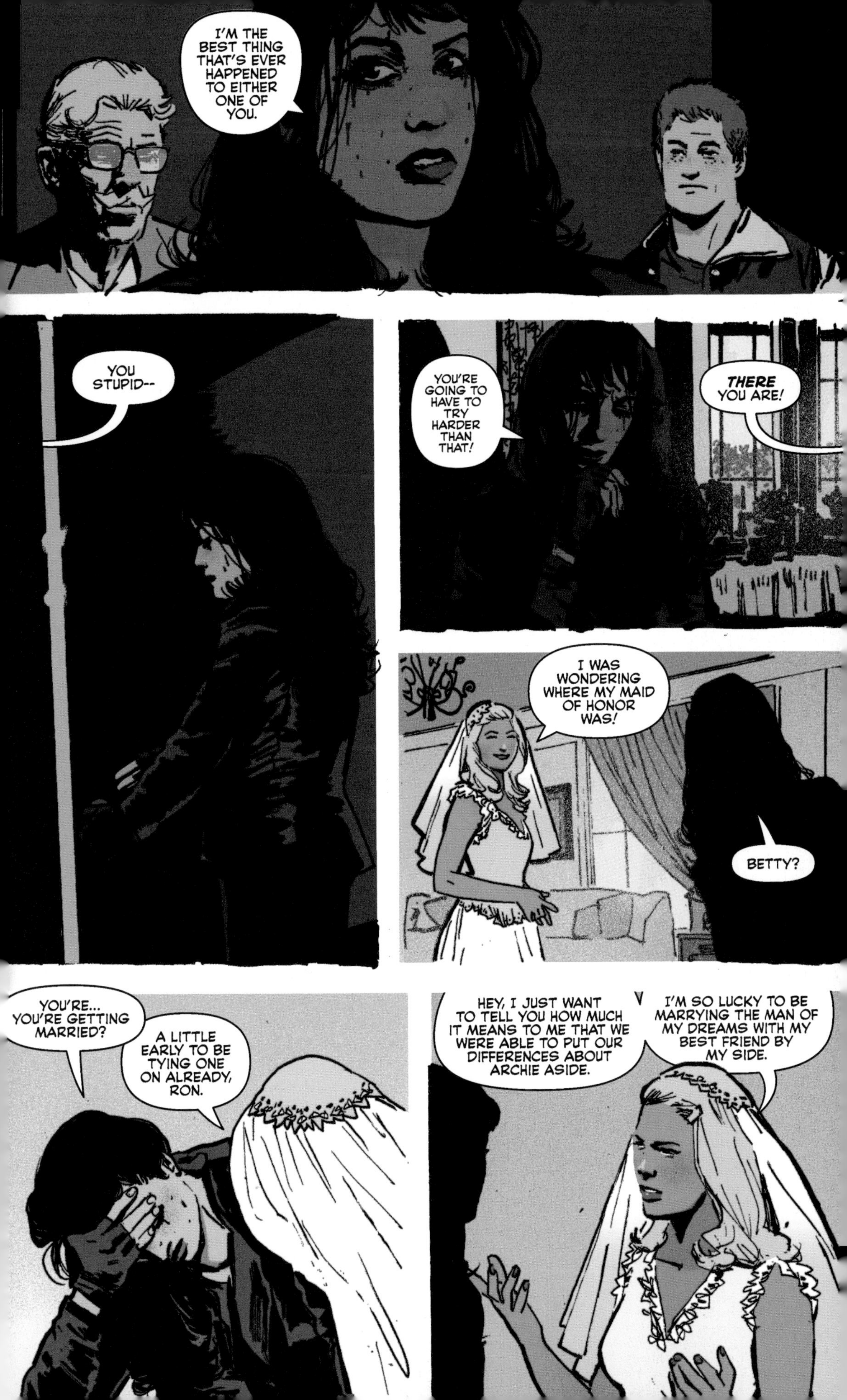
I'M THE BEST THING THAT'S EVER HAPPENED TO EITHER ONE OF YOU.
YOU STUPID--
YOU'RE GOING TO HAVE TO TRY HARDER THAN THAT!
THERE YOU ARE!
I WAS WONDERING WHERE MY MAID OF HONOR WAS!
BETTY?
YOU'RE... YOU'RE GETTING MARRIED?
A LITTLE EARLY TO BE TYING ONE ON ALREADY, RON.
HEY, I JUST WANT TO TELL YOU HOW MUCH IT MEANS TO ME THAT WE WERE ABLE TO PUT OUR DIFFERENCES ABOUT ARCHIE ASIDE.
I'M SO LUCKY TO BE MARRYING THE MAN OF MY DREAMS WITH MY BEST FRIEND BY MY SIDE.

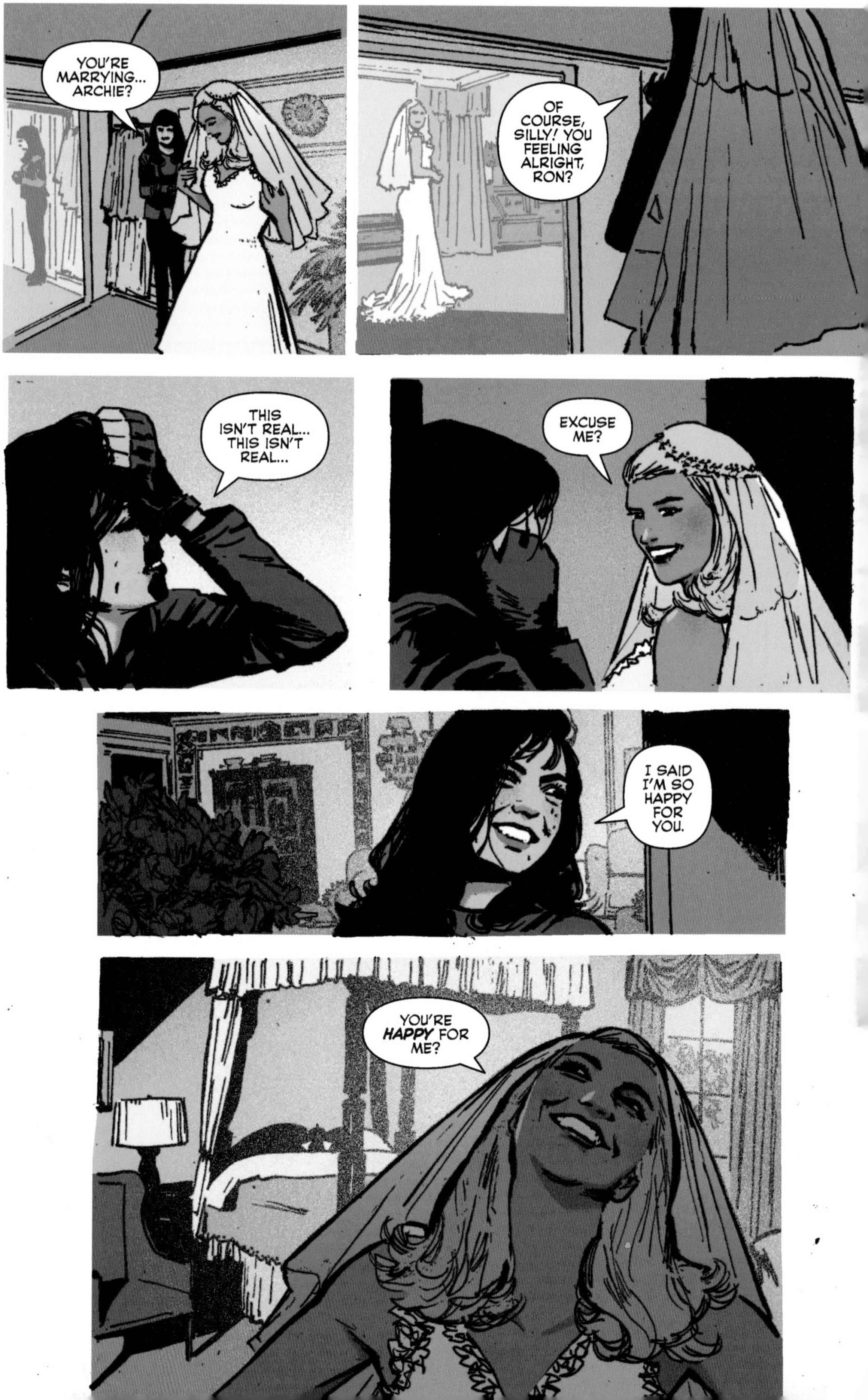
YOU'RE MARRYING... ARCHIE?
OF COURSE, SILLY! YOU FEELING ALRIGHT, RON?
THIS ISN'T REAL... THIS ISN'T REAL...
EXCUSE ME?
I SAID I'M SO HAPPY FOR YOU.
YOU'RE *HAPPY* FOR ME?

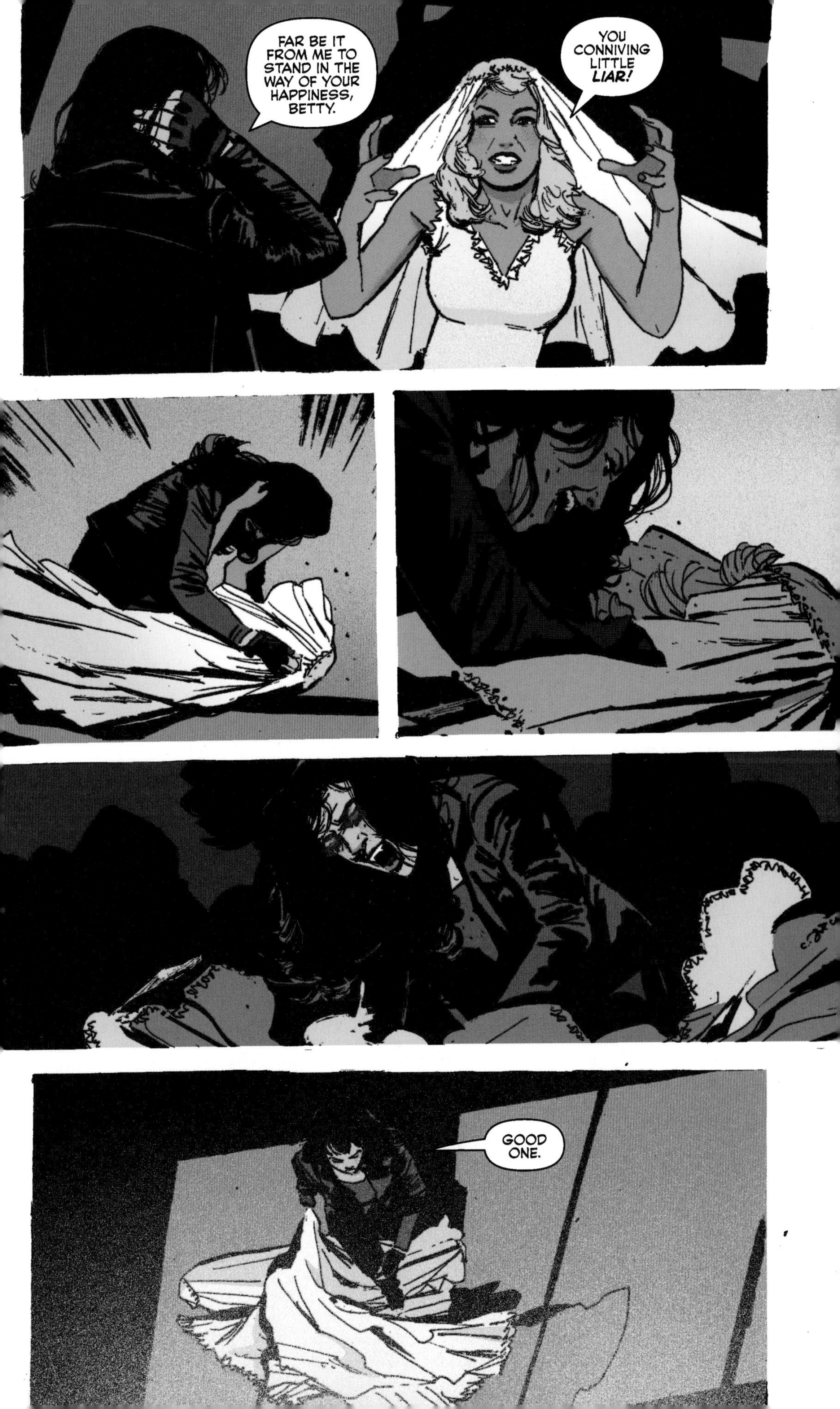
FAR BE IT FROM ME TO STAND IN THE WAY OF YOUR HAPPINESS, BETTY.
YOU CONNIVING LITTLE LIAR!
GOOD ONE.

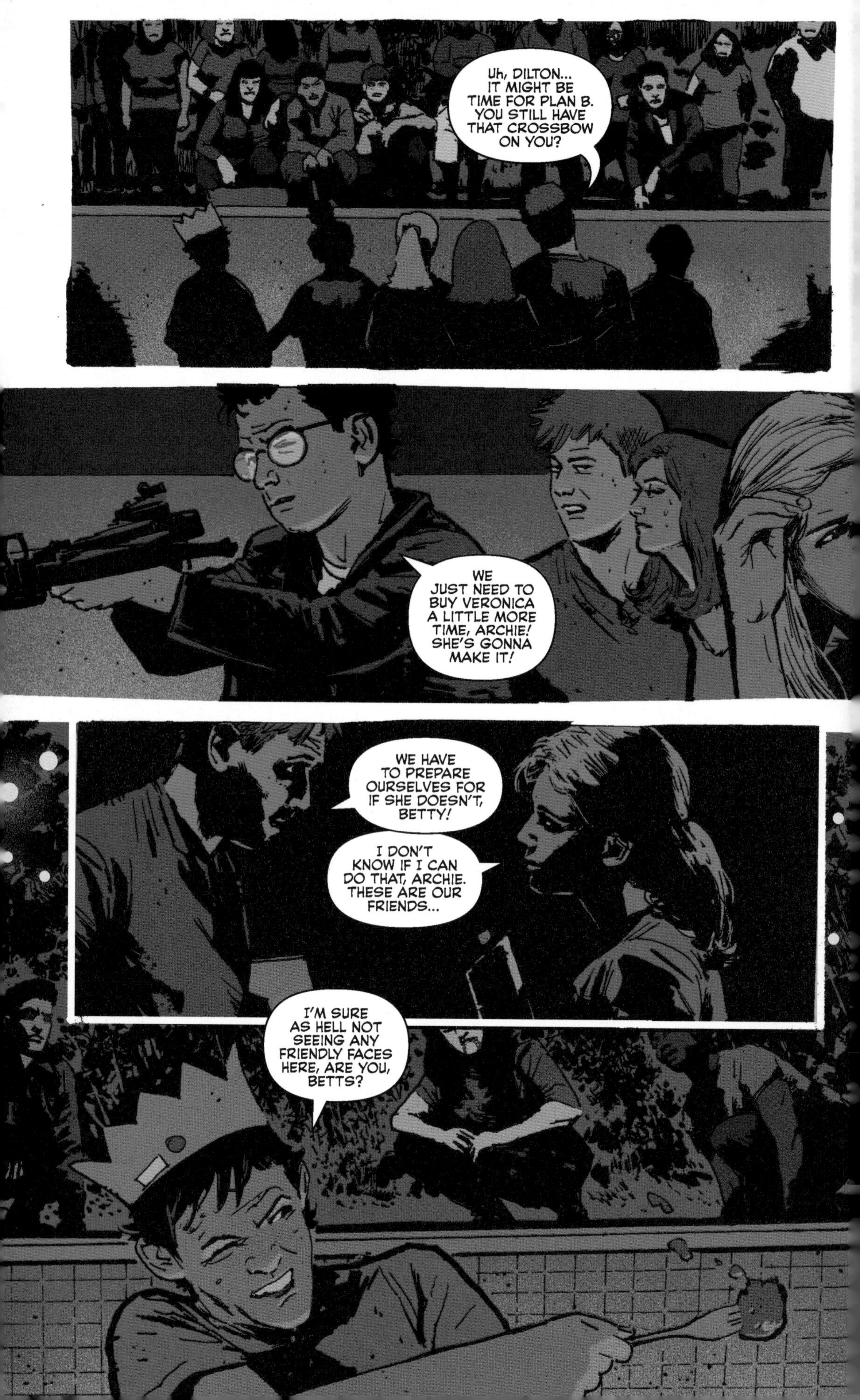
Uh, DILTON... IT MIGHT BE TIME FOR PLAN B. YOU STILL HAVE THAT CROSSBOW ON YOU?
WE JUST NEED TO BUY VERONICA A LITTLE MORE TIME, ARCHIE! SHE'S GONNA MAKE IT!
WE HAVE TO PREPARE OURSELVES FOR IF SHE DOESN'T, BETTY!
I DON'T KNOW IF I CAN DO THAT, ARCHIE. THESE ARE OUR FRIENDS...
I'M SURE AS HELL NOT SEEING ANY FRIENDLY FACES HERE, ARE YOU, BETTS?

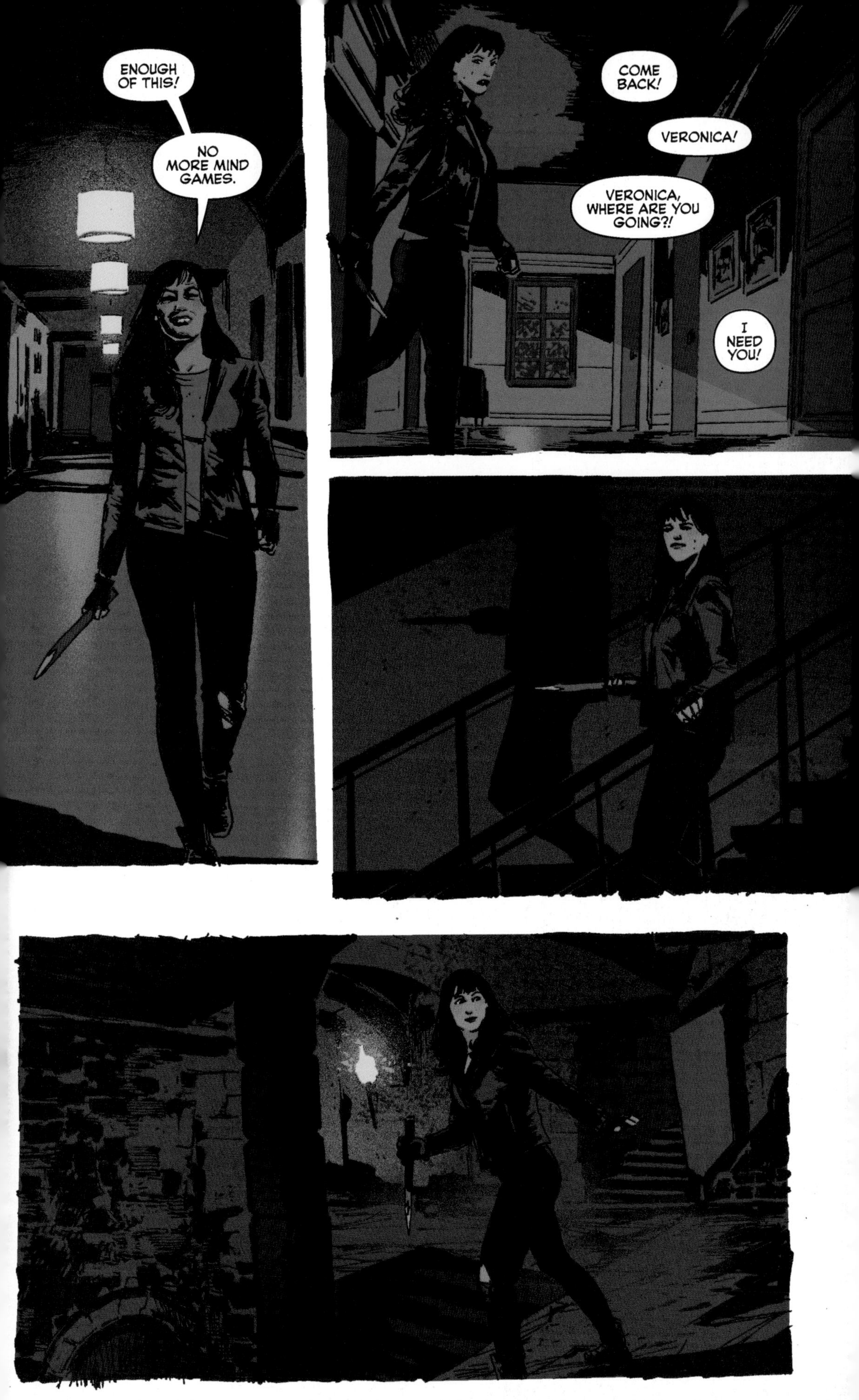
ENOUGH OF THIS!
NO MORE MIND GAMES.
COME BACK!
VERONICA!
VERONICA, WHERE ARE YOU GOING?!
I NEED YOU!

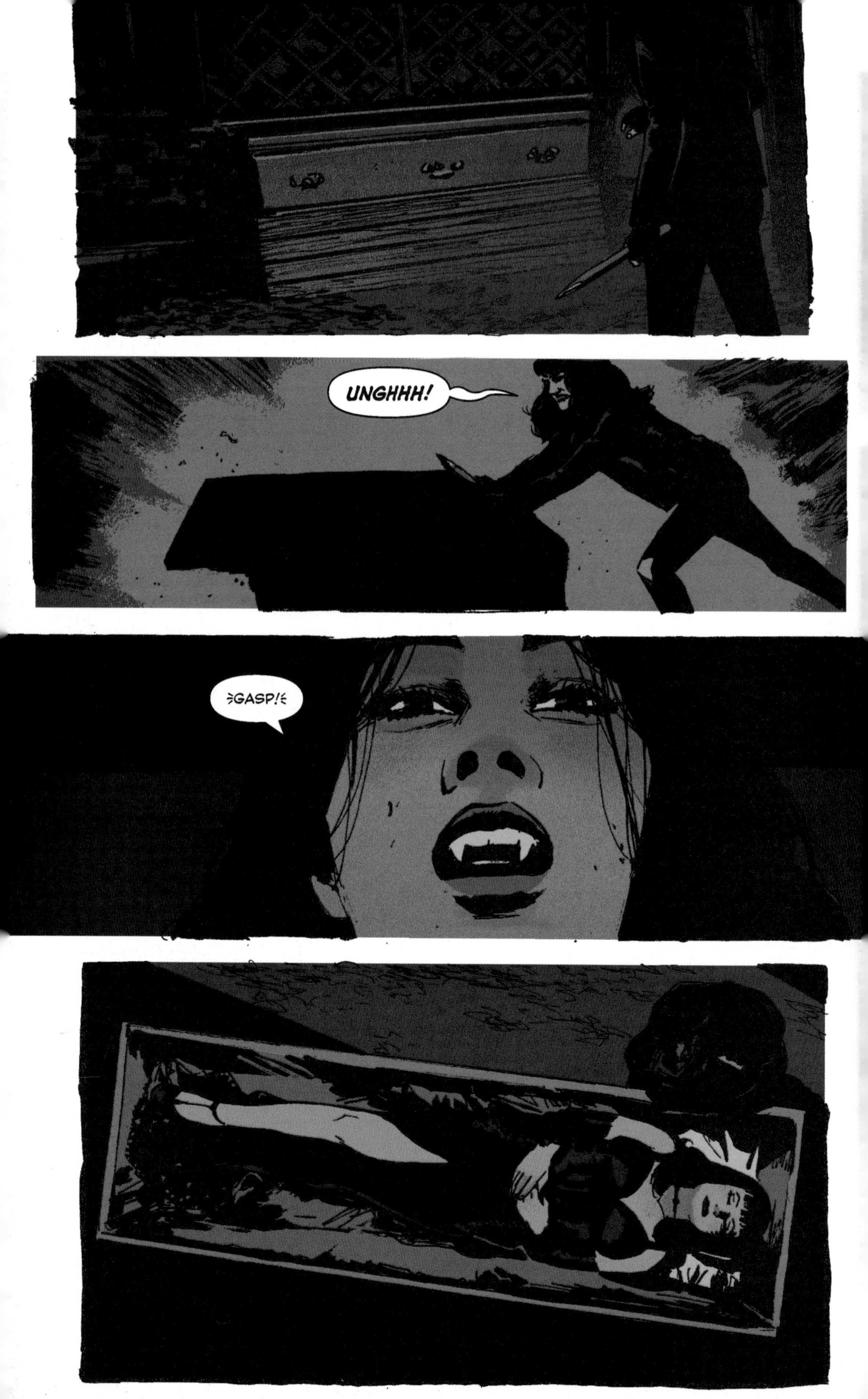
UNGHHH!
GASP!

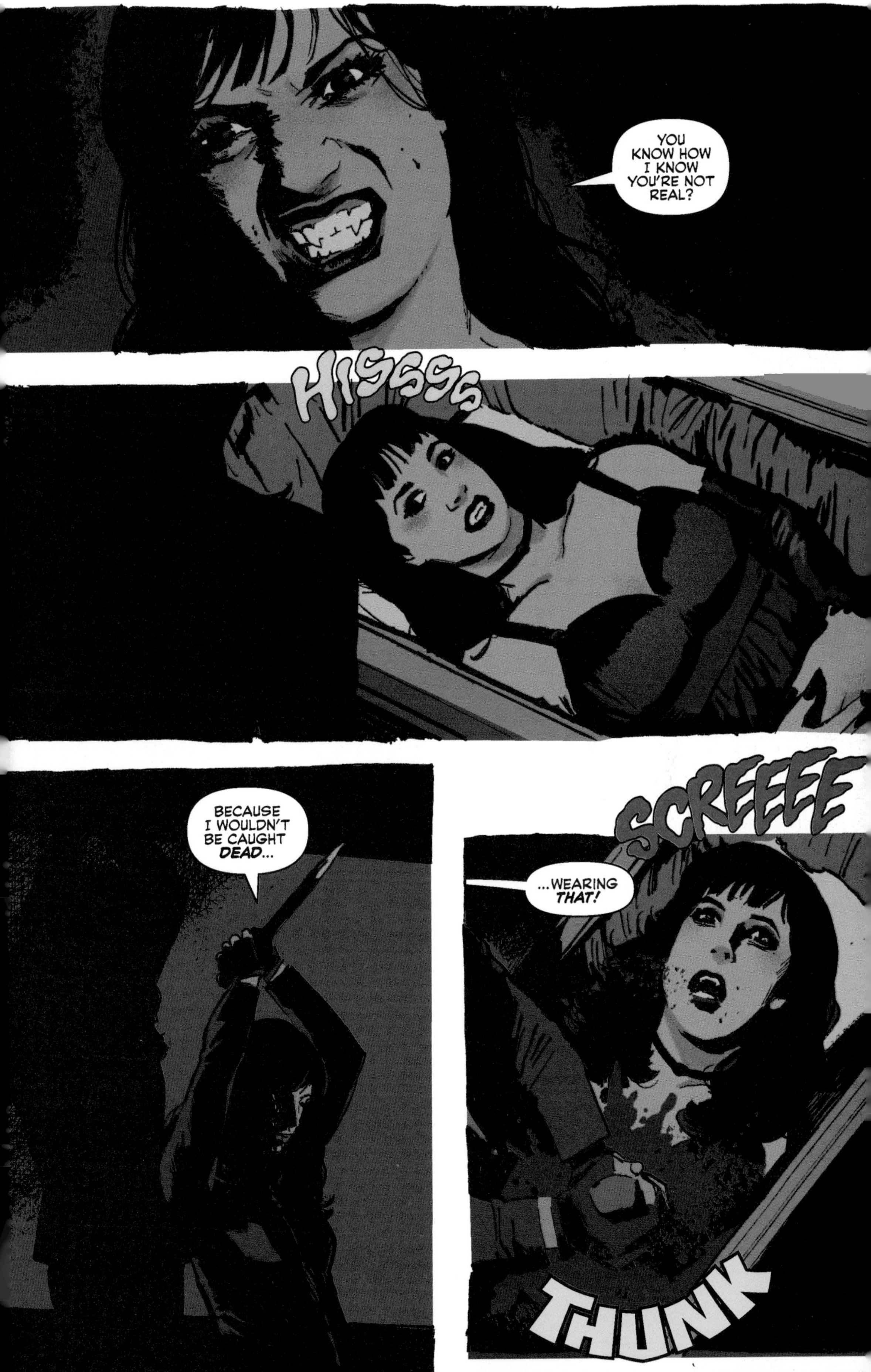
YOU KNOW HOW I KNOW YOU'RE NOT REAL?
HISSSS
BECAUSE I WOULDN'T BE CAUGHT *DEAD*...
SCREEEE
...WEARING *THAT!*
THUNK

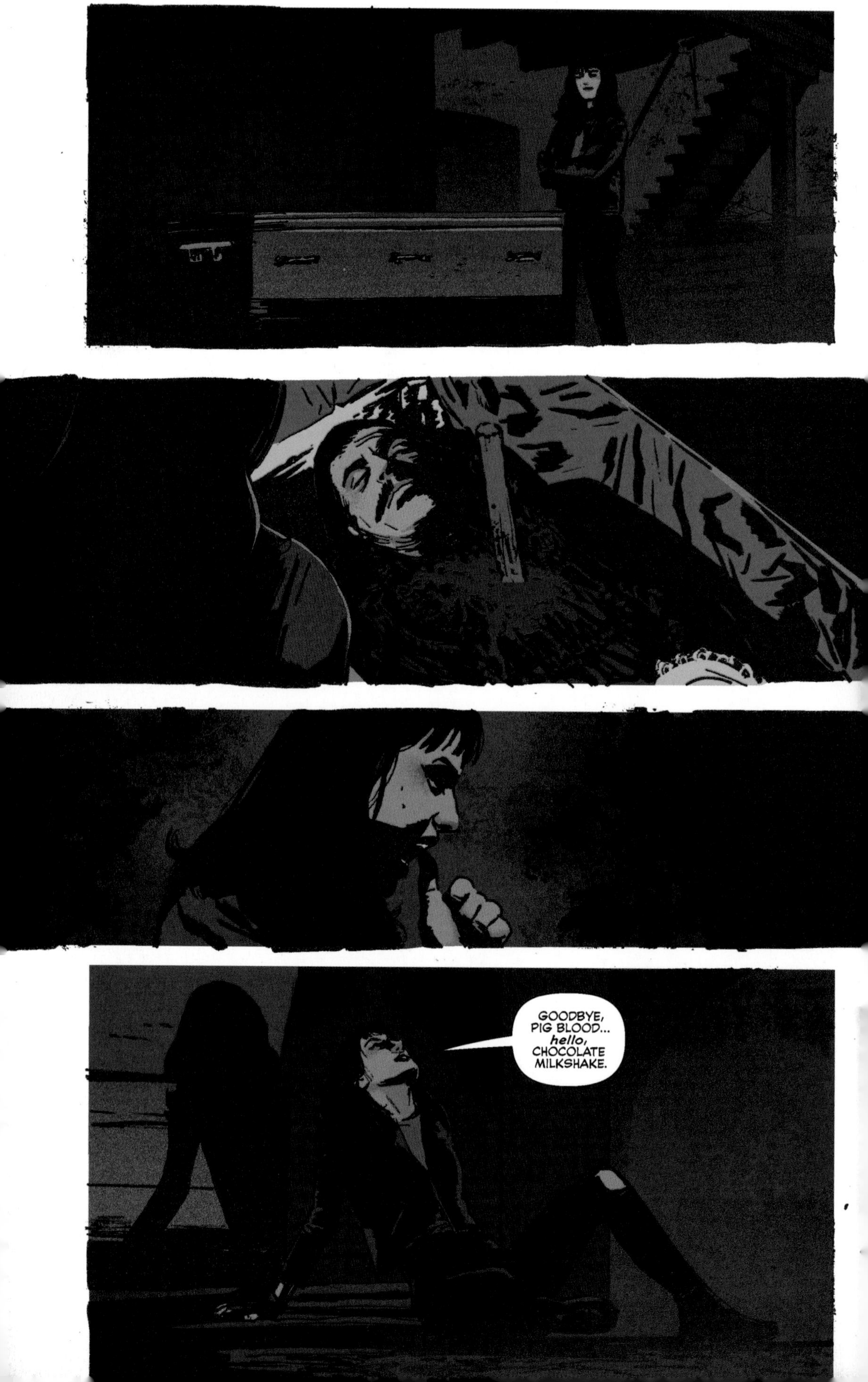
GOODBYE, PIG BLOOD... *hello,* CHOCOLATE MILKSHAKE.

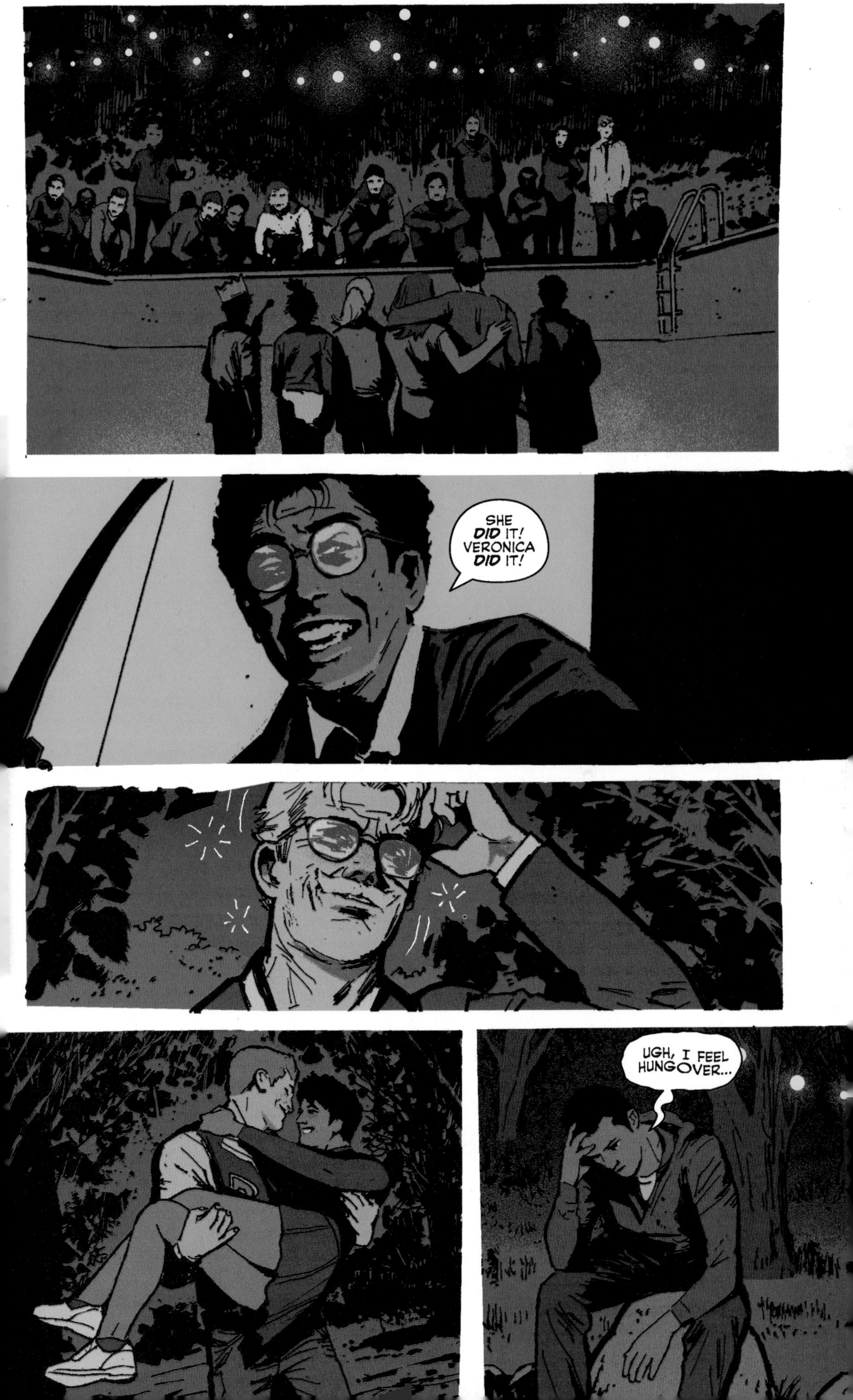
SHE *DID* IT! VERONICA *DID* IT!
UGH, I FEEL HUNGOVER...

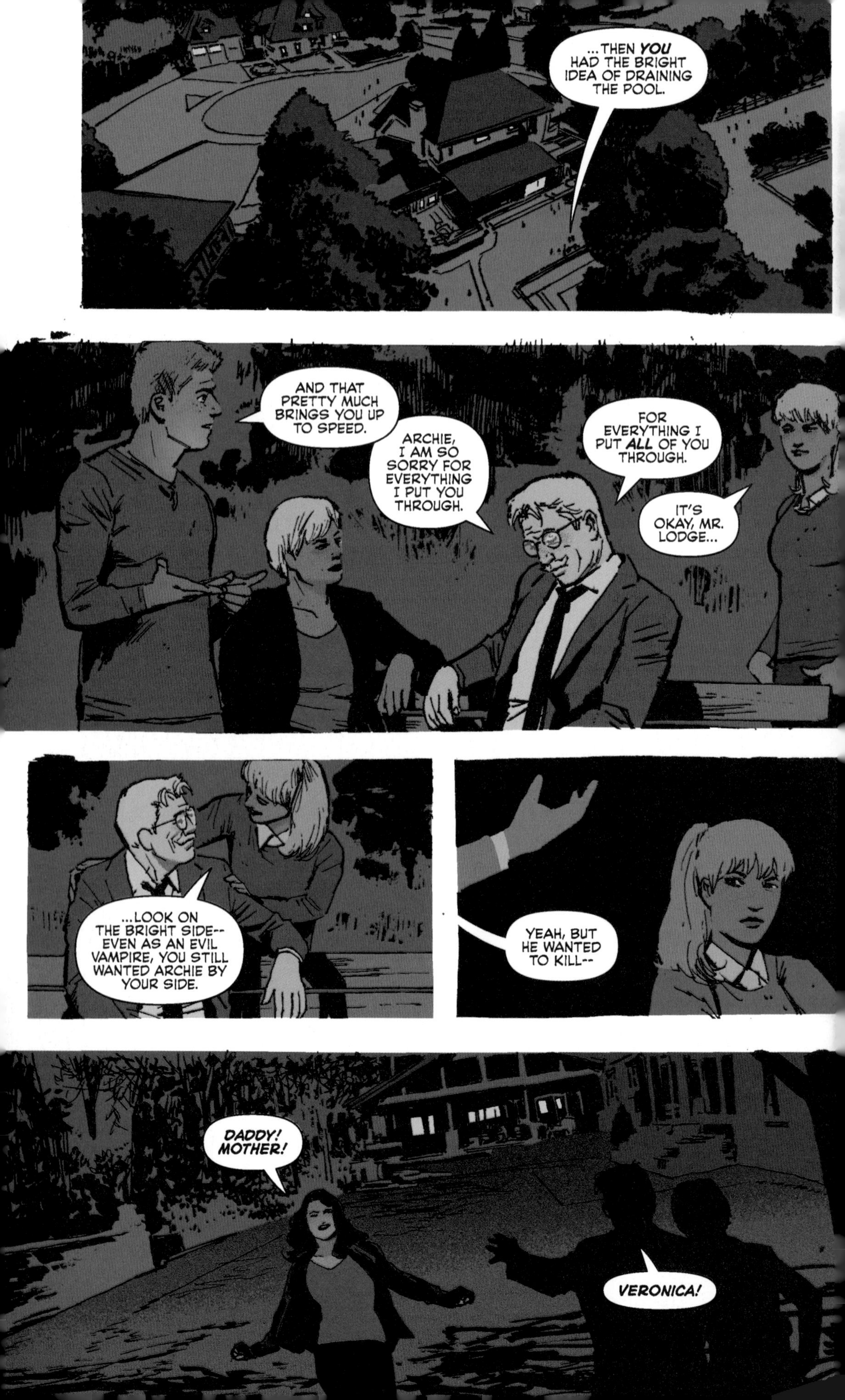
...THEN *YOU* HAD THE BRIGHT IDEA OF DRAINING THE POOL.
AND THAT PRETTY MUCH BRINGS YOU UP TO SPEED.
ARCHIE, I AM SO SORRY FOR EVERYTHING I PUT YOU THROUGH.
FOR EVERYTHING I PUT *ALL* OF YOU THROUGH.
IT'S OKAY, MR. LODGE...
...LOOK ON THE BRIGHT SIDE-- EVEN AS AN EVIL VAMPIRE, YOU STILL WANTED ARCHIE BY YOUR SIDE.
YEAH, BUT HE WANTED TO KILL--
DADDY! MOTHER!
VERONICA!

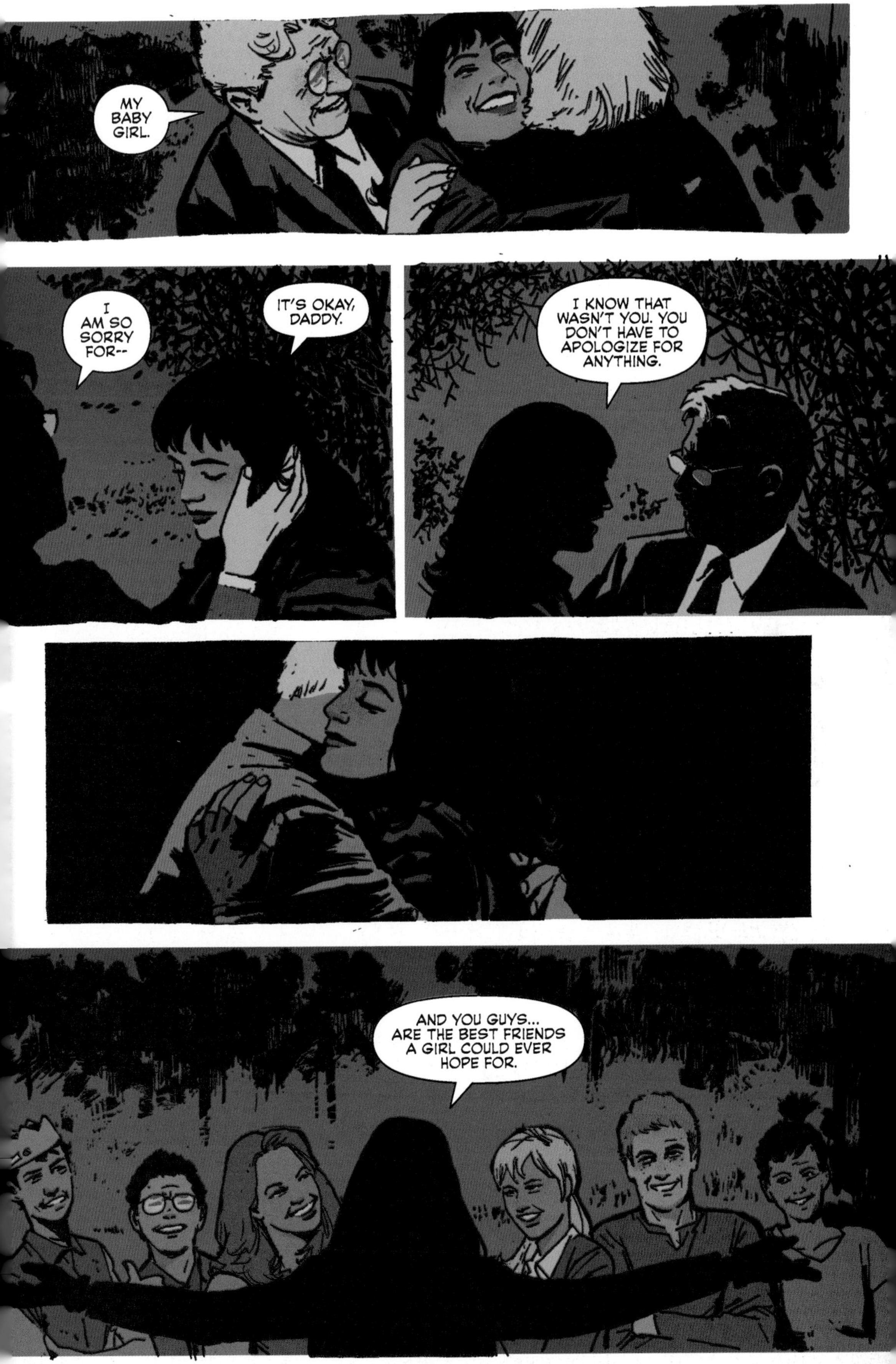
MY BABY GIRL.
I AM SO SORRY FOR--
IT'S OKAY, DADDY.
I KNOW THAT WASN'T YOU. YOU DON'T HAVE TO APOLOGIZE FOR ANYTHING.
AND YOU GUYS... ARE THE BEST FRIENDS A GIRL COULD EVER HOPE FOR.

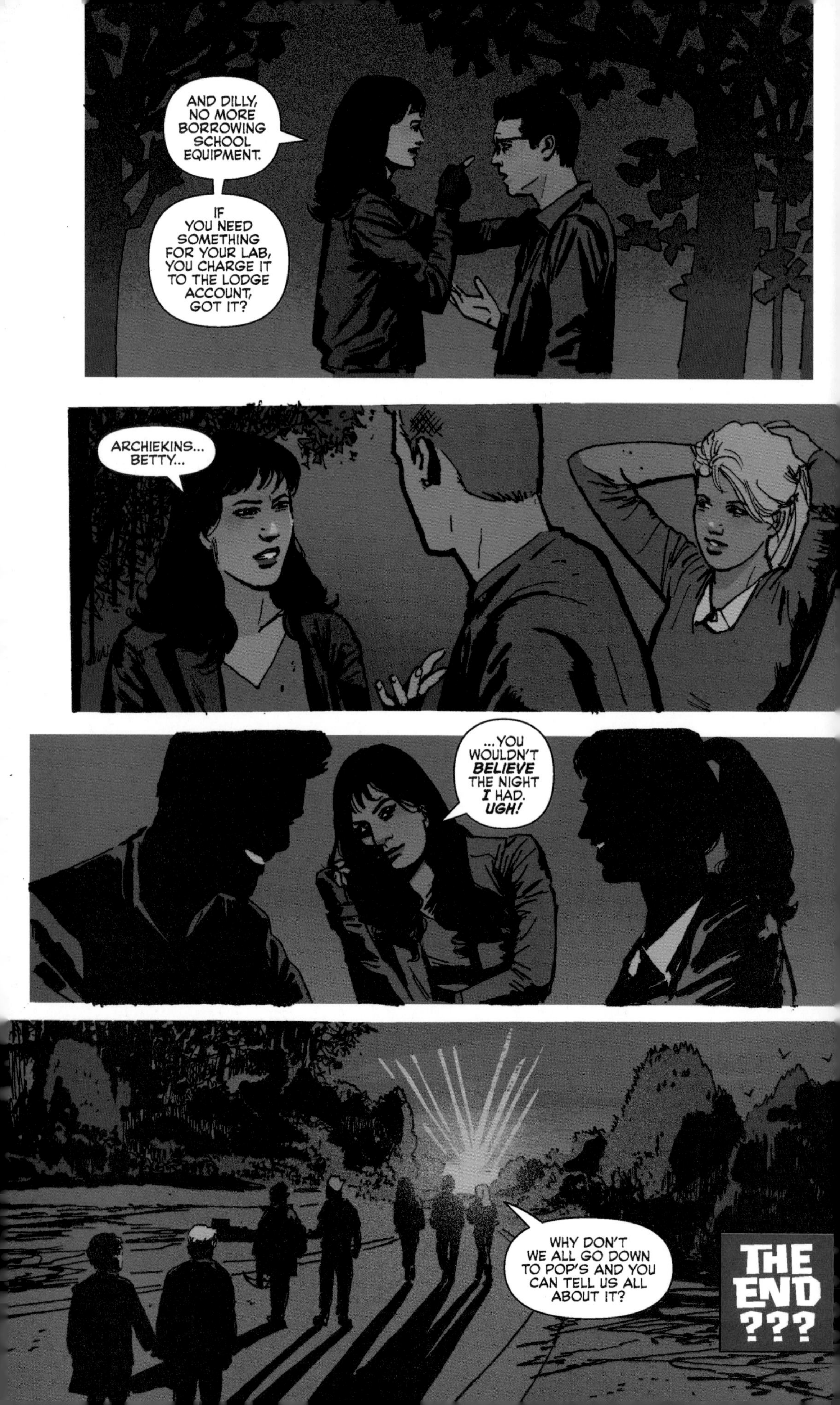
AND DILLY, NO MORE BORROWING SCHOOL EQUIPMENT.
IF YOU NEED SOMETHING FOR YOUR LAB, YOU CHARGE IT TO THE LODGE ACCOUNT, GOT IT?
ARCHIEKINS... BETTY...
...YOU WOULDN'T BELIEVE THE NIGHT I HAD. UGH!
WHY DON'T WE ALL GO DOWN TO POP'S AND YOU CAN TELL US ALL ABOUT IT?
THE END ???

SPECIAL FEATURES

VARIANT COVER GALLERY

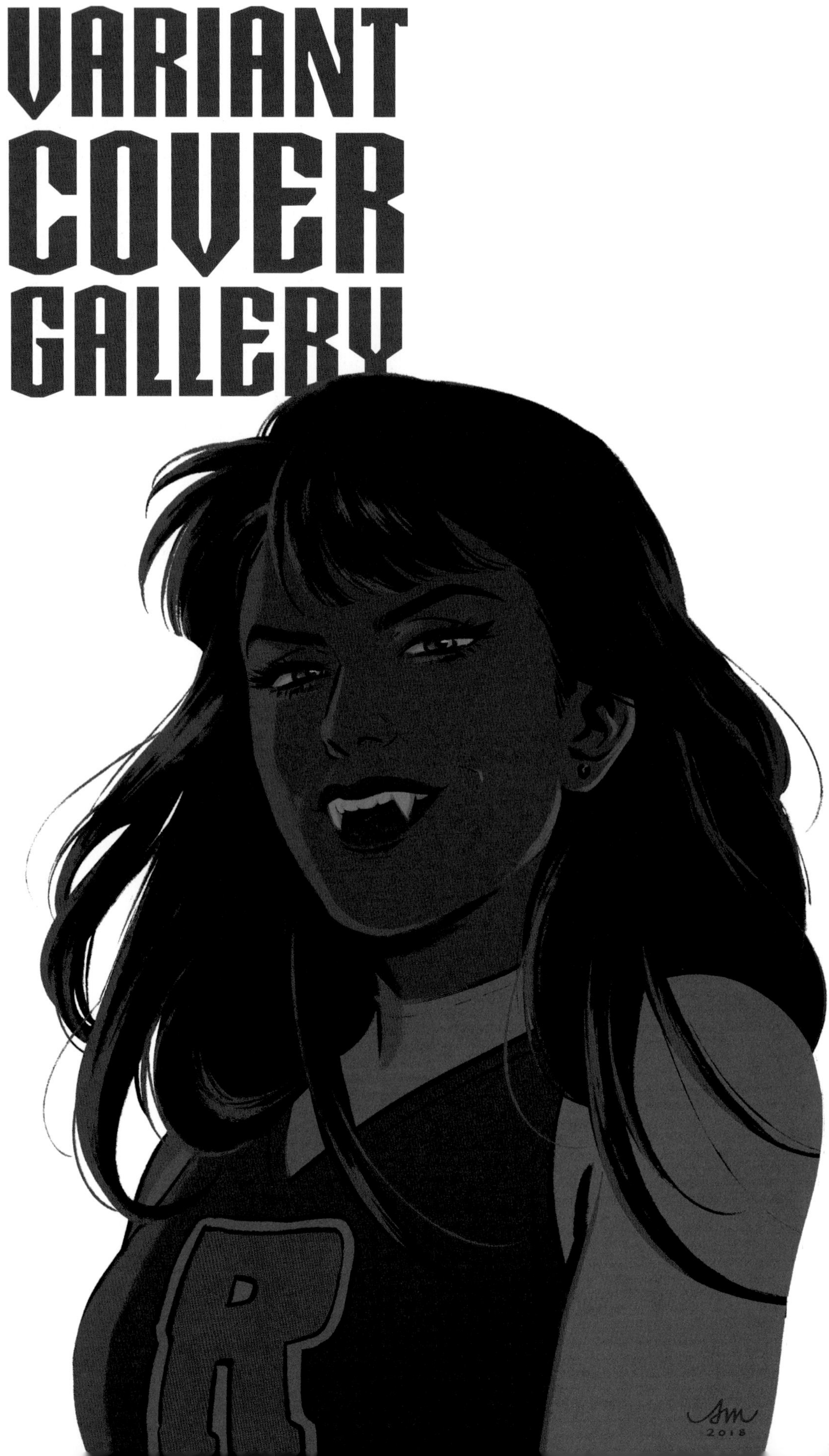

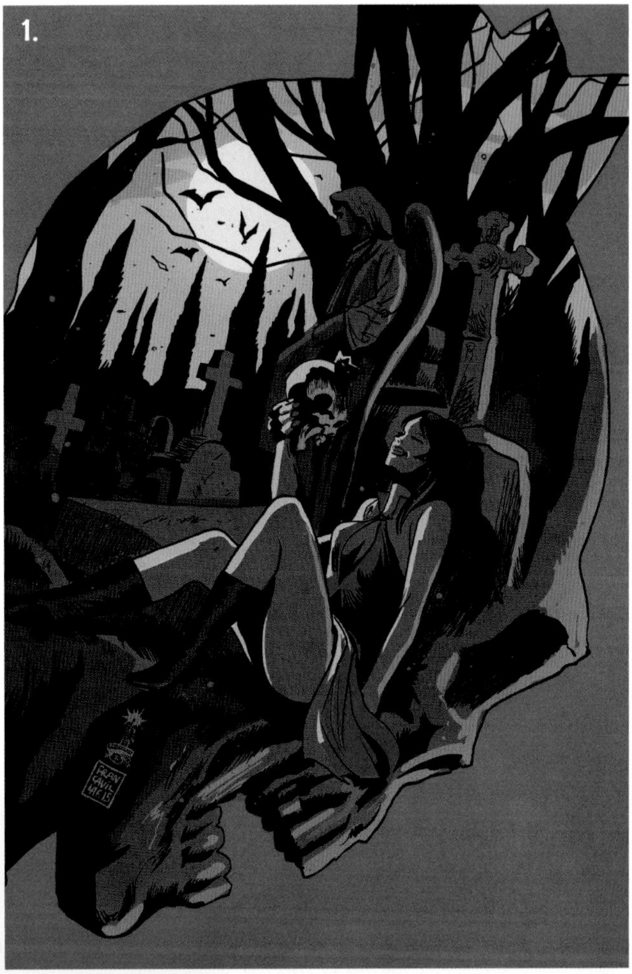
1.

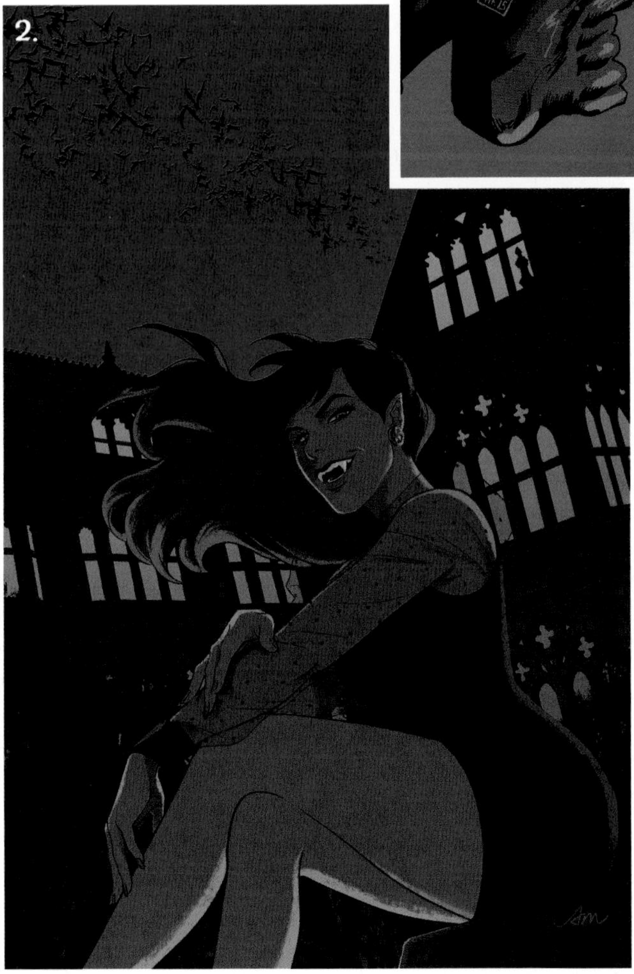
2.

ISSUE ONE VARIANT

1. FRANCESCO FRANCAVILLA
2. AUDREY MOK

ISSUE ONE VARIANT

3. DJIBRIL MORISSETTE-PHAN

4. MARGUERITE SAUVAGE

3.

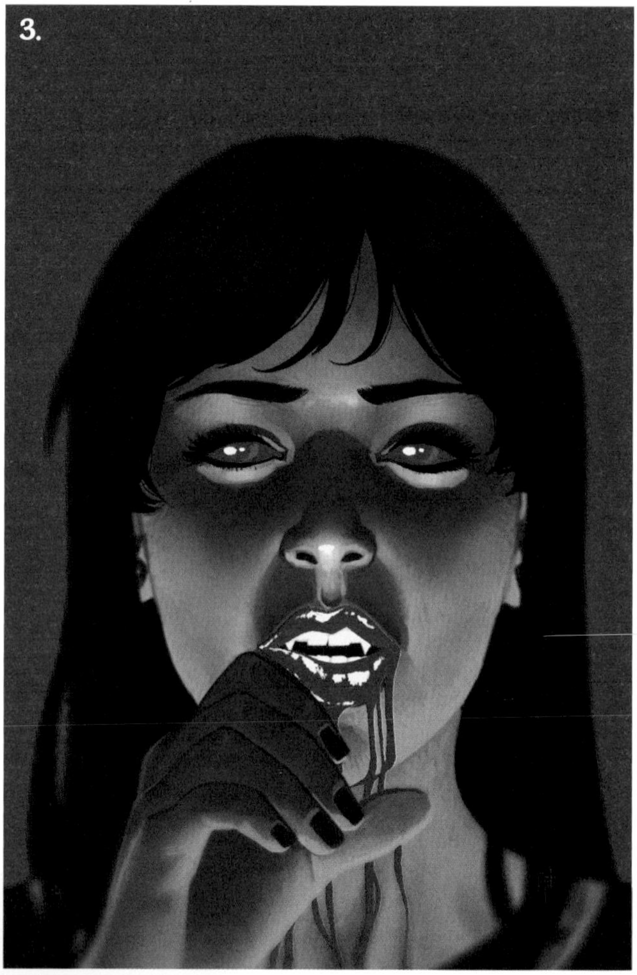

4.

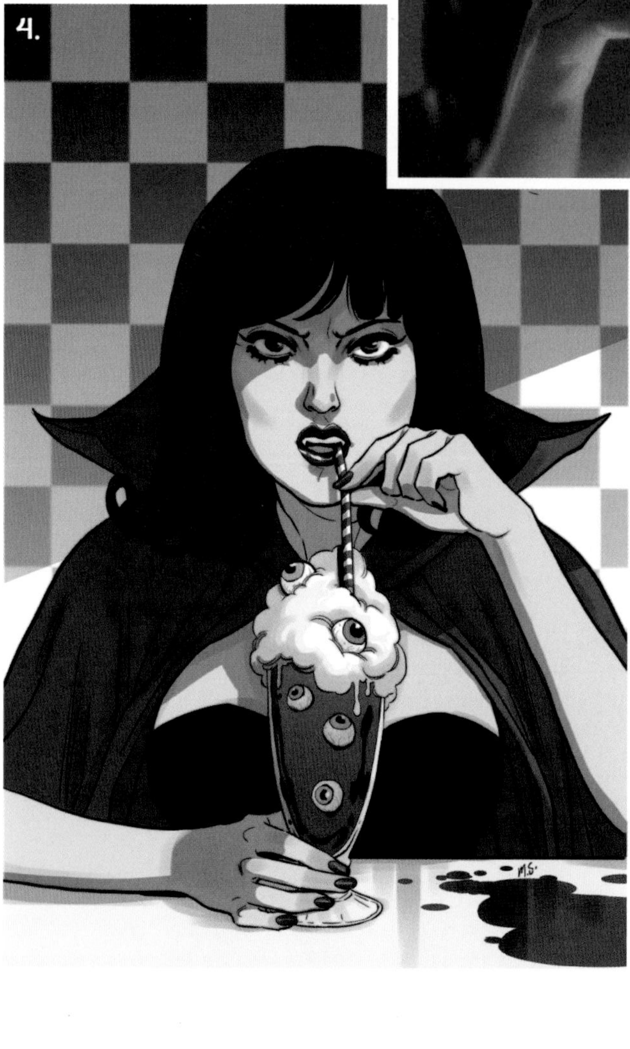

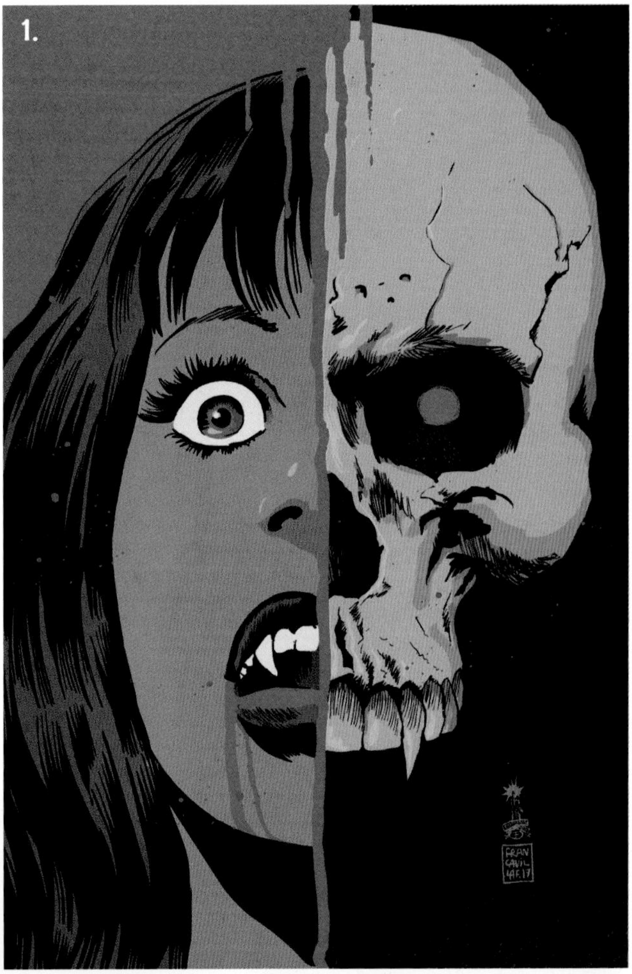
1.

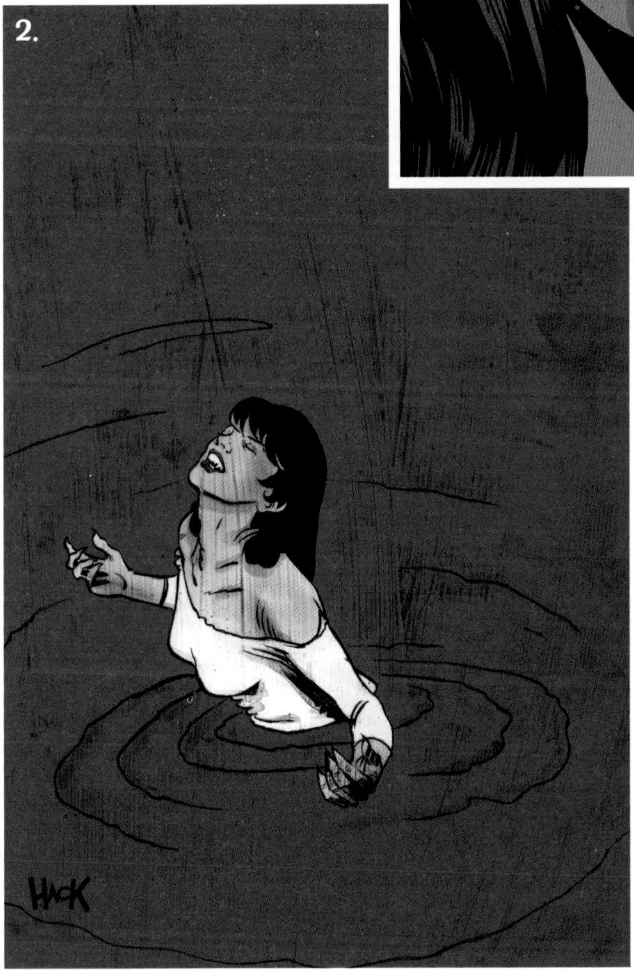
2.
HACK

ISSUE TWO VARIANT

1. FRANCESCO FRANCAVILLA
2. ROBERT HACK

ISSUE THREE VARIANT

1. FRANCESCO FRANCAVILLA
2. AUDREY MOK

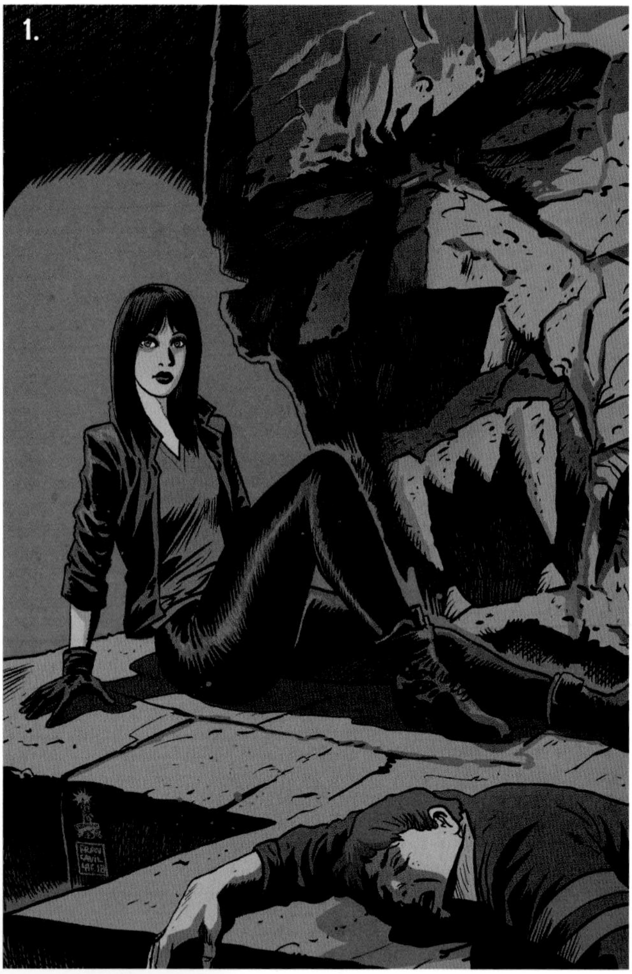

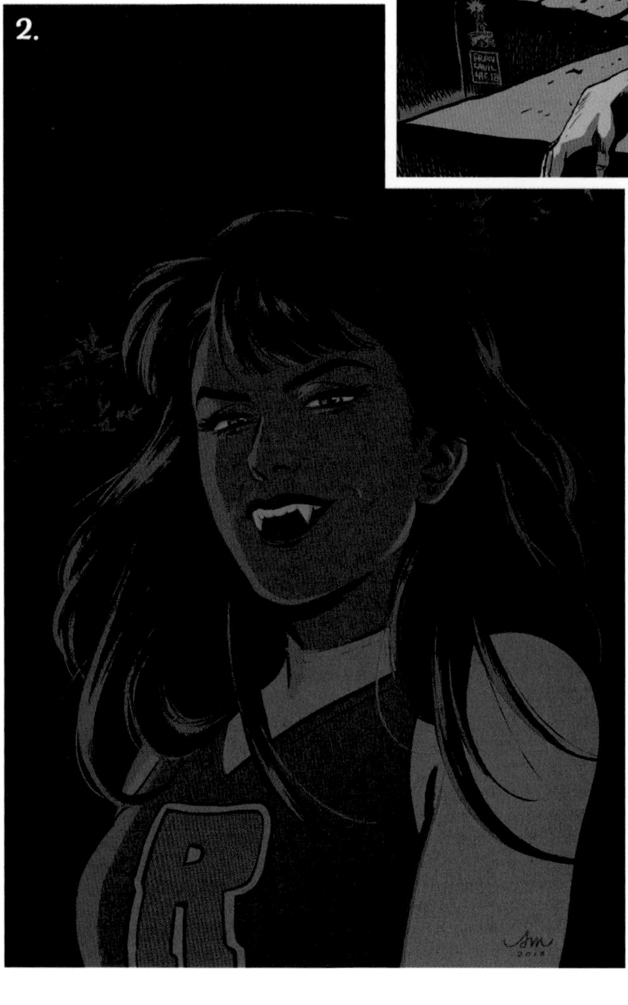

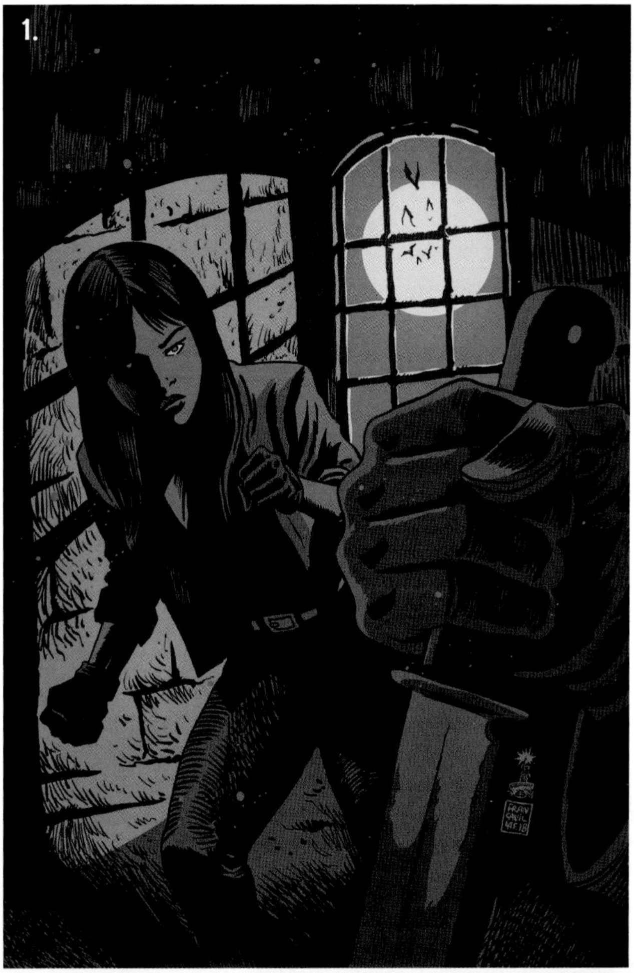
1.

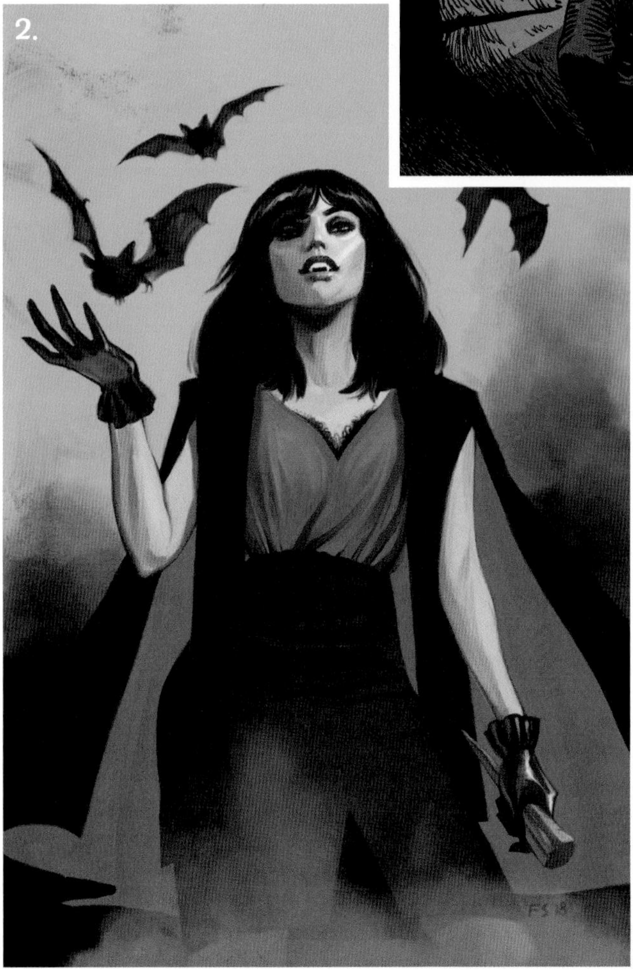
2.

ISSUE FOUR VARIANT

1. FRANCESCO FRANCAVILLA

2. FIONA STAPLES

ISSUE FIVE VARIANT

1. FRANCESCO FRANCAVILLA

2. MATTHEW TAYLOR

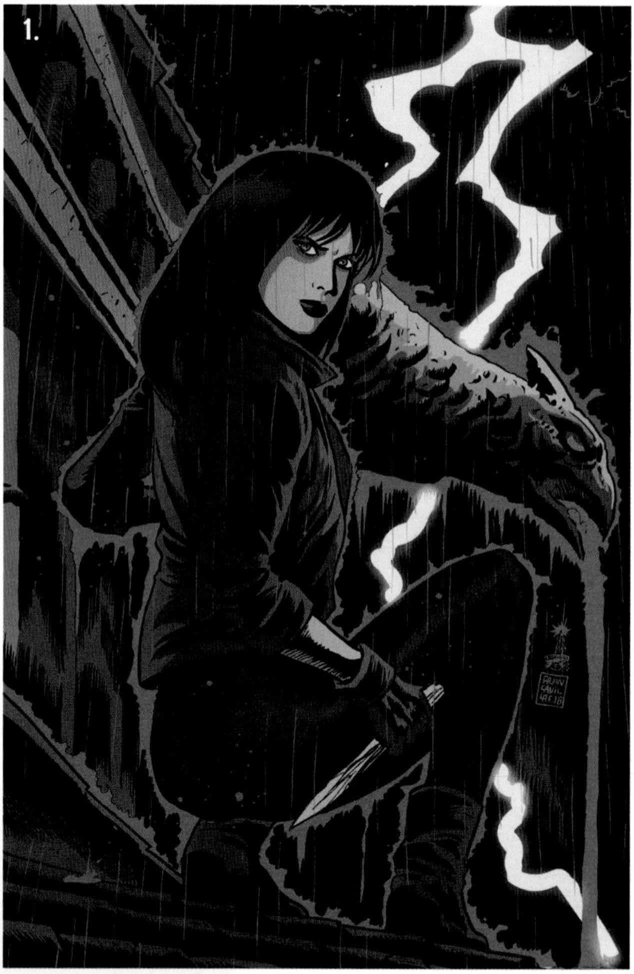

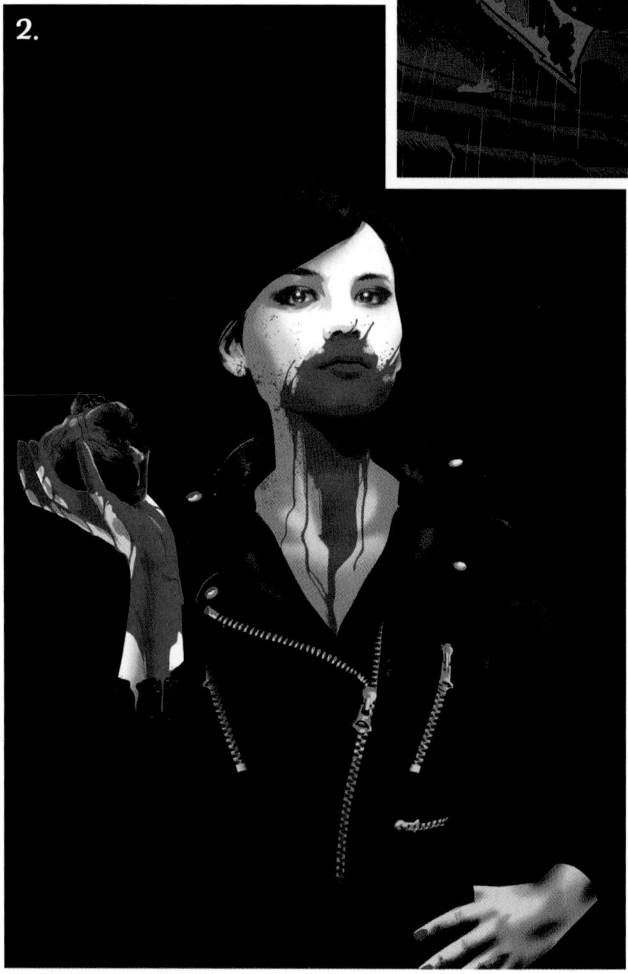

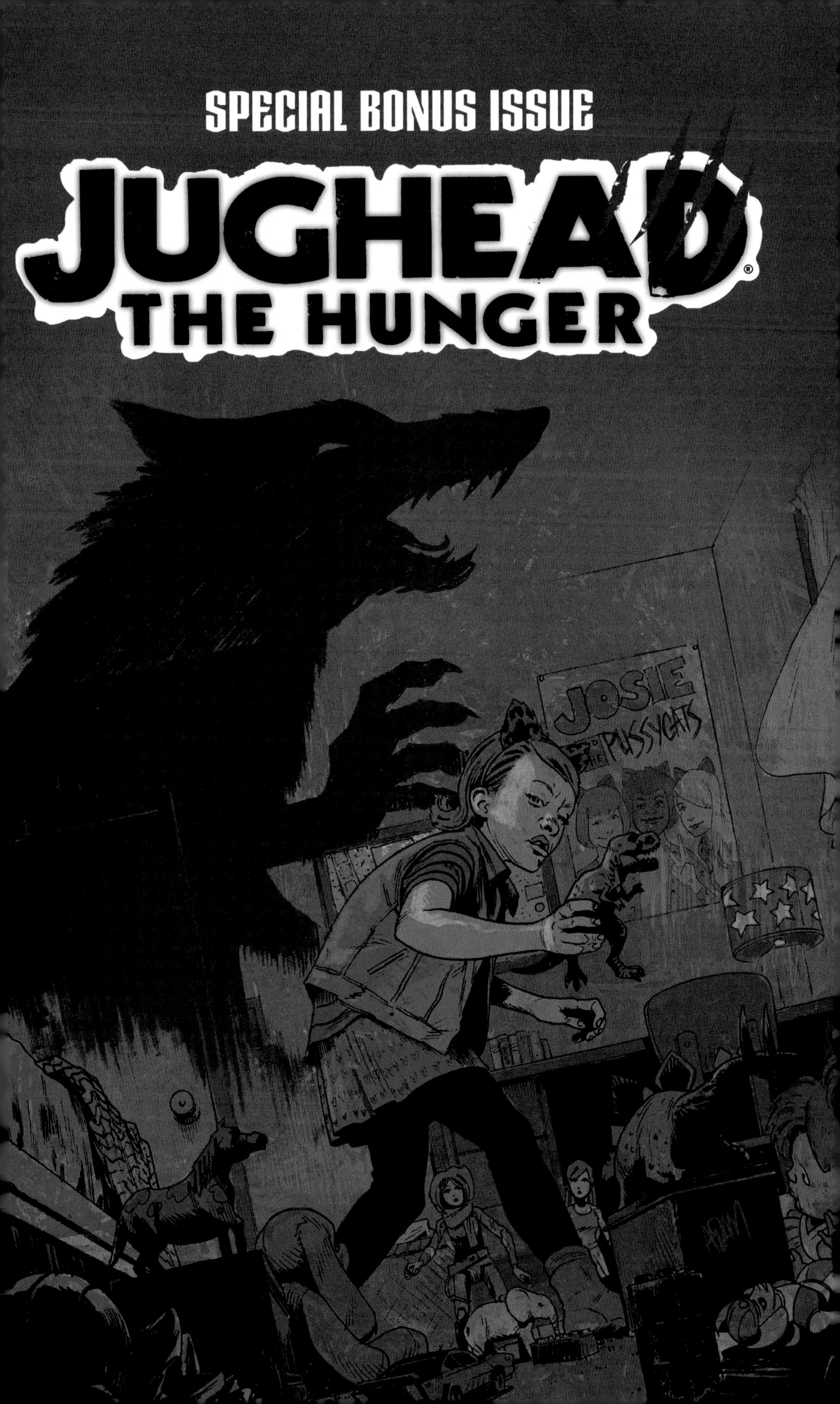
SPECIAL BONUS ISSUE
JUGHEAD®
THE HUNGER
JOSIE
PUSSYCATS

CHAPTER FOUR

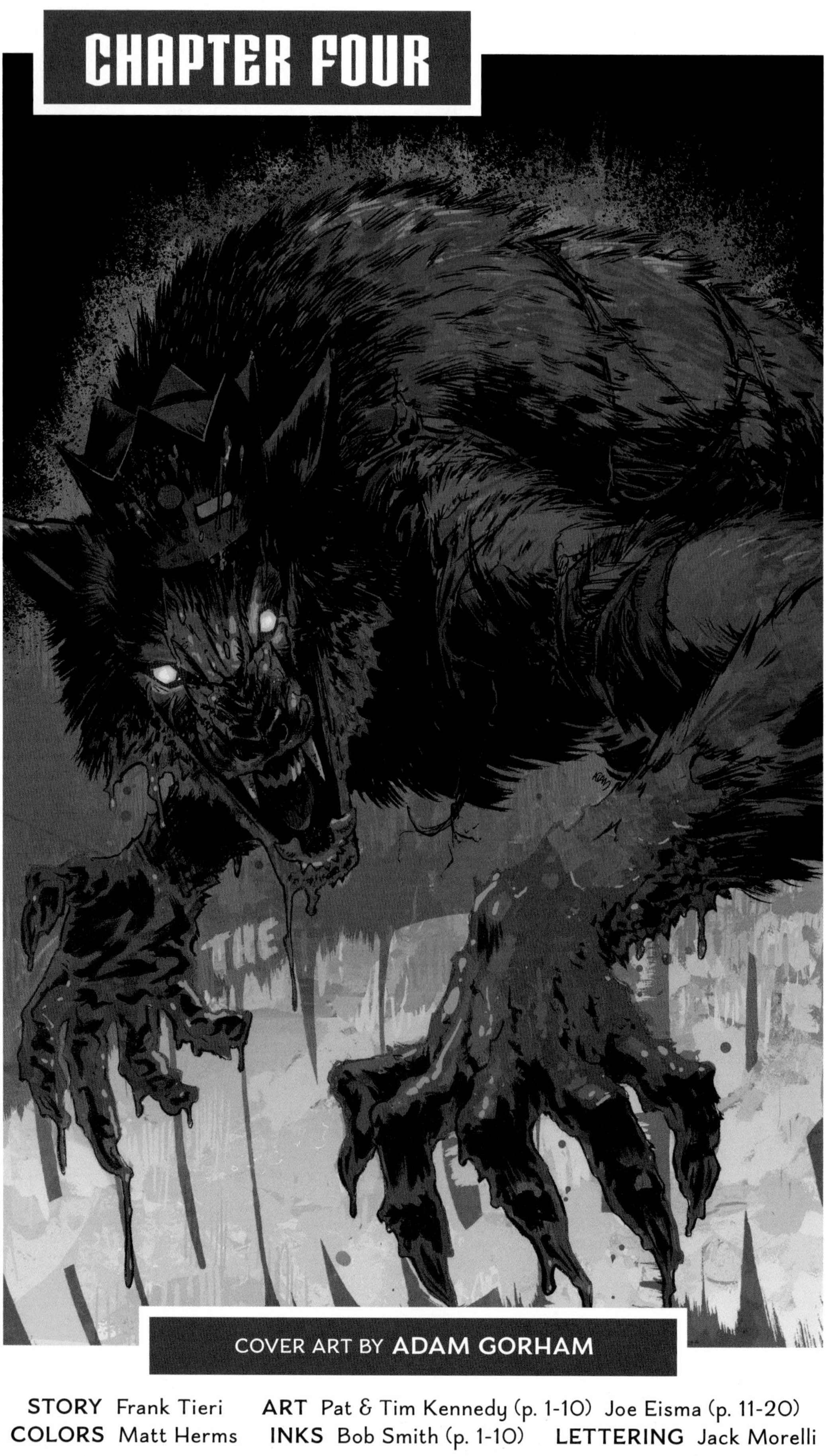
THE

COVER ART BY **ADAM GORHAM**

STORY Frank Tieri **ART** Pat & Tim Kennedy (p. 1-10) Joe Eisma (p. 11-20)
COLORS Matt Herms **INKS** Bob Smith (p. 1-10) **LETTERING** Jack Morelli

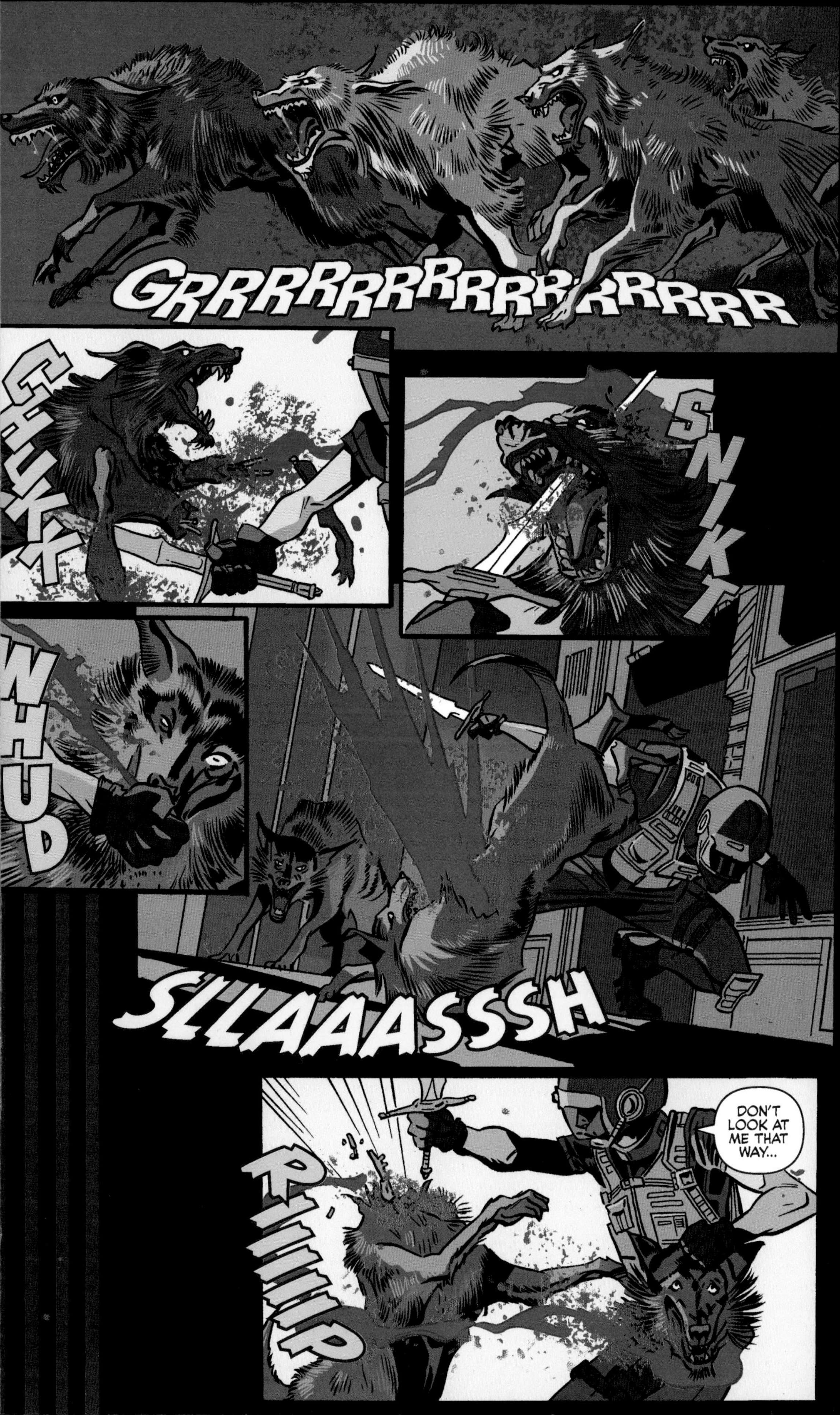
GRRRRRRRRRRRRRRR
CHUKK
SNIKT
WHUD
SLLAAASSSH
DON'T LOOK AT ME THAT WAY...
RIIIIIIP

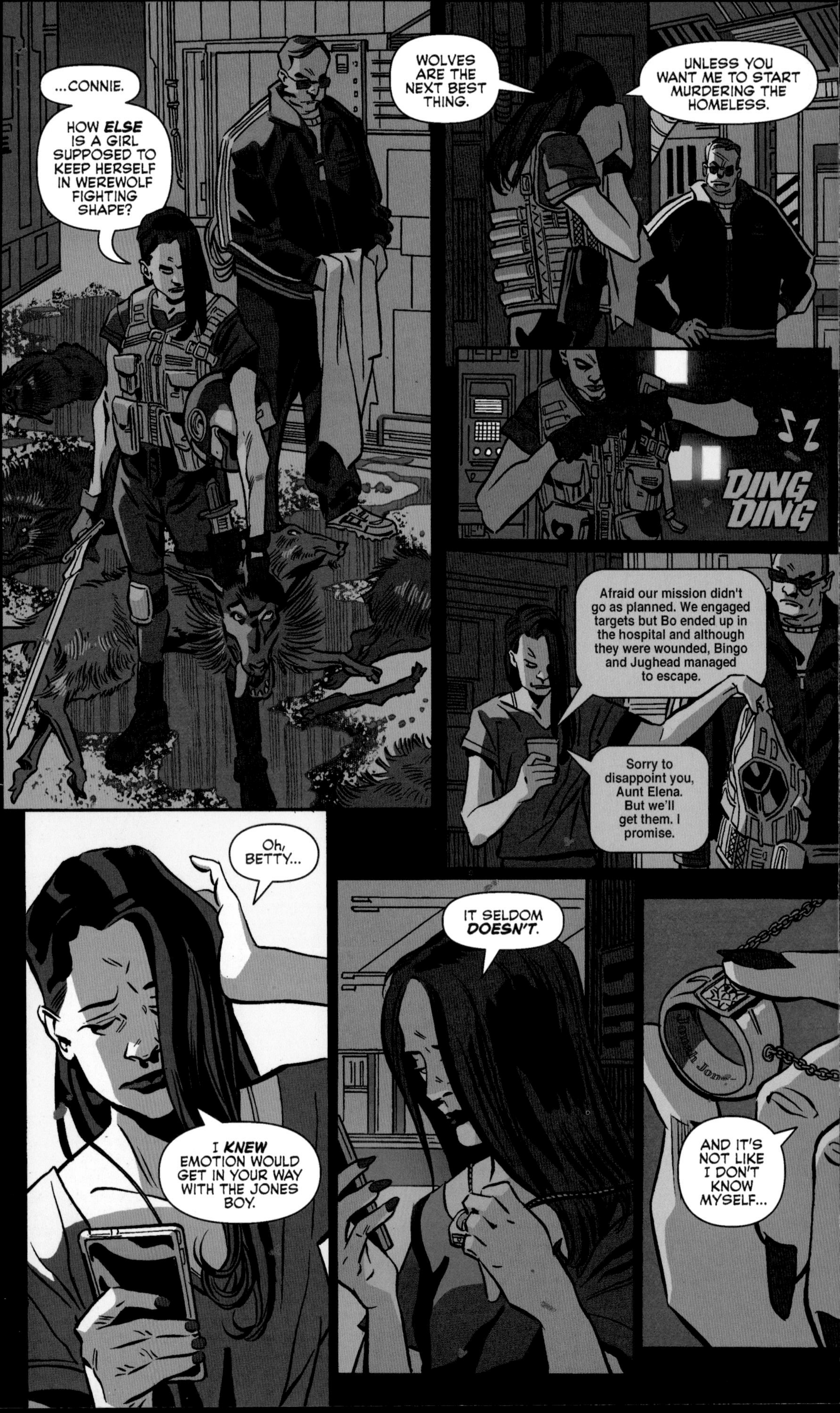
...CONNIE.
HOW ELSE IS A GIRL SUPPOSED TO KEEP HERSELF IN WEREWOLF FIGHTING SHAPE?
WOLVES ARE THE NEXT BEST THING.
UNLESS YOU WANT ME TO START MURDERING THE HOMELESS.
DING DING
Afraid our mission didn't go as planned. We engaged targets but Bo ended up in the hospital and although they were wounded, Bingo and Jughead managed to escape.
Sorry to disappoint you, Aunt Elena. But we'll get them. I promise.
Oh, BETTY...
I KNEW EMOTION WOULD GET IN YOUR WAY WITH THE JONES BOY.
IT SELDOM DOESN'T.
AND IT'S NOT LIKE I DON'T KNOW MYSELF...

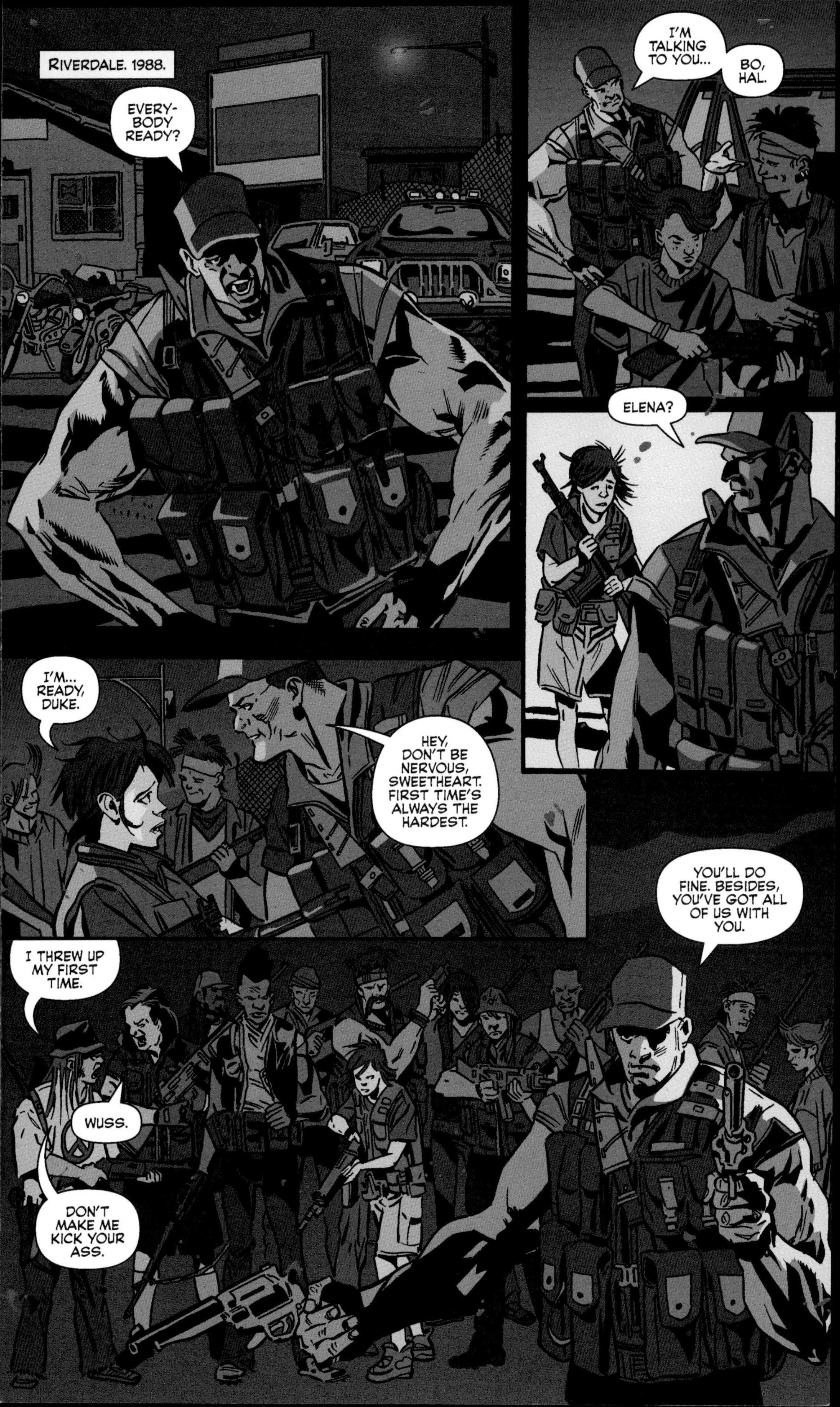
RIVERDALE. 1988.
EVERY-BODY READY?
I'M TALKING TO YOU...
BO, HAL.
ELENA?
I'M... READY, DUKE.
HEY, DON'T BE NERVOUS, SWEETHEART. FIRST TIME'S ALWAYS THE HARDEST.
YOU'LL DO FINE. BESIDES, YOU'VE GOT ALL OF US WITH YOU.
I THREW UP MY FIRST TIME.
WUSS.
DON'T MAKE ME KICK YOUR ASS.

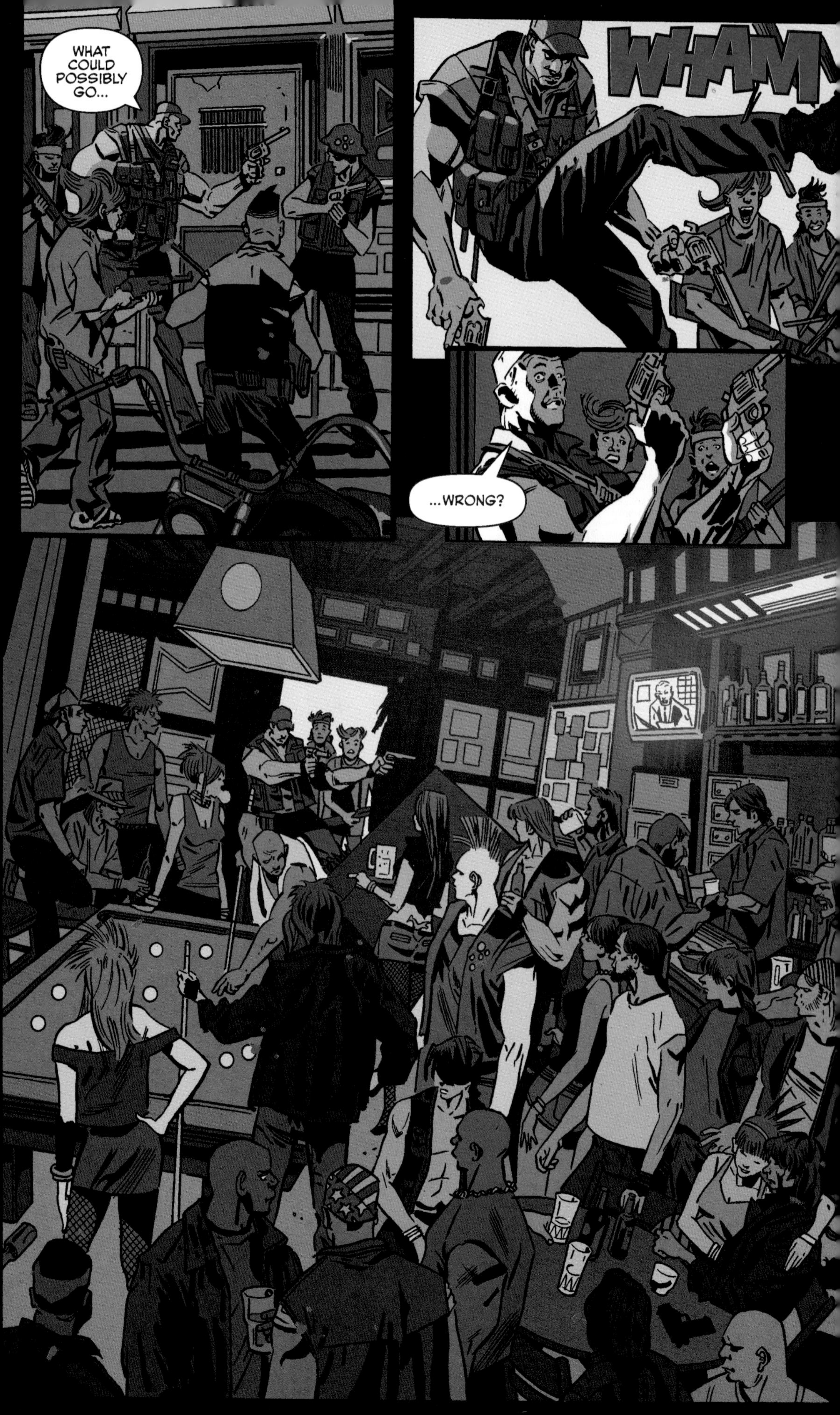
WHAT COULD POSSIBLY GO...
WHAM
...WRONG?

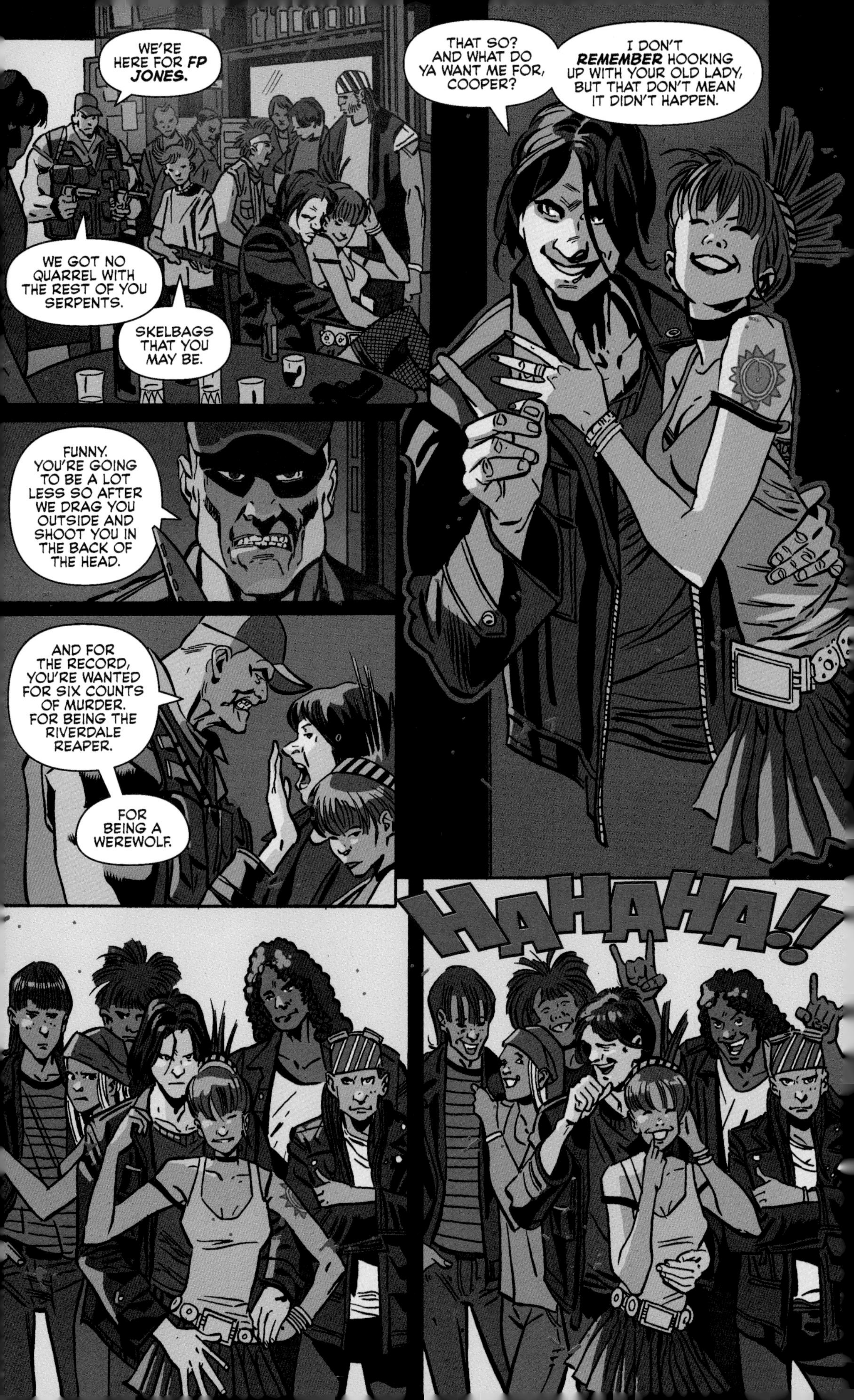
WE'RE HERE FOR FP JONES.
WE GOT NO QUARREL WITH THE REST OF YOU SERPENTS.
SKELBAGS THAT YOU MAY BE.
THAT SO? AND WHAT DO YA WANT ME FOR, COOPER?
I DON'T REMEMBER HOOKING UP WITH YOUR OLD LADY, BUT THAT DON'T MEAN IT DIDN'T HAPPEN.
FUNNY. YOU'RE GOING TO BE A LOT LESS SO AFTER WE DRAG YOU OUTSIDE AND SHOOT YOU IN THE BACK OF THE HEAD.
AND FOR THE RECORD, YOU'RE WANTED FOR SIX COUNTS OF MURDER. FOR BEING THE RIVERDALE REAPER.
FOR BEING A WEREWOLF.
HAHAHA!!

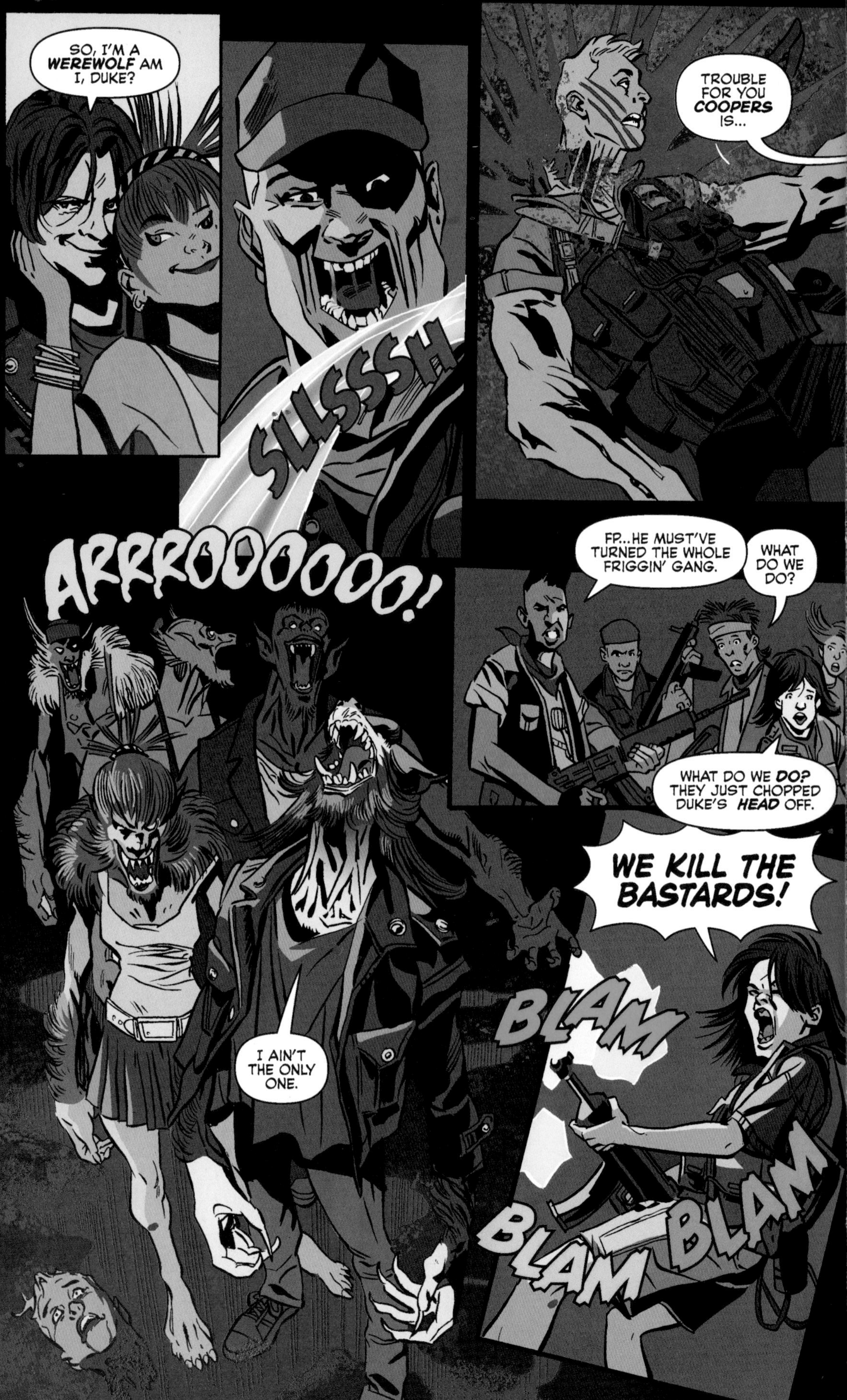
SO, I'M A WEREWOLF AM I, DUKE?
SLLSSSH
TROUBLE FOR YOU COOPERS IS...
ARRROOOOOOO!
I AIN'T THE ONLY ONE.
FP...HE MUST'VE TURNED THE WHOLE FRIGGIN' GANG.
WHAT DO WE DO?
WHAT DO WE DO? THEY JUST CHOPPED DUKE'S HEAD OFF.
WE KILL THE BASTARDS!
BLAM
BLAM
BLAM
BLAM

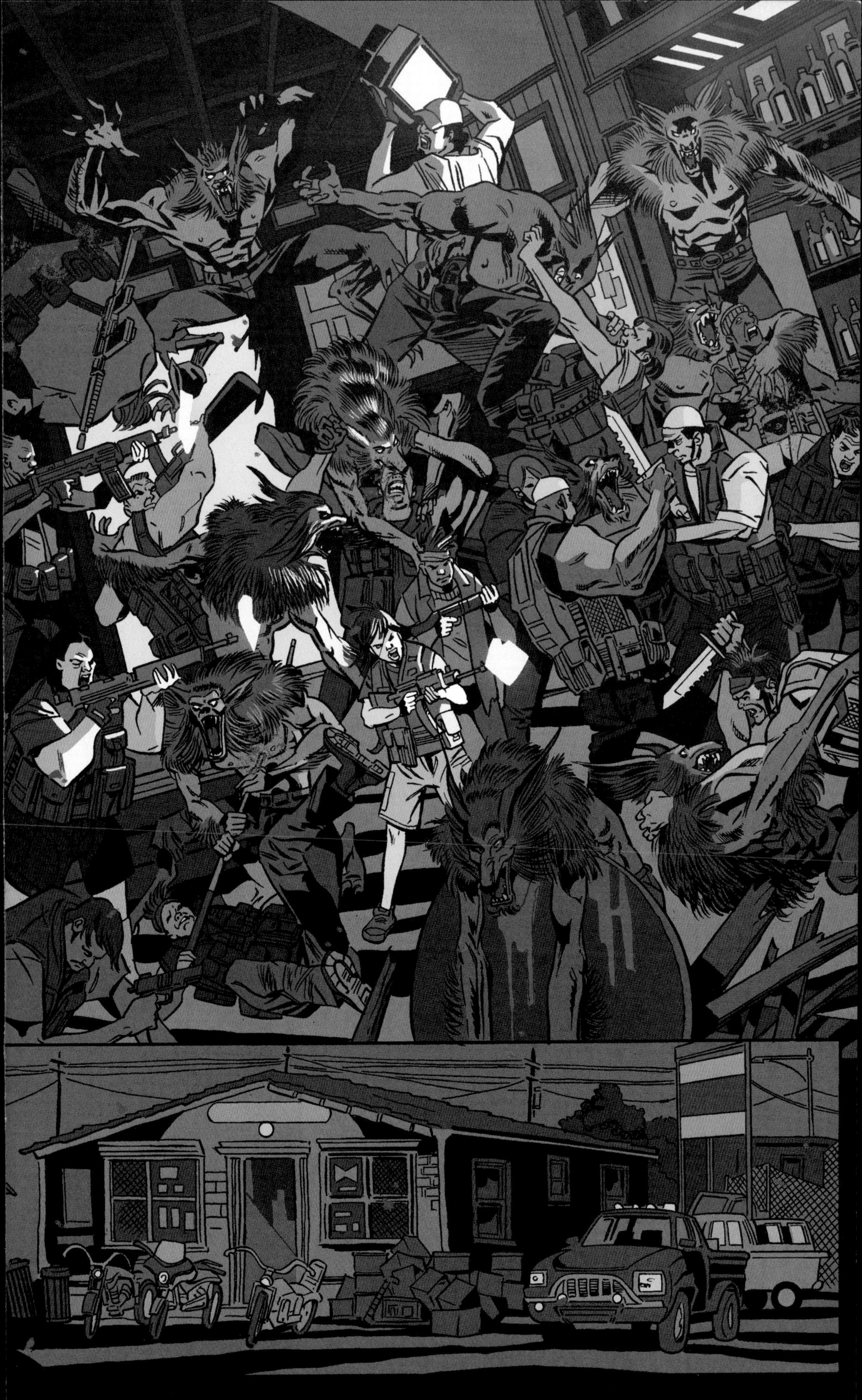

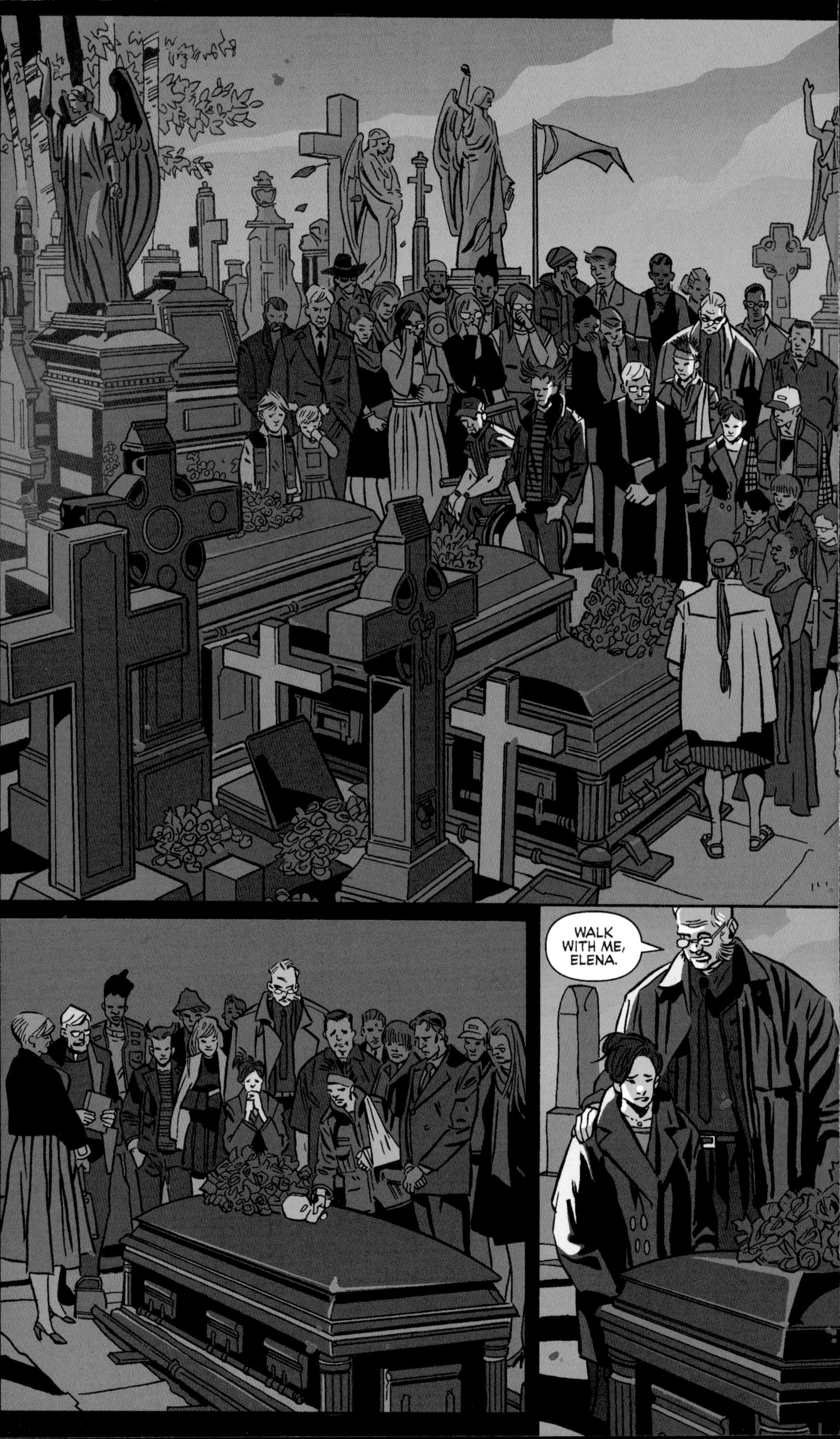
WALK WITH ME, ELENA.

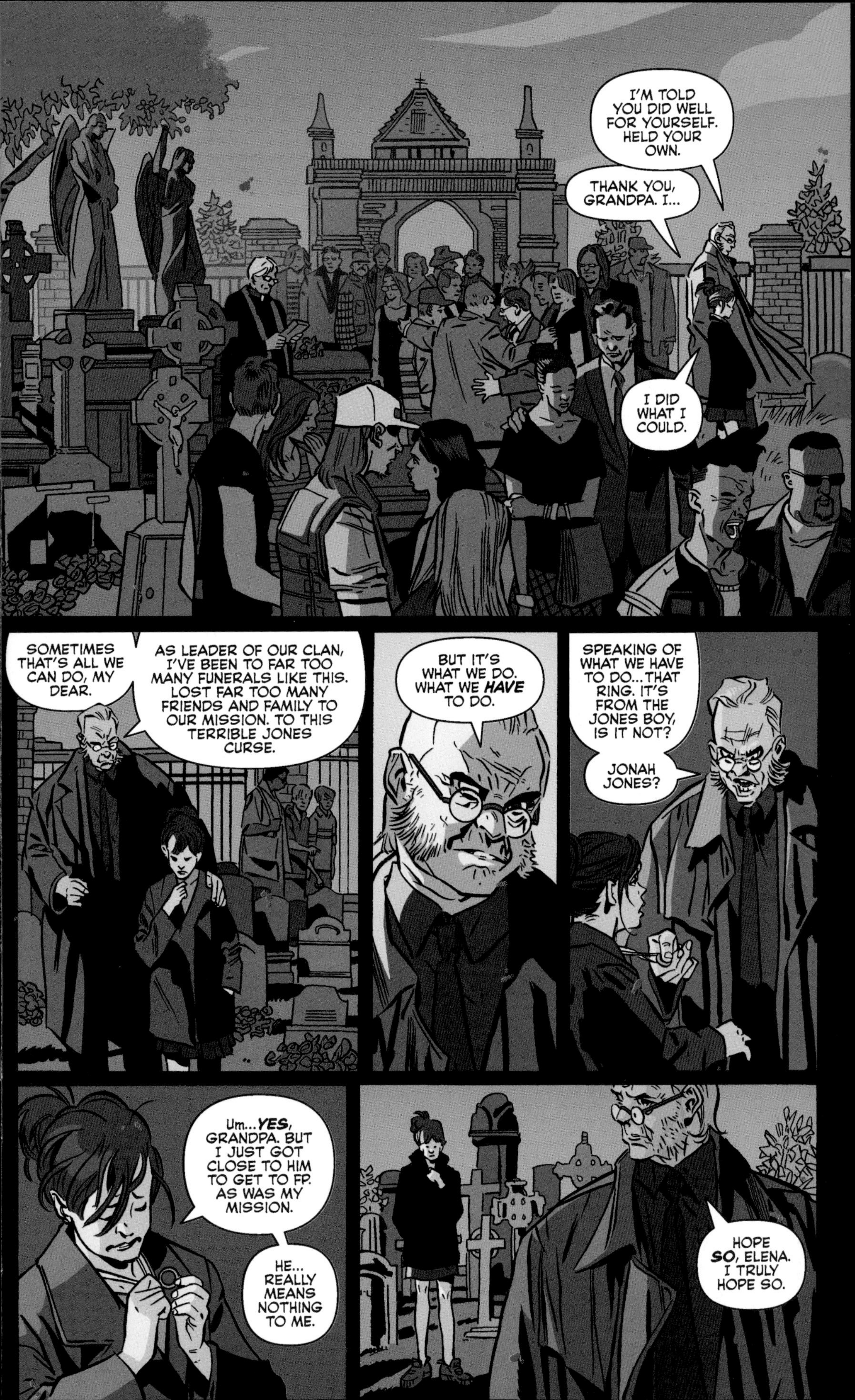
I'M TOLD YOU DID WELL FOR YOURSELF. HELD YOUR OWN.
THANK YOU, GRANDPA. I...
I DID WHAT I COULD.
SOMETIMES THAT'S ALL WE CAN DO, MY DEAR.
AS LEADER OF OUR CLAN, I'VE BEEN TO FAR TOO MANY FUNERALS LIKE THIS. LOST FAR TOO MANY FRIENDS AND FAMILY TO OUR MISSION. TO THIS TERRIBLE JONES CURSE.
BUT IT'S WHAT WE DO. WHAT WE *HAVE* TO DO.
SPEAKING OF WHAT WE HAVE TO DO...THAT RING. IT'S FROM THE JONES BOY, IS IT NOT?
JONAH JONES?
Um...*YES*, GRANDPA. BUT I JUST GOT CLOSE TO HIM TO GET TO FP. AS WAS MY MISSION.
HE... REALLY MEANS NOTHING TO ME.
HOPE **SO**, ELENA. I TRULY HOPE SO.

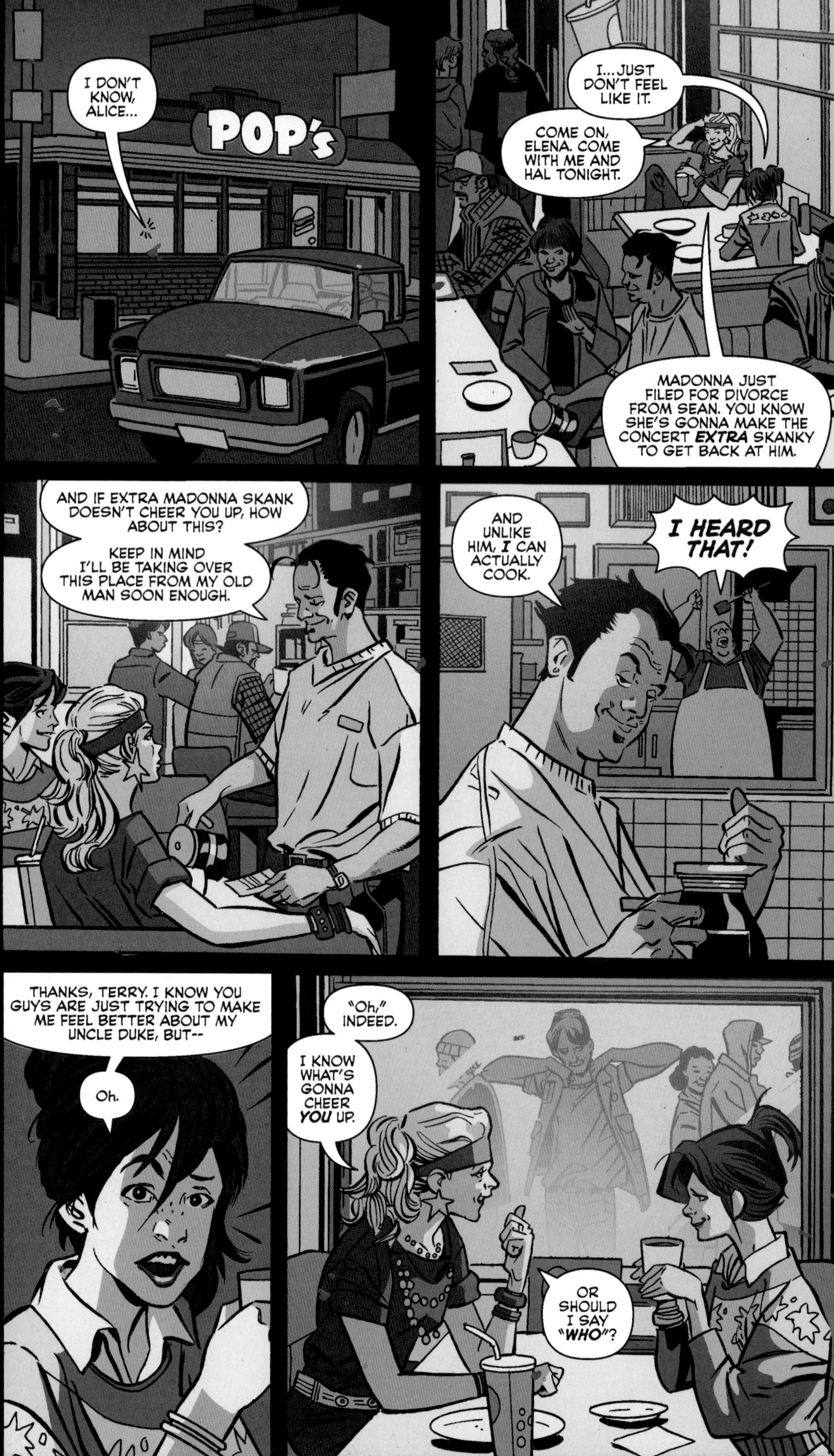
I DON'T KNOW, ALICE...
POP's
I...JUST DON'T FEEL LIKE IT.
COME ON, ELENA. COME WITH ME AND HAL TONIGHT.
MADONNA JUST FILED FOR DIVORCE FROM SEAN. YOU KNOW SHE'S GONNA MAKE THE CONCERT EXTRA SKANKY TO GET BACK AT HIM.
AND IF EXTRA MADONNA SKANK DOESN'T CHEER YOU UP, HOW ABOUT THIS?
KEEP IN MIND I'LL BE TAKING OVER THIS PLACE FROM MY OLD MAN SOON ENOUGH.
AND UNLIKE HIM, I CAN ACTUALLY COOK.
I HEARD THAT!
THANKS, TERRY. I KNOW YOU GUYS ARE JUST TRYING TO MAKE ME FEEL BETTER ABOUT MY UNCLE DUKE, BUT--
Oh.
"Oh," INDEED.
I KNOW WHAT'S GONNA CHEER YOU UP.
OR SHOULD I SAY "WHO"?

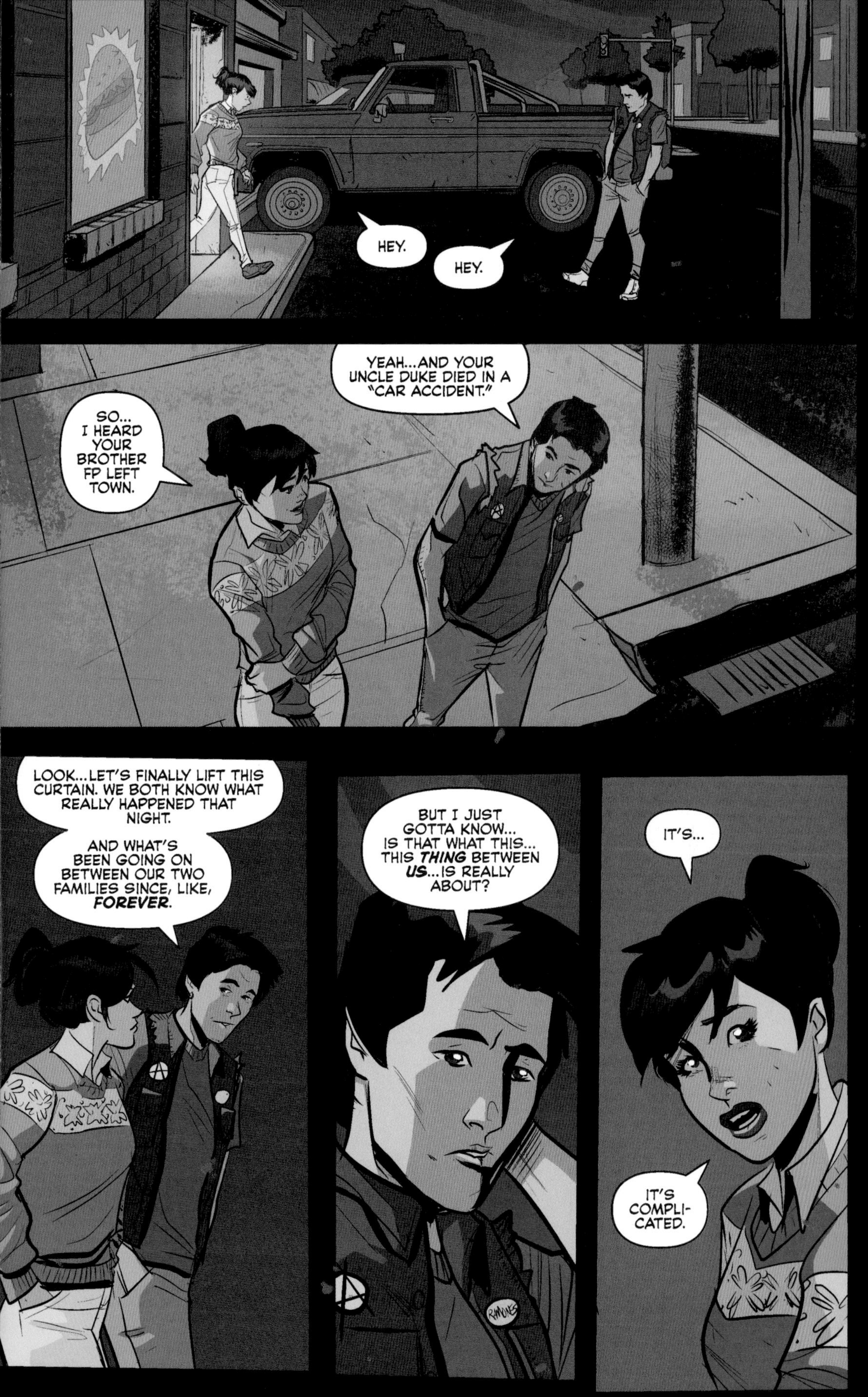
HEY.
HEY.
SO... I HEARD YOUR BROTHER FP LEFT TOWN.
YEAH...AND YOUR UNCLE DUKE DIED IN A "CAR ACCIDENT."
LOOK...LET'S FINALLY LIFT THIS CURTAIN. WE BOTH KNOW WHAT REALLY HAPPENED THAT NIGHT.
AND WHAT'S BEEN GOING ON BETWEEN OUR TWO FAMILIES SINCE, LIKE, **FOREVER**.
BUT I JUST GOTTA KNOW... IS THAT WHAT THIS... THIS ***THING*** BETWEEN ***US***...IS REALLY ABOUT?
RAMONES
IT'S...
IT'S COMPLI-CATED.

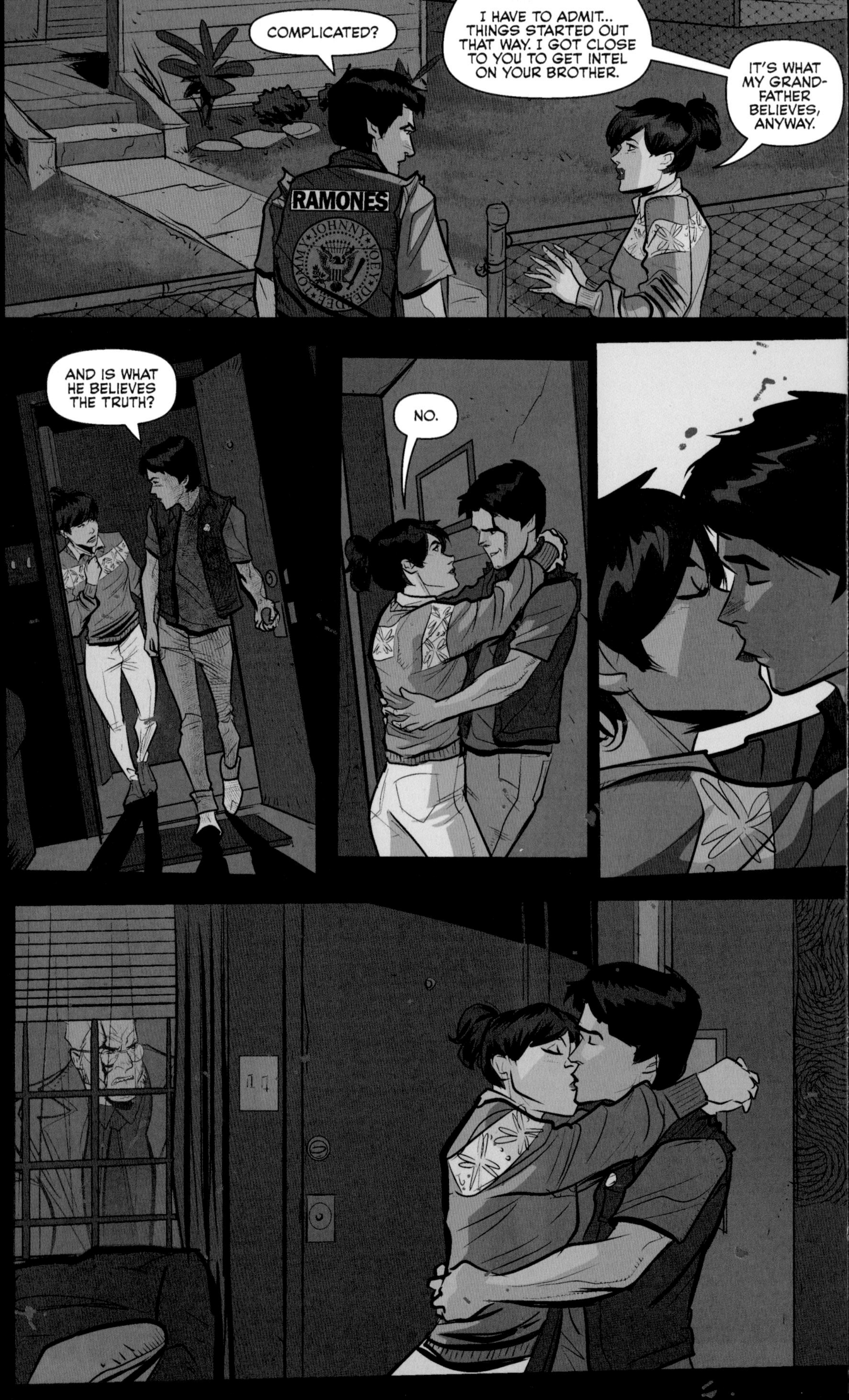
COMPLICATED?
I HAVE TO ADMIT... THINGS STARTED OUT THAT WAY. I GOT CLOSE TO YOU TO GET INTEL ON YOUR BROTHER.
IT'S WHAT MY GRAND-FATHER BELIEVES, ANYWAY.
RAMONES
JOHNNY JOEY DEE DEE TOMMY
AND IS WHAT HE BELIEVES THE TRUTH?
NO.

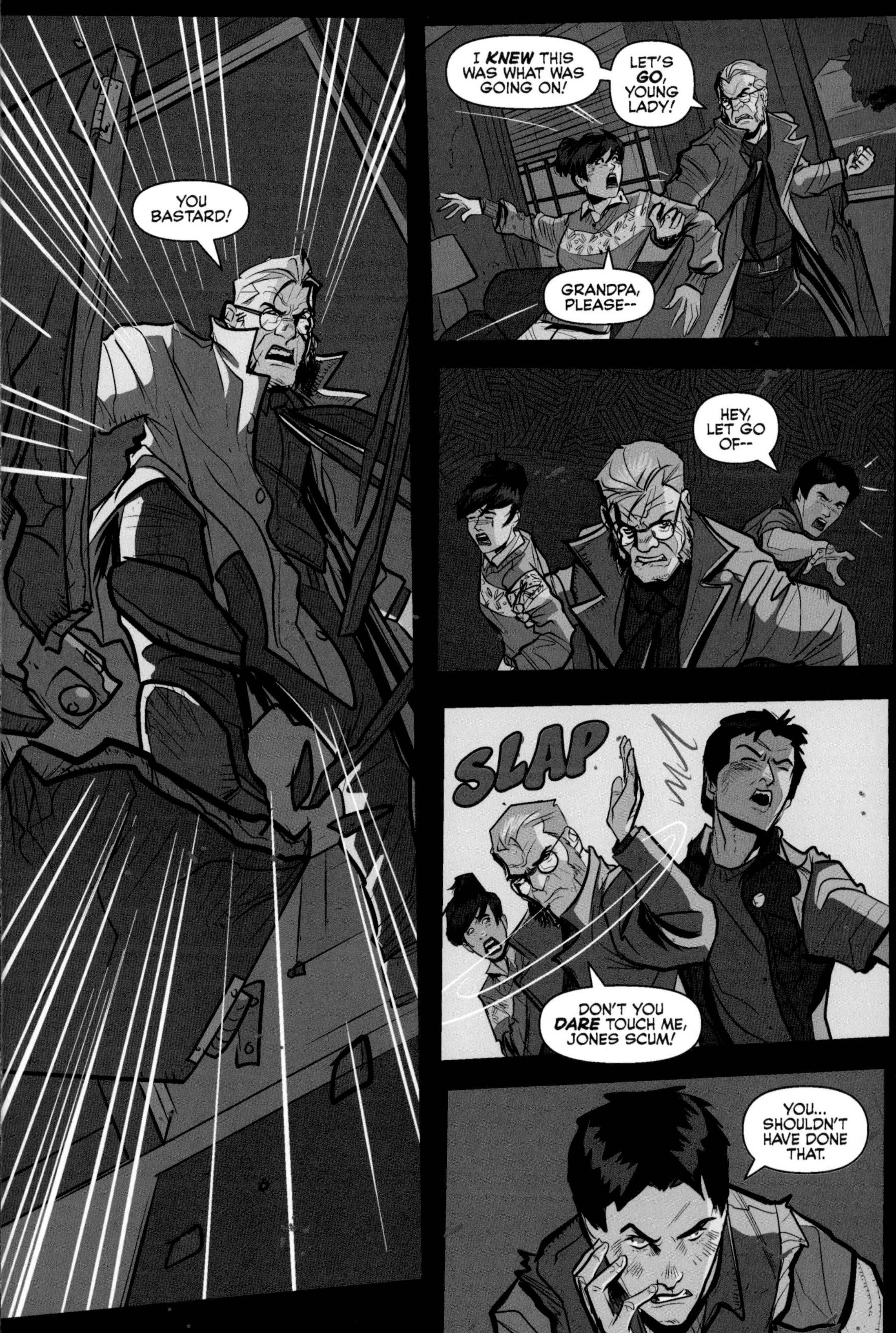
YOU BASTARD!
I KNEW THIS WAS WHAT WAS GOING ON!
LET'S GO, YOUNG LADY!
GRANDPA, PLEASE--
HEY, LET GO OF--
SLAP
DON'T YOU DARE TOUCH ME, JONES SCUM!
YOU... SHOULDN'T HAVE DONE THAT.

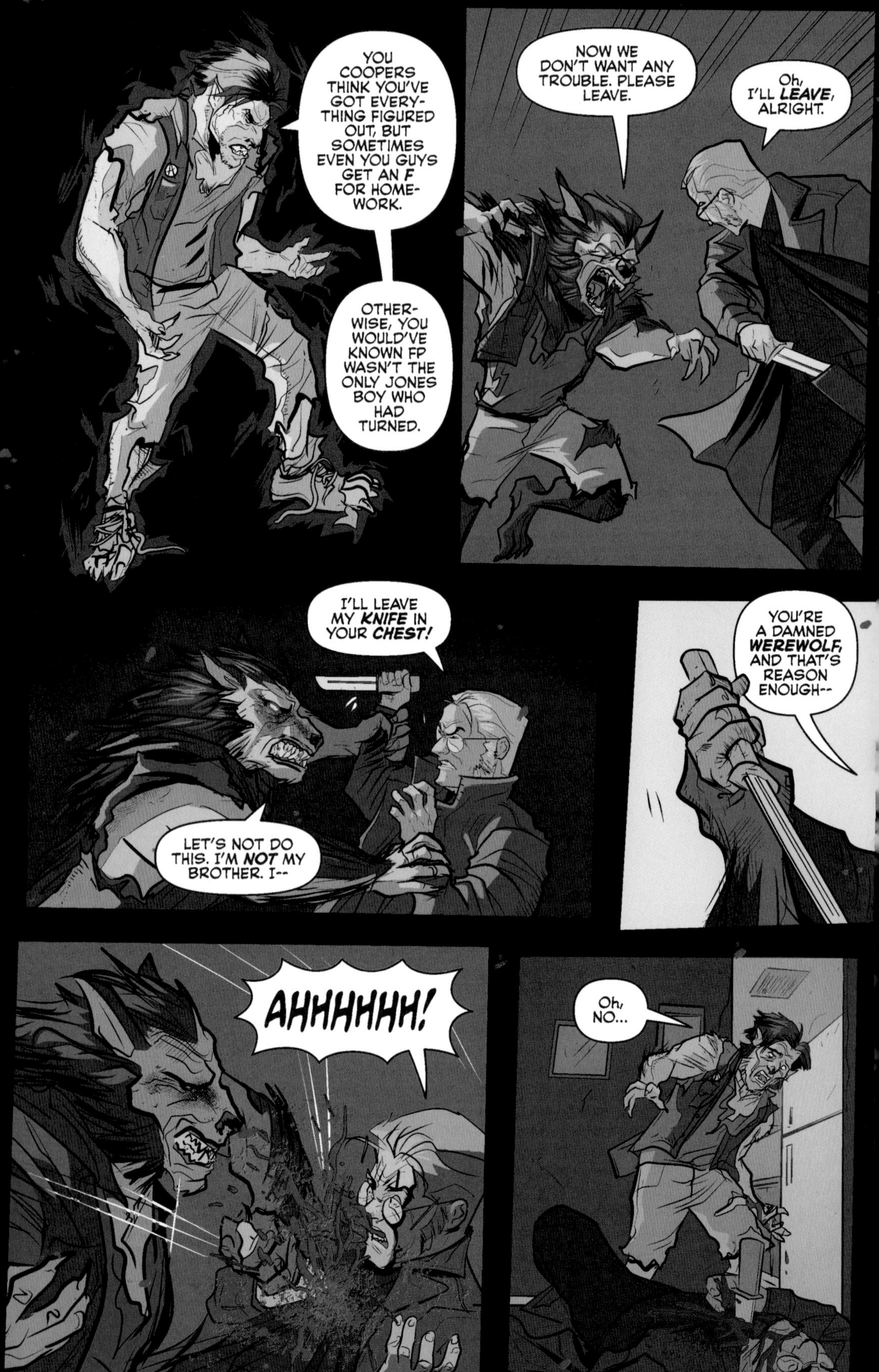
YOU COOPERS THINK YOU'VE GOT EVERY-THING FIGURED OUT, BUT SOMETIMES EVEN YOU GUYS GET AN F FOR HOME-WORK.
OTHER-WISE, YOU WOULD'VE KNOWN FP WASN'T THE ONLY JONES BOY WHO HAD TURNED.
NOW WE DON'T WANT ANY TROUBLE. PLEASE LEAVE.
Oh, I'LL LEAVE, ALRIGHT.
I'LL LEAVE MY KNIFE IN YOUR CHEST!
LET'S NOT DO THIS. I'M NOT MY BROTHER. I--
YOU'RE A DAMNED WEREWOLF, AND THAT'S REASON ENOUGH--
AHHHHHH!
Oh, NO...

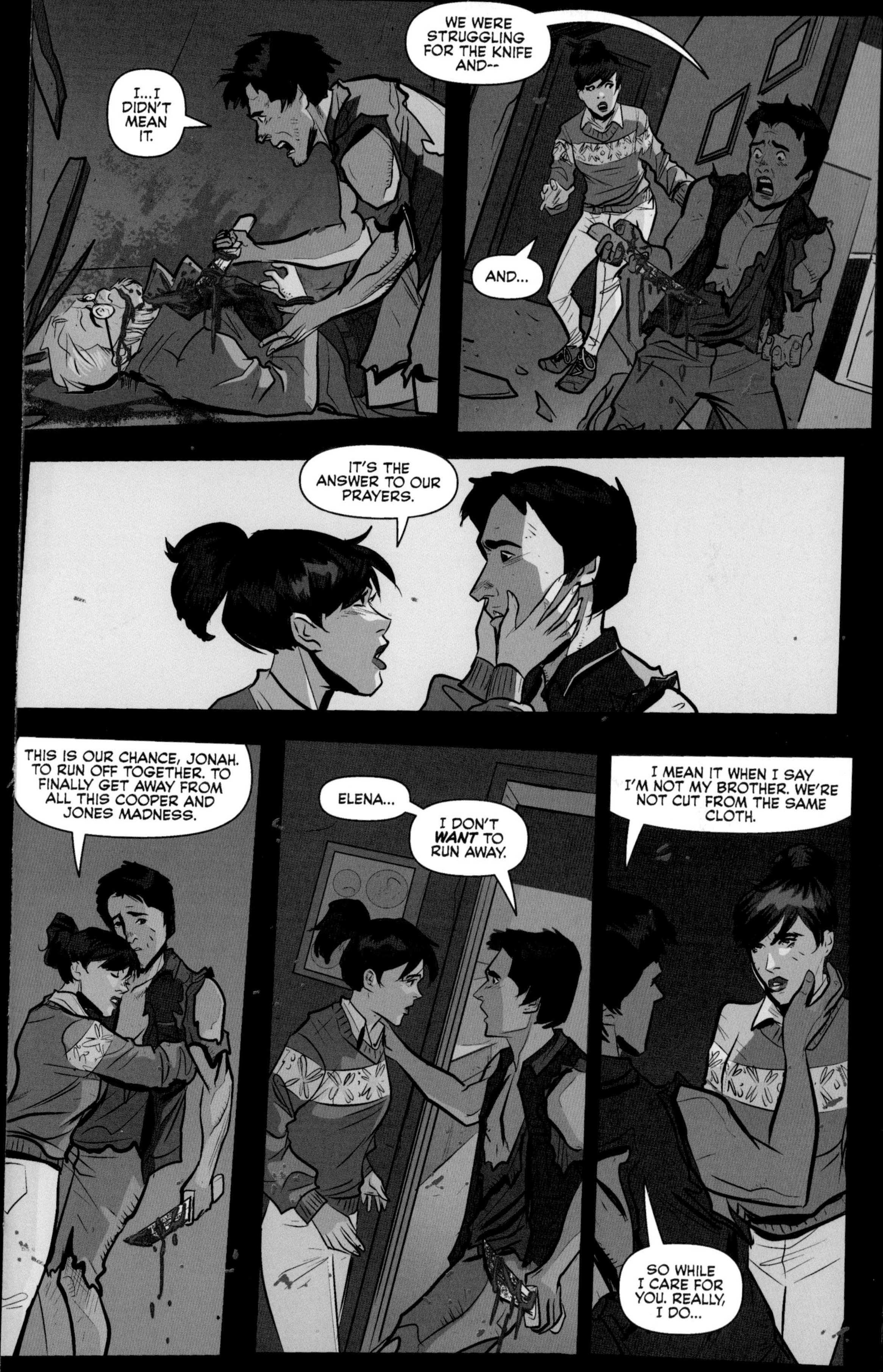
I...I DIDN'T MEAN IT.
WE WERE STRUGGLING FOR THE KNIFE AND--
AND...
IT'S THE ANSWER TO OUR PRAYERS.
THIS IS OUR CHANCE, JONAH. TO RUN OFF TOGETHER. TO FINALLY GET AWAY FROM ALL THIS COOPER AND JONES MADNESS.
ELENA...
I DON'T *WANT* TO RUN AWAY.
I MEAN IT WHEN I SAY I'M NOT MY BROTHER. WE'RE NOT CUT FROM THE SAME CLOTH.
SO WHILE I CARE FOR YOU. REALLY, I DO...

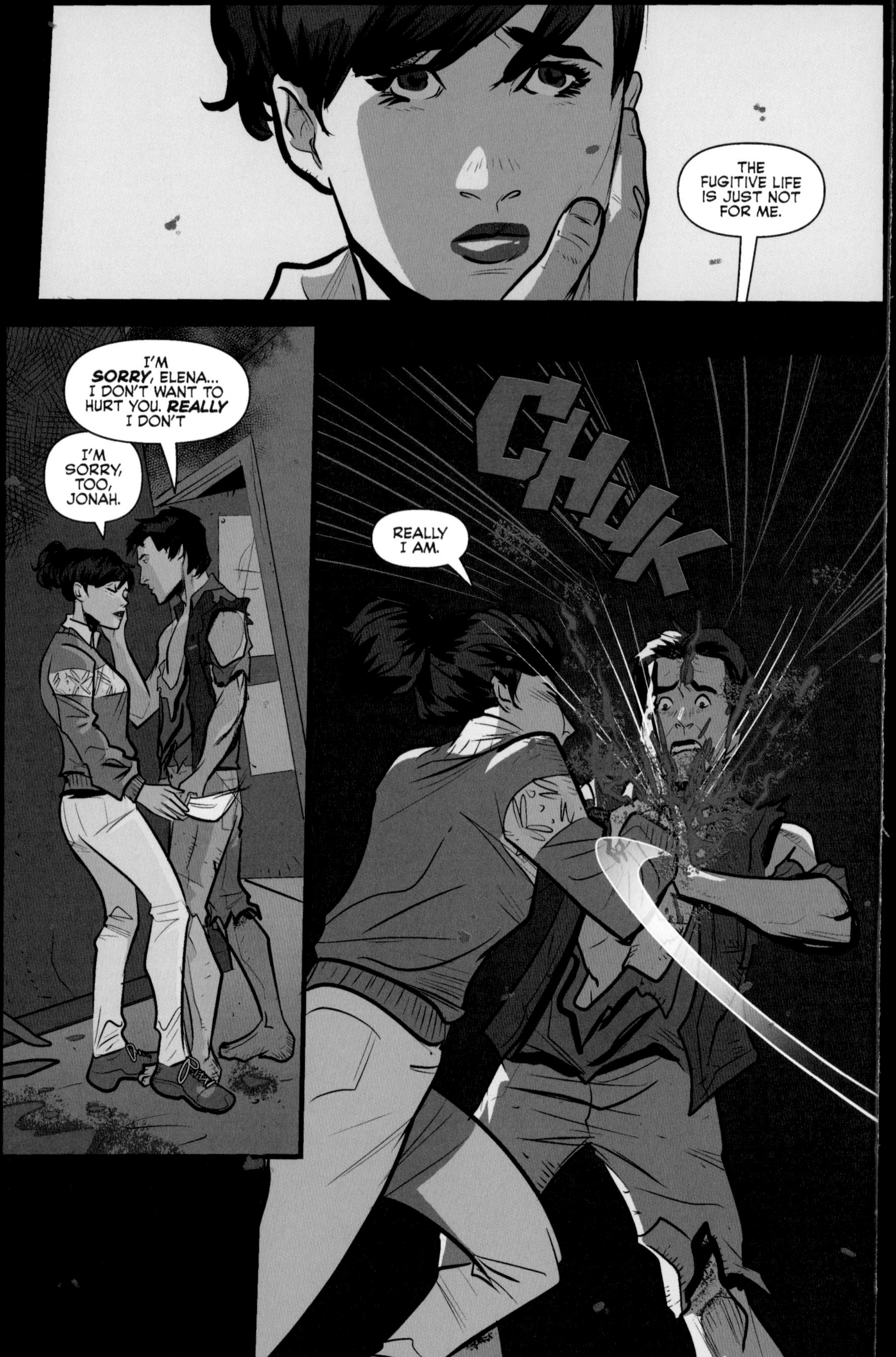
THE FUGITIVE LIFE IS JUST NOT FOR ME.
I'M **SORRY**, ELENA... I DON'T WANT TO HURT YOU. **REALLY** I DON'T
I'M SORRY, TOO, JONAH.
CHUK
REALLY I AM.

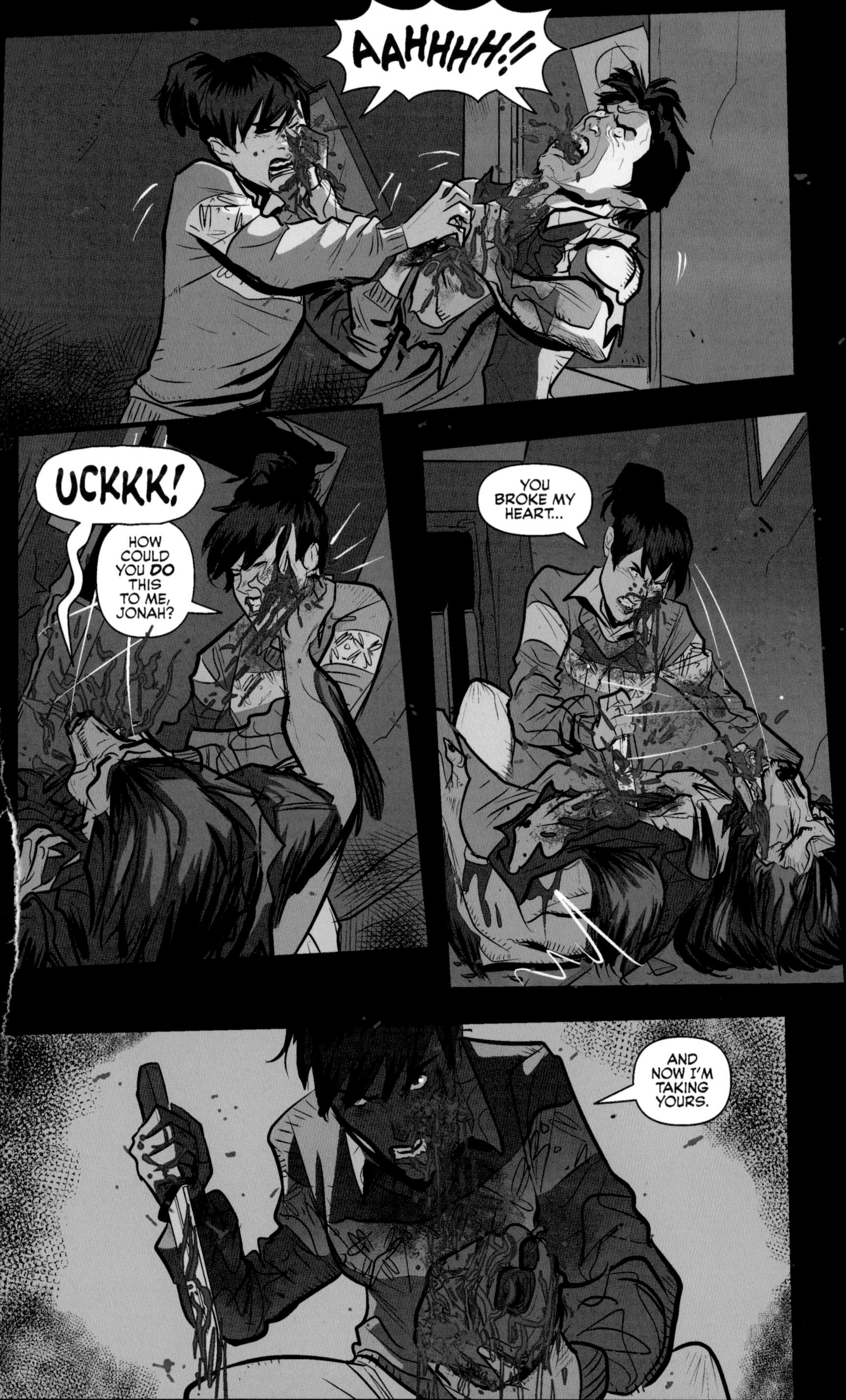
AAHHHH!!
UCKKK!
HOW COULD YOU DO THIS TO ME, JONAH?
YOU BROKE MY HEART...
AND NOW I'M TAKING YOURS.

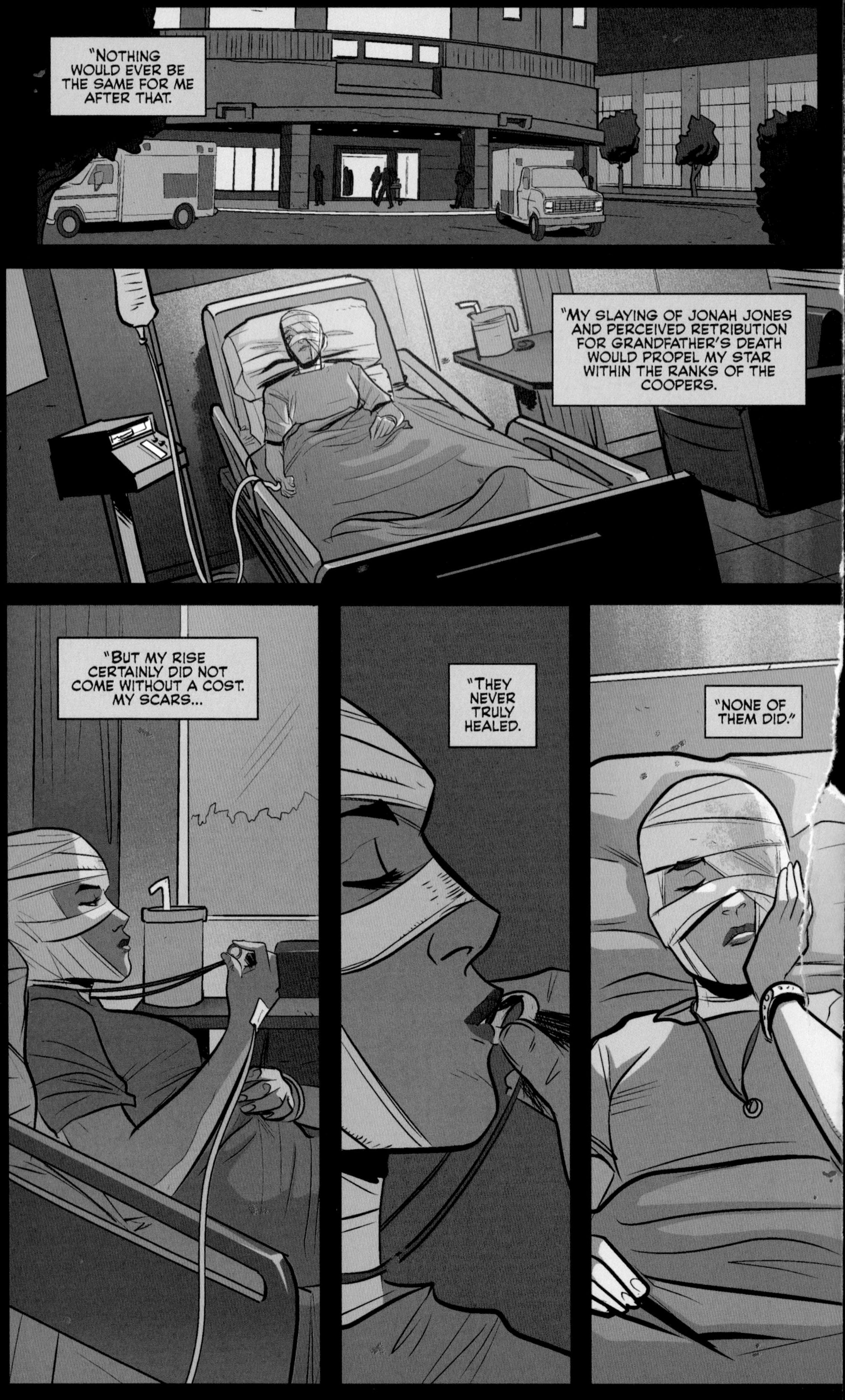
"NOTHING WOULD EVER BE THE SAME FOR ME AFTER THAT.
"MY SLAYING OF JONAH JONES AND PERCEIVED RETRIBUTION FOR GRANDFATHER'S DEATH WOULD PROPEL MY STAR WITHIN THE RANKS OF THE COOPERS.
"BUT MY RISE CERTAINLY DID NOT COME WITHOUT A COST. MY SCARS...
"THEY NEVER TRULY HEALED.
"NONE OF THEM DID."

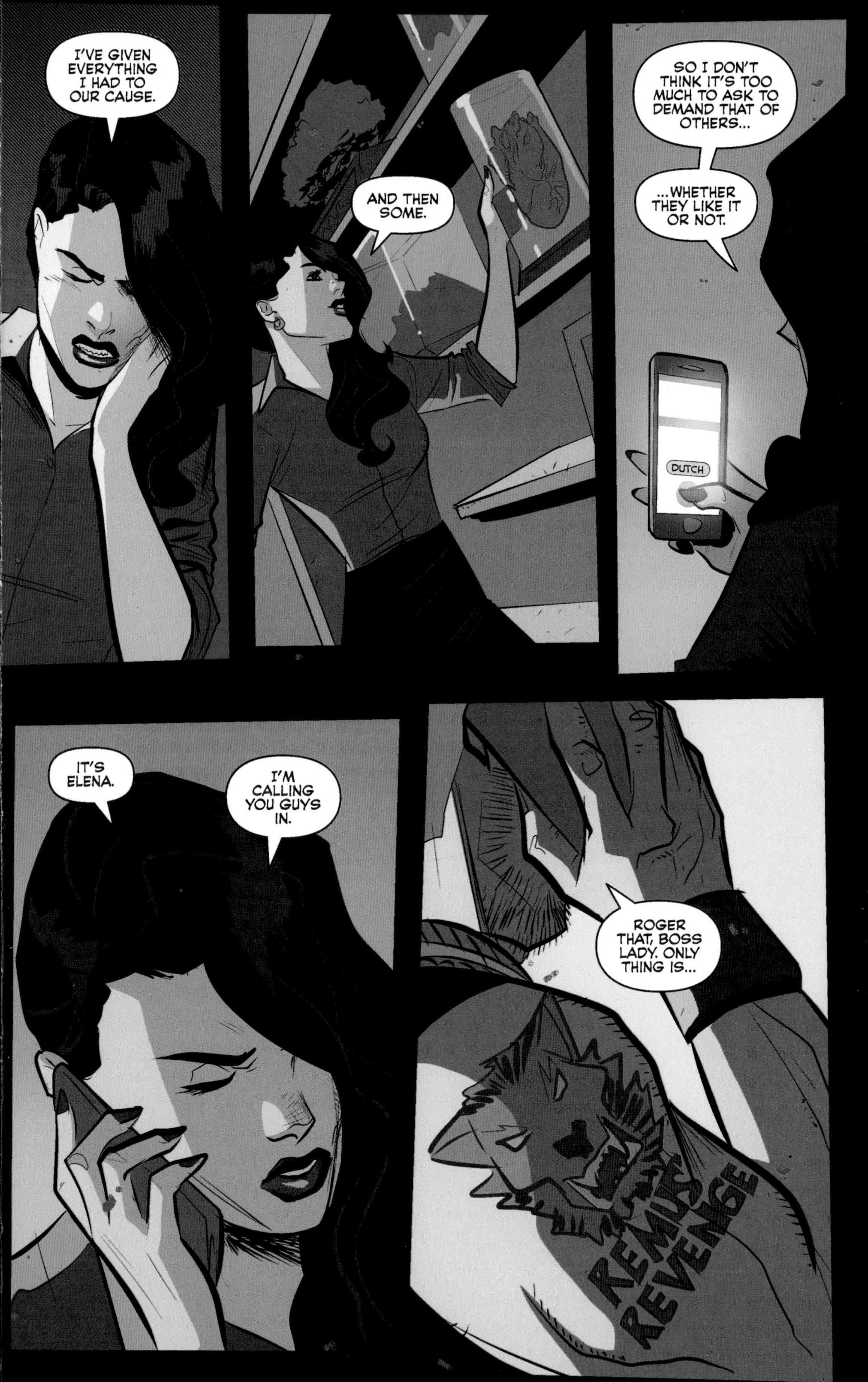
I'VE GIVEN EVERYTHING I HAD TO OUR CAUSE.
AND THEN SOME.
SO I DON'T THINK IT'S TOO MUCH TO ASK TO DEMAND THAT OF OTHERS...
...WHETHER THEY LIKE IT OR NOT.
DUTCH
IT'S ELENA.
I'M CALLING YOU GUYS IN.
ROGER THAT, BOSS LADY. ONLY THING IS...
REMUS' REVENGE

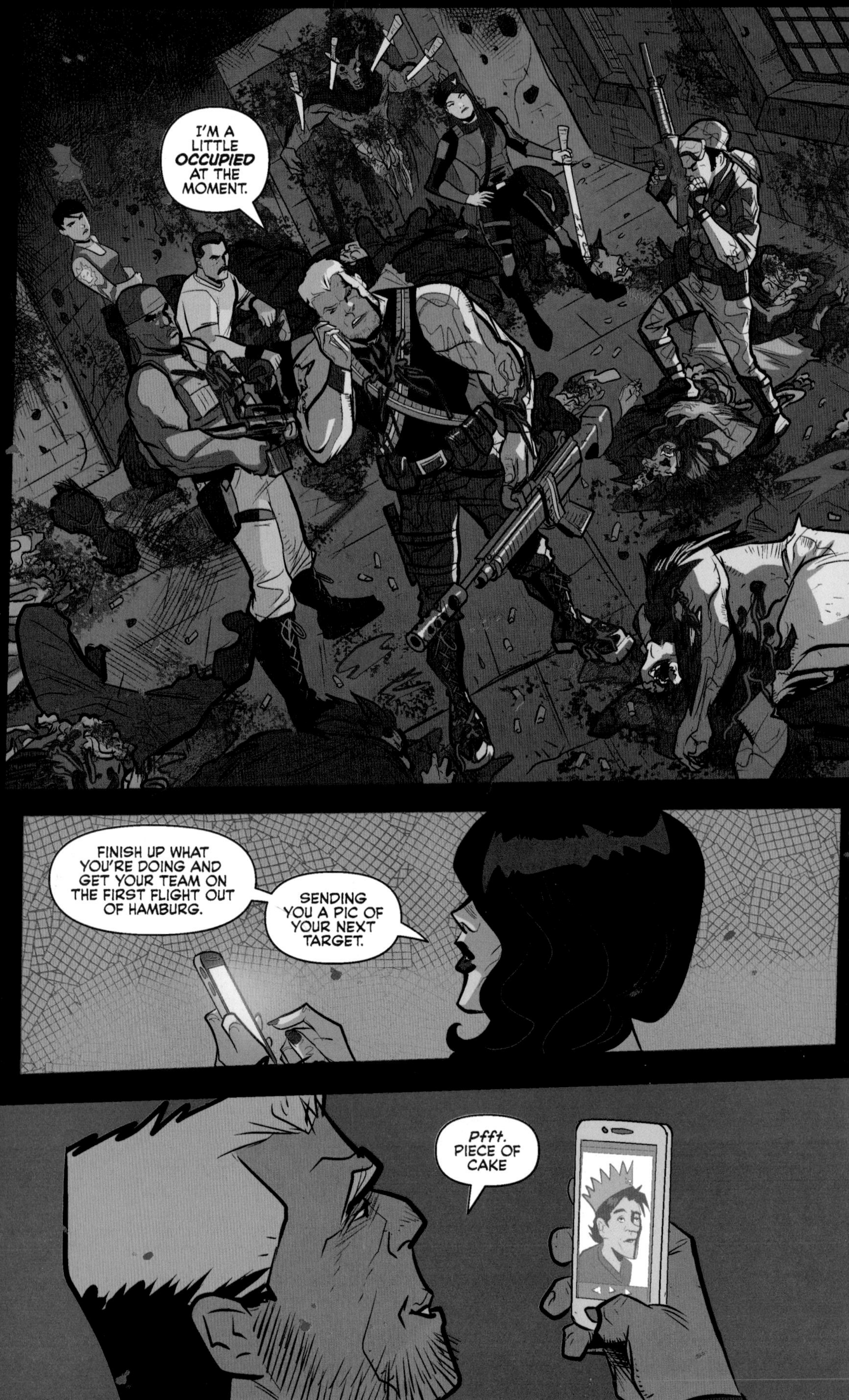
I'M A LITTLE OCCUPIED AT THE MOMENT.
FINISH UP WHAT YOU'RE DOING AND GET YOUR TEAM ON THE FIRST FLIGHT OUT OF HAMBURG.
SENDING YOU A PIC OF YOUR NEXT TARGET.
Pfft. PIECE OF CAKE